Curriculum development

a comparative study

P.H. Taylor and
M. Johnson

NFER Publishing Company Ltd.

Published by the NFER Publishing Company Ltd.,
Book Division, 2 Jennings Buildings,
Thames Avenue, Windsor, Berks, SL4 1QS
Registered Office: The Mere, Upton Park, Slough, Berks, SL1 2DQ
First Published 1974
© P. H. Taylor and M. Johnson, 1974
85633 035 3

Printed in Great Britain by
John Gardner (Printers) Ltd., Hawthorne Road, Bootle, Merseyside L20 6JX

Distributed in the USA by Humanities Press Inc.,
450 Park Avenue South, New York, NY 10016, USA

Contents

Foreword

Our purpose in producing this book was not to evaluate the efficiency of the curriculum development process in different national contexts, though we know that such assessments are possible[1] but not how reliable or valid they are. Our purpose was altogether less ambitious. It was simply to make available to those interested in the process of curriculum development data on how it is handled in countries other than their own and so enable them, if this was their interest, to see to what extent it is possible to make generalizations about it, and to what extent it is an historically and culturally embedded process.

In trying to serve this purpose we invited all the contributors to deal with four basic issues:

A. the meaning given to 'curriculum' in their country;
B. the style of curriculum development employed;
C. an appraisal of curriculum developments; and
D. the future of curriculum development;

and though not all contributors have conformed to this plan exactly, nor dealt in the same detail with the issues, we believe they have sufficiently to make comparsions possible. Of course we cannot claim that each contributor's views are completely authoritative. But we do believe that each has attempted to be objective in so far as it is possible to be objective about such a socio-political process as curriculum development.

If this book does serve the purpose intended it will be more because our colleagues in our own and other countries were readily responsive to our solicitations than to what we have been able to bring to the enterprise, and we are grateful to them. We hope that we have represented their views as they would wish. We have not always found the translation of their ideas easy, but we enjoyed the challenge.

Philip H. Taylor *Mauritz Johnson*
Birmingham *Albany*
 January 1974

---

[1] See for example ALKIN, M. (1973) 'A theoretical framework for the analysis of curriculum and instructional reform', *Int. Rev. Educ.*, XIX, 2, 195–207,

CHAPTER 1

Bases for Comparing Approaches to Curriculum Development

Mauritz Johnson

It must have been exciting to have had the means and the leisure to travel abroad in those bygone days when each country still had its own distinctive style of living and customs which to outlanders seemed quaint. Inevitable it probably was, but ironical it surely is, that the advent of widespread international jet travel made it easier to get somewhere that, becoming more and more like home, became less and less interesting to get to. Of course, Europe's cultural monuments are still there, demanding that homage be paid to them, and the natural monuments of the New World's vast spaces have not eroded away. But one modern city is much like another, wherever located, with the same impossible traffic congestion, the same shiny new hotels and office buildings, and the same merchandise, similarly packaged, offered in the stores. Moreover, it has become increasingly difficult to guess people's nationalities, so similar have we all become.

Comparing educational systems

Education has not been immune to the trend toward homogenization. Educational researchers from Europe regularly present papers at the annual meetings of the American Educational Research Association. Americans in droves, and probably other foreigners as well, descend on the British primary schools. A dozen countries collaborate in an International Evaluation of Educational Achievement under the auspices of UNESCO, whose Institute of Education further contributes to comparative educational understanding through its publication of the *International Review of Education*. Informative documents on various national systems of education emanate from the Organization for Economic Co-operation and Development. Instructional materials developed under grants from the Nuffield Foundation in Great Britain and from the National Science

Foundation in the United States are well known in many countries and used in the schools of some of them.

Although detailed analytical data are not available, it seems probable that the curricula and the instructional procedures of the various national systems have grown increasingly similar during the second half of this century. As a number of European nations have adopted policies promoting less exclusive secondary education through a more comprehensive institutional format, they have encountered problems somewhat like those with which educators grappled in the United States several decades earlier. Paradoxically, the efforts of American schools have recently been directed at achieving some of the intellectual rigour associated with the more exclusive European schools. Quite apart from the closer contacts, therefore, these trends have also served to reduce some of the more striking differences among systems.

Nevertheless, despite the forces tending toward uniformity, each nation has its own peculiar ways of arriving at its educational decisions and carrying them out. Tradition is a powerful determinant of what is taught, but it also influences how a national system goes about changing what is taught. Just as flora are not always transplantable to other environments, not all educational practices are exportable to other cultures. The interplay of tradition and internationalism within each national context produces interesting variations in the way that curriculum development is accommodated to situational characteristics.

Nevertheless, even with the utmost respect for cultural differences and for the solutions that education authorities and curriculum workers in each country have worked out for indigenous problems, the student of curriculum development is impelled to search for generalizations and to see if, at some level of generality, common issues can be identified. The diversity is fascinating, but the regularities may be more enlightening. Noting differences reminds one that procedures considered virtually sacred in one's own system constitute only one way of solving particular problems. But, noting similarities helps one to see more clearly what the essential tasks are. To become aware of a wide range of alternatives without simultaneously recognizing that there are some differences which do not make any difference is like noting the uniqueness of each individual person without seeing that all people are very much alike, or like observing the rapidity of change without noticing that the more things change the more they remain the same.

The meaning of curriculum

If an international symposium were to be held on prison reform or heart disease, it is unlikely that any participants would assume that the topic was space exploration or cancer. But even within a single country an educational term like 'curriculum' often has so many interpretations that it would be surprising if its meaning did not vary from one national system to another. In comparing various approaches to curriculum development, therefore, one needs above all to satisfy oneself that the same phenomenon is under discussion in each instance. When explicit definitions are not provided, one must infer from the text what is meant by the term.

Clues to the nature of a thing come from references to its substance, form, and function. Curriculum is viewed by some as a plan and by others, as actual occurrences or effects. As a plan, a curriculum document would be prescriptive and serve as a guide to action; under the second interpretation it would be descriptive and serve as a report or record. When curriculum is viewed as a plan of some sort, it is significant to note whether it is a plan for a product, setting forth the results an educational programme is to achieve, or a process plan, indicating the instructional procedures and materials that teachers are to use and the learning experiences that students are to have.

Those who consider the curriculum to be a plan for the experiences that are to be provided for learners argue that what learners actually do is what is of most importance, that the events in the instructional situation are subject to direct control whereas their outcomes are not, and indeed are often unpredictable. Moreover, they feel that some experiences are worthwhile in themselves, regardless of what is learned through them. Those who take the opposing view argue that learning experiences are merely instrumental, that their worth depends on their effectiveness in producing desired learnings, and that any one of a number of experiences could be suitable to achieve an intended outcome. In their opinion, the choice of learning experiences and instructional materials and procedures belongs to teachers, not curriculum developers.

At the higher levels of generality, almost all statements about curriculum are phrased in terms of categories, such as subjects, and it is difficult to tell without further analysis, whether the category represents (1) certain things that are to be learned by whatever means may be devised, or (2) certain experiences through which specified learnings are to be achieved, or (3) certain experiences that are to be provided without regard to the learning which results.

Obviously, the function which curriculum serves is related to what it is perceived to be. If it is a report, rather than a plan, it cannot be used as a basis for planning instruction. If it is a plan that specifies the experiences to be provided, it leaves little further instructional planning to be done. If it is a statement of what learning is to be achieved, it indicates to instructional planners and developers only what is to be accomplished through whatever learning experiences and instructional materials they select or design.

Participants in curriculum development

Who can and should engage in curriculum development depends in part upon how curriculum is defined and how its function is perceived. Potential participants include lay citizens and political officials on the one hand and professional educators, specialists, scholars, and educational authorities on the other. These participants may function at various degrees of remoteness from the instructional setting, ranging all the way to the highest national levels. They can be classified as having final decision-making authority, as having responsibility for initiating proposals for higher approval, as contributing knowledge or expert opinion to decision makers, and as influencing decisions through persuasion or the exercise of power without official authority.

Depending on the national system, teachers may play any or all of these roles for one or more types of decision, being actually involved in making decisions individually or as members of official committees and influencing decisions as individual experts or through their professional associations.

The role of the students themselves with respect to curriculum decisions is a matter of controversy, both as to the options that should be granted them as individuals and the extent to which they should participate in making decisions regarding the requirements to be imposed upon them collectively and the opportunities to be made available to them.

Because disagreement exists concerning the limits of curriculum development, it is useful to recognize that there are, in any event, three major categories of decision in educational planning: (1) *what* is to be taught (and intended to be learned), (2) *why* it is to be learned, and (3) *how* it is to be taught. The second category entails the setting of broad educational goals, anticipating the qualities desired in the educated person, citizen, or worker which justify teaching whatever is included in Category 1. Since both categories deal with objectives or anticipated results at different levels of specificity, some prefer to consider them aspects of a single goal-setting process. Others would combine Categories 1 and 3 on the grounds that deciding what is to be learned and how it can best be learned are inseparable aspects of instructional planning. The fact that both of these views are held indicates that, whether separated or not in practice, the three categories are distinguishable, at least for purposes of analysis,

Therefore, in any context is it instructive to ask the following questions concerning participation in curriculum planning:

1. who, at what level, decides what broad educational results are desired and assigns priorities to them?
2. who, at what level, decides what areas of study will be required or offered in various components of the system in order to achieve the broad educational goals?
3. who, at what level, decides what specific learning outcomes are most important to achieve within each area of study in order both to reach the identified goals and facilitate further study within that area to achieve other goals?
4. who, if anyone, issues directives to teachers regarding the materials and procedures they must use in achieving the identified learning outcomes?
5. who, if anyone, offers suggestions to teachers regarding instructional materials and procedures to achieve particular learning outcomes, or develops detailed materials and activity sequences which teachers may adopt if they wish?
6. who, at what level, decides the conditions under which instruction will occur: the qualifications of the teachers; the size and composition of schools and instructional groups; the allocation of time for various purposes; the type and amount of space, facilities, equipment, and materials that must or will be made available; and the manner in which students' achievement will be evaluated and the success of schools in attaining the identified goals will be determined?

Making and implementing decisions

Like the identity of the participants, the manner in which decisions are taken and then implemented can be expected to vary with the type of decision and to differ among countries. Moreover, which decisions, if any, need to be taken at any given time depends on the circumstances then existing in a particular country. One can imagine, though perhaps only with difficulty, a situation in which no controversy exists regarding educational goals, where there is complete agreement on what should be taught, where teachers have long since accepted or determined how they ought to teach, where no new materials are being developed to compete with those in use, and where the conditions of instruction are well-established by regulation or custom. In such a situation, few, if any, educational decisions would be needed outside the classroom itself. It is, of course, highly unlikely that this is the case in any country.

Even so some decisions are always pending in any national

context, there are differences in pace of change and there is a cyclical pattern of change such that in any particular period of time countries may be in different phases of the cycle. Thus, one country may make decisions one at a time, bringing about minor changes in the system, first in one sector and then in another. In another country, numerous far-reaching changes affecting large portions of the system simultaneously may be under consideration and eventually adopted all at once. But whether major or minor, frequent or occasional, decisions finally taken must be followed by a period of implementation, and once the change has been introduced and the new programme or practice has become firmly established, institutionalized in fact, a phase in the cycle is reached in which no decision is needed, unless the pace is such that further changes are decided upon before there has been enough time to implement previous decisions.

It will be noted, therefore, that in recent years there has been a gradual evolution in the education systems of some countries, while in others there has been extensive reform, often in response to some significant policy change, such as one concerning the length of compulsory schooling, racial de-segregation, or the comprehensiveness of secondary schools. Not all decisions are precipitated by shifts in social philosophy or political climate, of course. The relentless increase in available knowledge forces every nation to decide what new insights, if any, will be incorporated into educational programmes at various levels. Some countries may have better mechanisms than others for keeping the content of instruction abreast of contemporary scholarship. The pressures imposed upon students by the ever-increasing amount of knowledge to be acquired, along with the impersonalization associated with larger institutional settings and modern life, generally, have prompted efforts to 'humanize' schooling in many countries, and the problem has undoubtedly been viewed more seriously and solved more effectively in some countries than in others. A point of interest about each country, therefore, is not only what educational planning decisions have been taken, but what factors made those decisions necessary.

Mechanisms and procedures for educational planning differ in regard to the thoroughness with which needs are identified, alternatives are considered, and solutions are tested, as well as in regard to the extensiveness with which various segments of the society and particularly of the professional education community are consulted before a decision is taken. Very possibly, the more efficiently decisions can be arrived at the less effectively they can be implemented. A decision taken at a level other than that at which it is to be implemented can be promulgated, but the willingness and capacity to implement it cannot. It is of interest, therefore, to note how various nations solve this problem of introducing curriculum changes—how decisions are communicated, what methods of enforcement or persuasion are used, what help, if any, teachers are given in effecting the changes.

Influences and constraints

By whatever means curriculum development proceeds in a given country, it occurs in response to various forces. Likewise, there are other forces which tend to inhibit new curricular developments, serving to discourage initiatives in certain directions and making it more difficult to arrive at decisions and carry them out.

Some of these forces are well-established and characteristic of a particular national context, while others are symptomatic of the times, such that no country is immune from them. What are the factors that appear to have precipitated a flurry of curriculum revision in certain settings and what other factors explain a less frenetic level of activity elsewhere? Are any factors common to all situations? Are any unique?

The curriculum development process can have pressures exerted upon it directly, or it can be influenced indirectly, sometimes with considerable subtlety. Universities, for example, may have some official responsibility for the curricula of the lower schools, or they may unofficially exert some degree of influence through admissions requirements and authoritative persuasion or they may have no effect whatsoever. How influential are professional educators' associations, the news media, the textbook publishers, various civic organizations and special interest groups, and other segments of the society which may have no official part to play in the decision-making process?

Some of the same forces which can be credited with facilitating curriculum development can also be blamed for making it difficult. When many forces simultaneously tend in the same general direction, decisions can be quickly reached and efficiently put into operation. But when forces work against each other, disagreements, uncertainties, and resistances arise to forestall or retard progress. It can be assumed that no country is free of its share of difficulties and problems in getting on with its curriculum development, but it is instructive to discover the nature of the constraints encountered in each national context.

Recent curriculum developments

Quite apart from the procedures followed and the organizational structure in which they occur, it is also of interest to learn what kinds of product have resulted recently and are currently being developed in various countries. Has greater attention been given to the broad pattern of curricular offerings and requirements, or to the specific content of the categories constituting that pattern? Have efforts been concentrated more at one educational level, e.g., elementary or secondary, than another? Have certain subject areas had more emphasis than others, and if so, have these been the same ones in most countries? Has curriculum development focused on special categories of students, such as minority groups in the population or those at some particular level of learning ability, or have no such distinctions been made?

As was suggested earlier, various forces can provide impetus for curriculum development activity. Recent curriculum developments in various countries may have been prompted by roughly the same forces or, alternatively, circumstances peculiar to particular contexts may have been dominant. If a policy of periodic review exists, no other explanatory factors may be necessary, but where no such policy exists, one may properly look for the reasons why a given reported development effort was undertaken.

Looking ahead

It is most disconcerting to consider seriously following someone else's example only to find that he is himself considering abandoning the exemplary practice. Whatever we may learn about curriculum development from the past experiences of other countries, we could learn more from extrapolating those experiences into the future. Obviously, it is impossible to project the future accurately, but clues are available from trends already discernible. Speculations about future curriculum developments based on tendencies perceived in various countries have the dual value of giving added perspective to their current situations and at the same time providing added insight into the probable future facing one's own country.

In contemplating the future, one has, once again, both the curriculum development process and the curriculum itself to consider. There may appear to be a much greater possibility of changing the process in one country than in another, and some potential changes will be viewed as far more probable than others. Similarly, with or without changes in the development process, certain future developments in curriculum are already identifiable as more likely to occur than others.

Needs already in evidence in a culture will diminish or intensify; demands currently being expressed in the society will be satisfied or heighten. If the existing mechanism for curriculum development is adequate to meet these changing needs and demands, and others now unforeseen, then the curriculum will be appropriately modified. If the current procedures are not adequate for this purpose, then it can be expected that they themselves will be altered. Consideration might well be given to the problems that can be anticipated in trying to make the necessary curriculum modifications with existing mechanisms for curriculum development or in transforming that mechanism into a more effective one.

Summary
The descriptions of curriculum development in a number of countries presented in this volume offer the reader an opportunity to identify both similarities and differences in their approaches to educational planning. A starting point is to discern what aspect of educational planning is considered to be 'curriculum development', which in turn depends on what substance, form, and function are attributed to 'curriculum'. Once the process in question has been identified, certain questions can be raised concerning it:

1. who participates in the process?
2. what kinds of decisions does it entail?
3. how are decisions implemented?
4. what forces initiate and inhibit the process of curriculum development and influence its results?

Descriptions of some recent curriculum developments help to illustrate the general features of the process that emerges. Whether these developments have been wide-ranging or concentrated on certain levels, subjects, and types of learner sheds some light on the forces impinging on the system. But further, these examples help to clarify the roles various participants play, the nature of the decisions faced, and procedures by which decisions are taken and changes are introduced.

Finally, taken together the prospects for the future of curriculum development as seen by competent observers in each country suggest the outlines of the challenges lying ahead for curriculum developers everywhere. With a broadened perspective of the task and shared expertise on how to accomplish it, curriculum workers in each country should be better equipped to deal effectively with whatever challenges may arise.

CHAPTER 2

Curriculum Development in Belgium

R. Vandenberghe

Introduction

As a general introduction a brief outline of the Belgian school system is given to allow a better insight into the construction and the specific meaning of the curricula of primary and secondary schools in Belgium.

The system consists of four groups of schools, organized by different authorities, viz. the State schools, Free Catholic, Provincial, and Neutral-State-aided (i.e. Municipal) schools. The State and the Catholic Church are the most important organizing authorities as the ratios of pupils per school level given in the table below show.

Table 1: *The Percentage of Schools by Type and Organizing Authority 1958–9 and 1970–1*

| | AUTHORITIES | | | | | | | |
| | State | | Province | | Muncipality | | Cath. Church | |
SCHOOL LEVEL	1959	1970	1959	1970	1958	1970	1958	1970
Infant School	4·1	12·6	—	—	29·3	28·7	66·5	58·5
Primary School	8·0	16·0	0·1	0·1	39·0	32·8	52·8	50·8
Secondary School (general)	37·8	33·4	0·8	0·7	5·1	3·6	56·1	62·1
Secondary School (technical and professional)	11·5	18·2	10·0	9·7	14·6	9·5	49·7	55·3

In Belgium there are two language communities, the Flemish and the French. As a result, there are schools in which the language of teaching is Flemish (in Flanders) and others in which it is French (in Wallonia).

Compulsory education lasts until the age of 14 and begins on September 1 of the year of the child's sixth birthday, when he starts the first year of primary school. However, many children, (98 per cent of all five-year-olds) attend infant school.

The pupils remain at primary school for six years. At the age of

12 they proceed either to a general secondary school or to a technical and professional school. In the context of this article it is not necessary to investigate the differentiations within the secondary school system, which covers a six-year period, after which the pupils can go on to university or non-university higher education.

At present, a number of important changes are occurring in the school system. In various schools the so-called 'Renewed Secondary School' is being tested. As in most West European countries, Belgium is seeking an evolution towards the so-called 'Comprehensive School'. In addition a number of reforms for primary schooling are in preparation. These changes inevitably have an effect on teachers, with the result that there is an enormous interest in the reform of teacher training and of in-service education. They have also led to a somewhat different conception of the curriculum. This last change will be discussed below.

General characteristics of Belgian curricula
1. *The curricula before 1970*
   a. *Curricula directed towards subject-matter.* In Belgium, the term 'curriculum' means 'a well-ordered description of content', i.e. the subject-matter to be taught to the various classes. For both primary and secondary schools a catalogue is given, per class, of the content which should be taught. Thus, Belgian curricula should be understood in a very traditional and rather narrow sense.

This implies that the description of the content to be taught is based on the internal structure of a certain subject or science. For strictly sequential subjects such as mathematics, this may be an appropriate and necessary method, but for non-sequential subjects such as geography or biology, this extreme orientation towards the inner logic of the subject may rightly be questioned.

Such an overemphasis on subject-matter is, it may be argued, the result of insufficient consideration of one of the essential relationships in didactics, i.e. that between objectives and content. So far, Belgian curricula have given insufficient consideration to the fact that content is determined by *a priori* established objectives.

However, this should not lead to the conclusion that curricula in Belgium do not have any aims at all. In the general introduction to the entire curriculum for each school level as well as in the introduction to each separate subject, these aims are defined, but this is done in a relatively general manner, so that the users of the curriculum, the teachers, are not able to establish a clear relationship between objectives and subsequent content. In other words, the fact that the objectives are defined at a highly abstract level causes the teachers to be ignorant of the exact behaviour which the pupils should be able to perform after having taken the course. This, of course, leaves ample scope for fairly individual and diverse interpretations.

b. Curricula as a guide to teaching. The foregoing paragraphs probably create a rather negative impression. However, if curriculum is defined as a 'well-ordered description of the subject-matter to be taught', the Belgian curricula provide a valuable guide to the teaching method to be adopted. It is considered that in primary as well as secondary schools the curricula actually influence teaching methods to a very high degree. Every teacher is relatively well-informed about the contents of the curricula. This means that primary school teachers are acquainted with the contents of the various subjects which they must teach in their classes. Secondary school teachers are familiar with the curricula relative to their subject or speciality. In fact, teacher training devotes much attention to the various curricula. Every teacher is confronted and becomes familiar with the existing curricula.

The very considerable influence of the curricula may also be seen in the fact that a textbook for classroom use is considered of greatest value when it is an accurate reflection and further development of the subject matter listed in the curricula. In other words, the content of the curriculum and the manner in which it is treated are the principal criteria for the evaluation of a textbook.

The influence of existing curricula should of course be seen in relation to the highly centralized character of Belgian school policy. The above-mentioned organizing authorities maintain a central framework for the various curricula (see section B, below) in order to ensure a certain uniformity in what is taught. Thus, for example, the curricula for primary schools are edited by the Ministry of National Education, and teachers in State primary schools are expected more or less to conform to this curriculum. The same is true for the curricula of the Catholic primary schools, which are also distributed to the teachers from a central source by the Central Council of Catholic Primary Schools.

The pros and cons, the advantages and disadvantages of such centralization are not a point at issue here. What matters is that there is an effort to ensure a certain uniformity in what is taught in schools by means of centrally-designed curricula, and that this is a traditional element in the Belgian school policy.

However, it would be wrong to identify this pressure for centralized curricula with a *dirigiste* one. In practice there is divergence from the official curricula. The actual elaboration of the curricula in the various textbooks, which the teachers are relatively free to choose, the teachers' individual interpretations of the curriculum, the decisions of a team of teachers in a certain school, the effects of contacts with the inspectors, the propositions of the directorate, the publication of criticism on the curricula[1], etc., are all factors preventing a strict *dirigisme*. It is clear that there is room for a flexible approach to the proposed subject-matter[2].

c. The curricula of Belgian schools are relatively diversified. A comparison of the various curricula shows that there are clear differences, in both quality and elaboration, which are primarily related to the differentiation and specification of objectives, the more or less structured description of content, and the number of concrete examples provided to guide teaching. These and other factors finally determine the differences in the quality of the curricula—differences which are not always desirable and lie in the manner in which the curricula are constructed. Their quality is, for the most part, dependent on the committee which is set up *ad hoc* in order to construct the curriculum concerned.

It is often maintained that this diversity should be considered a positive feature. However, some doubt should be entertained as to whether, due to the strong influence of the curricula on what is taught, the differences in the quality of curricula do not lead to differences in the quality of teaching. There are no data available concerning the exact relationship between the curriculum prescribed and what is taught, its quality and character, so one may only speculate on the relationship.

d. Timing. For a long time it was common for the whole curriculum for primary schools to be changed at one time. This happened last in 1958. Now the procedure is different: change takes place for each separate subject and the changes are published at different times. This has the advantage that changes are undertaken more easily, confined as they are to a small part of the curriculum. And teachers are able gradually to accommodate their teaching to the desired changes. However, when the curriculum of primary schools is modified piecemeal, there is the risk that the general purpose which it serves may be overlooked. A further danger is that for a time teachers may devote too much attention to the subject which was most recently modified to the detriment of other subjects of the curriculum.

---

[1] In various journals which the teachers regularly consult, the existing and newly published curricula are discussed, often quite amply. Usually this is done from personal experience, anecdotally by the teachers, and does not represent a systematic evaluation of the proposed curricula.

[2] On the other hand, it is observed that many teachers use the curriculum as an alibi for concerning themselves with proposed reforms. This is shown by such statements as: 'If we regularly split our class in groups, we can't get through the curriculum'.

2. The curricula after 1970

Together with the structural reforms which, from the school year 1970–71 became effective in the State schools, various curricula were drastically reformed[1]. Although these changes mainly applied to the content of courses it is striking that new procedures of curriculum construction were sought.

The reform of curricula was related primarily to the considerable changes in the basic aims of secondary schooling: the change from a sharply selective school structure to a more comprehensive structure. Such changes called for efforts to adapt old curricula to new purposes. In the first year of the new secondary schools the emphasis is on giving the pupil a gradual orientation in a field of study by providing him, on the basis of sufficient information, with careful and systematic experience of subject matter. Both the method of learning and its outcome for the pupil critically affect the form of curricula that is appropriate. An exclusive use of subject matter which is a complete, logical elaboration of the subject would be inappropriate. Teaching should rather start with exemplary elements of a speciality, which will adequately illustrate its specific ways of thinking and its methodology.[2]

By means of numerous publications, formally organized meetings, informal contacts, the establishment of special committees, and so on, attempts were made to integrate the new curricula into the repertoire of teachers. How successful these and the introduction of new curricula have been it is not yet possible to say, nor may it be because the construction, introduction and evaluation of curricula are done in much too unsystematic a manner. This does not imply that the curricula are worthless, but they may be still too strongly committed to traditional procedures. The greatest deficiency is that there are no systematic evaluation data available which could form the basis for a future, more deliberated reconstruction of curricula[3].

[1]   These structural reforms only applied to secondary schools; in Belgium the school years start on September 1 and end on June 30 of the following year.

[2]   In the framework of this article we cannot discuss all aspects of these structural reforms. A more detailed description can be found in C. C. DE KEYSER, (1969) 'Nadenken over de structuren van het secundair onderwijs'. ('Reflections on the structure of secondary schools'). *Gids op maatschappelijk gebied*, 60, 555–8.

[3]   A critical reflection on this matter can be found in W. DECONINCK (1971), 'Het nieuw biologieleerplan in de observatiecyclus van het Vernieuwd Secundair Onderwijs' (The new biology curriculum in the observation grade of the Renewed Secondary School). *Tijdschrift Belg. Nationale Vereniging der Leraren in de Biologie*, 17, 175–88.
C. C. DE KEYSER (1973) 'Het Belgisch secundair onderwijs op een beslissend keerpunt. Van hiërarchische over multilaterale naar comprehensieve structuren',(From hierarchic and multilateral to comprehensive structures) *Pedag. Forum*, 7, 4–38.

B. The style of curriculum development

1. *Participants in the process*

The general procedure of curriculum construction for both primary and secondary schools, and who is involved in this process, are described below.

The organizing authority sets up an *ad hoc* committee which is asked to modify the existing curriculum or, as was the case recently, to construct a new one. Since these curricula deal with separate subjects, the committee consists chiefly of subject experts, usually inspectors and experienced teachers who have taught or supervised the subject for a long time. The chairman of the committee will more than likely be an inspector.

The committee procedure for the construction or modification of a curriculum undoubtedly has a number of advantages. The curriculum committee usually consists of persons who are in close contact with current practices in the schools, and who clearly know which ideas are in vogue and, therefore, to what extent they may propose certain changes. This again reveals the central role of the inspectorate in the Belgian school system. A second advantage consists of the manner in which the modified curriculum is presented. The members of the committee know what language to use in order to influence the teachers, and in their role as inspectors, are able to observe how the new or modified curriculum is realized and what specific difficulties occur. However, it should be emphasized that this is a personal view, though one which is not entirely without foundation.

This method of construction and modification of curricula on the basis of *ad hoc* committee also has a number of disadvantages. There is no question here of curriculum development in the technical sense; no specification of objectives and the selection of appropriate subject matter to meet them; no pilot testing of new curricula, nor any summative and formative evaluation, nor other essential aspects of modern curriculum development. Such cannot be found in the way in which a committee goes about its task.

In addition, many teachers are not involved at all in the construction of curricula. The changes to existing curricula and their final shape are decided by the appointed committee. On the other hand, it should be emphasized that teachers and the methods which they have developed have a certain influence on the modification of curricula. It often happens that the decision to modify a curriculum is taken at a moment when new approaches to teaching are gaining currency. In other words, one of the functions of a new curriculum is officially to confirm and so legitimize what has already gained a hold in the classroom. However, this does not mean that there is always a confirmation of innovations which are already in general use. The development of new curricula, while it may accept innovations already being practiced, is more concerned with the implementation of central policy.

In addition to accepting changes in practice already established in the schools, it would, however, seem necessary in the future to consider the possibilities of more direct participation by teachers in the process of curriculum reform and development. This will only be possible when Belgium has created an appropriate infrastructure for the closer involvement of the teachers concerned in curriculum reform.

Not only does Belgium need to develop means for bringing teachers more closely into the process of curriculum change but it would also be desirable to develop permanent means for bringing more scientific procedures to bear on the process.

2. *Nature of the decisions taken*

It has already been indicated that Belgian curricula primarily describe subject-matter. As a result, the principal decisions which are taken by all curriculum committees chiefly concern the selection of content. The main question is what knowledge from existing disciplines and fields of study qualifies for inclusion or what should be taught in a particular subject. Indirectly what may be called the 'educational value' of the subject matter and its possible transfer potential are also discussed but usually not as a matter of primary importance.

A second group of decisions deals with the distribution of the selected contents among the various classes in both primary and secondary schools. This means that the committee tries to find the optimal sequencing of subject matter over the various classes. Since classes in the Belgian school system are closely related to age, it can also be said that the committee is looking for a distribution of the subject matter selected *a priori* to the various age groups. In this, some consideration of developmental psychology is involved, though rarely explicitly.

3. *Means of implementation*

In order to present the new or modified curricula to teachers and to introduce the curricula into what the schools teach, a variety of means are used.

For the primary schools it is customary to publish so-called 'appendices' in which the curriculum is presented in considerable

detail. Such 'appendices' often make comparisons with the former
editions of the curriculum, give directions concerning how the
curriculum is to be translated into work in the classroom and indicate
possibilities for the evaluation of the results of the work done. Most
also contain references to additional reading. The curriculum
committee expects the individual teacher, on the basis of this
suggested literature, to examine and assess the curriculum quite
thoroughly.

The 'appendices' are often the result of the yearly action of the
inspectorate. The organizing authorities instruct their inspectors
to aim their activities, their visits, conferences and pedagogic work,
in any one school year specifically at one particular curriculum. A
report of the results of the inspectors' acitivities is then included in
the 'appendix' to the curriculum.

Immediately before and after publication, the curricula are
frequently and elaborately described and commented upon in the
journals which are taken by most teachers. To what extent these
articles are actually read and how much this affects the teachers'
classroom practice, are two important questions to which no reliable
answers are available. There is, however, evidence to suggest that
teachers do not read very widely[1]; rather they read slectively, and
primarily about what they already know. Even so it is likely that
these articles do actually meet the demand for information on the
part of the teachers.

Another important means for presenting the new curricula are the
so-called 'pedagogic conferences' conducted by an inspector. Primary
school teachers are obliged to attend these conferences once or twice
a school year. Teachers from various schools of the same region
gather for a whole day and can use this opportunity, for example,
to examine the practical implications of the new curriculum. It is
also possible during these conferences for other topics to be discussed
and in this way general issues to be raised.

For secondary school teachers, the situation is somewhat different.
Systematically organized conferences do not take place, though some
inspectors take individual initiatives but there is no obligation laid
on secondary school teachers to attend these meetings.

So far, the value of the pedagogic conferences has not been
thoroughly examined. Some research has shown that the teachers do
not have a very favourable opinion of these conferences and seriously

---

[1] R. VANDENBERGHE, Wetenschappelijke begeleiding van de onderwijs-
vernieuwing. *Tijdschrift Opvoedkunde*, 1967–68, 13, 257–9.

doubt their effectiveness.¹ They also feel that they provide insufficient opportunities for in-service education.² Nevertheless, some authorities consider that they are a very efficient means in the framework of continuous school reform.

Every year, during the Easter holidays, the Minister of National Education organizes a pedagogic week. This is a very valuable opportunity to present and discuss new curricula and possibly to demonstrate certain parts of them in operation. The pedagogic weeks are presided over by a number of inspectors and teachers are not obliged to attend the meetings. Although general themes can be dealt with during the week, it is noteworthy that usually one curriculum or other is thoroughly discussed. There is no such opportunity for secondary school teachers.

In addition to the official meetings of pedagogic conferences and organized weeks, many inspectors and local or national teachers' organizations take certain initiatives with respect to in-service education of teachers. In these informal meetings, attention is often focused on the new or modified curricula. Provisional and unsystematic observation has shown that these local and regional meetings can have a great effect. As such, they are important means of implementation and realization of the curricula.

Finally, a very important means provided by the Belgian school system is the opportunity which inspectors have to introduce new curricula during their visits to schools. Unfortunately, one can only speak of 'opportunities' since little is known about the actual effect of these visits. This is a large issue and research has yet to be developed to illuminate it. What is the inspectors' concept of their function, what do teachers expect from them, how do they experience the inspector's action, do they consider them supervisors or advisors? These and other questions are very relevant to the curriculum reform movement.

Clearly the Belgian school system has at its disposal a variety of means for implementing the curricula. However, it is a source of concern that very few research results are available which enable

R. Vandenberghe and S. Janssen, De houding van leerkrachten uit het Lager Onderwijs tegenover de onderwijsverandering, (Primary school teachers' attitude towards school reform), *Tijdschr. Opvoedk.*, 1971–72, 209–231.

P. Vermeulen (1973) 'Bijscholing van leerkrachten uit het Lager Onderwijs. Een exploratie-onderzoek naar verlangens en wensen bij de leerkrachten uit het Lager Onderwijs in verband met organisatie vormgeving en inhoud van de bijscholing'. (In-service education of primary school teachers. An explorative investigation into desires and wishes of primary school teachers with respect to the organization, shape, and contents of in-service education). Univ. Leuven, unpublished licenciate dissertation, p. 96 ff.

one to obtain an insight into the validity and effectiveness of these means. Increasingly, hopes are being expressed suggesting that there is a desire for certain changes in traditional procedures and that thought be given to forms of assistance more appropriate to the contemporary educational scene. It is therefore highly desirable that information from research studies should be available to make possible more rational decisions.

C. Conclusions and future perspectives

It is obvious that the curriculum, narrowly defined as content or subject matter, plays an important role in the Belgian school system, and school reform is primarily, if not invariably, considered in terms of new curricula. But the narrow definition is clearly an inhibiting factor. In the current international literature curricula are understood in a much wider sense to include considerations of educational objectives, the construction of learning experiences and the evaluation of outcomes. In the near future, Belgium may well need to create a number of possibilities for curriculum development which adopt the more contemporary model. This will necessitate the education, at both the initial and the in-service stages, of teachers in the use of this model, and it would be desirable for a number of research projects to be started which exemplify the process of curriculum development suggested by the model.[1]

However, in spite of many deficiencies, much interesting work is already being undertaken though a more systematic approach to curriculum development and evaluation is becoming necessary especially as the wider view of curriculum is becoming understood.

[1] A good start is made by the project 'Menswetenschappen' (Human Sciences) which is conducted under the supervision of Prof. C. C. De Keyser at the Institute for Pedagogic Sciences of the Catholic University of Leuven.

CHAPTER 3

Curriculum Development in Canada

John Herbert and Naomi Hersom

Introduction

Curricula can only be understood as part of the society in which they originate. Canadian conditions, particularly its regionalism and pluralism, are not widely understood outside Canada. Before looking at curriculum development from the official and the student perspective and making some predictions for the future, we will describe the combination of geographic, economic, political, and social patterns which form the unique Candian environment which curricula in Canada reflect.

The national setting

Canadian society is shaped by the country's size, the geographic features which divide it into vast regions with different economic interests, its political structure, its cultural diversity and policy, and the distribution and composition of its population.

Canada is the second largest country in the world. St. John is 1735 miles east, and Vancouver 2865 miles west, of Ottawa, the nation's capital. Most of the population of about 21 million live in separate, densely populated centres along the southern border, the rest are spread out thinly over the 500-mile wide band north of this area. This distribution of population hinders national cohesion. School administrators, school board trustees, teachers, and curriculum developers rarely meet or exchange ideas with their peers from across the country; sometimes they are even inaccessible to their own provincial services. Communication is often easier North-South than East-West. Many Canadian curriculum developers can more easily attend professional meetings in the United States and publish in American, rather than Canadian, journals. This has delayed the development of indigenous curriculum organizations and made the exchange of intra-national information difficult. When collecting up-to-date information for this chapter we kept hearing from our informants across the country that they did not know, or were unsure, about what was happening in the next province, or even a few hundred miles away in their own province[1].

There are other reasons for this lack of communication. Vast areas such as the northern Territories, the Prairies, the Maritime Provinces, and the areas west of the Rocky Mountains, each the size of a large country, are separated from other regions of Canada by great natural barriers, by differences in their climate, resources and wealth, and by occupational and economic interests. Forestry, mining, the growing of wheat or fruit, fisheries, manufacturing, banking, and business tend to be specific to regions whose citizens identify with the needs of their local industry. Contrasting regional views of laws, tariffs, freight rates, ecological measures, and taxes accentuate differences. In some areas, Canada is an industrial nation; in others it is underdeveloped, though literate. Prime Minister Elliot Trudeau has compared it to a dinosaur—messages from the tail take so long to reach the centre, it cannot respond quickly to problems. The Canadian solution, at least for internal affairs, is regionalism. Citizens from each region tend to be more concerned with curricula to suit their local needs than with ensuring similarity across the nation.

Geographic factors are not the only divisive forces. The political structure subdivides each of these regions and so adds to the differences. There are 10 Provinces and two Territories, set up by the British North America Act, the Constitution of Canada. Each of the 10 provinces has a premier and a cabinet on the parliamentary model. As a result, provinces may differ in their official language, income and sales taxes, police forces, political parties, and in almost every way in which one parliamentary country can differ from another.

The administrative structure for education reflects the geographic, economic, and political divisions. Each province has a Minister of Education: 10 ministers of Education for a population smaller than that of Belgium and the Netherlands combined! Each Minister has complete legal power and responsibility for education, and a ministerial staff formulating curricula and regulations. Some provinces do, and others do not, have policies of decentralization, making the structure even more complex.

The length of schooling, the influence of the church, the substantive content of curricula and the rigour with which they are prescribed, the resources available, the examination system, the extent of community participation in decision making, and the power and influence of students and teachers are but some of the educational characteristics which differ among provinces.

[1] Antoinette Oberg and Eric Hillis of the University of Alberta and Anne Johnston of the University of Toronto assisted in the collection of information.

Since Ministers of Education are politicians elected every four years or so, they tend to be highly sensitive to the need for reflecting public opinion, and are not adverse to being seen as innovators and effective administrators. This has tended recently to produce rapid official changes in some provinces. But since four years is not long enough to develop, implement, and test major curricular or administrative changes, these have not always been reflected in the schools. Civil servants and teachers have sometimes been left behind or have quietly resisted changes, so that the rate of implementation in the schools has deviated to an unpredictable extent from official policy.

Because universities, colleges, professional schools, and other institutions of higher learning, as well as museums and educational television and radio stations, are provincially financed and administrated, they also differ in many respects from province to province.

Unlike the United States, curriculum development in Canada has not undergone 'nationalization' by the establishment of institutes or national curriculum projects. The federal government in Canada has no curriculum development function, moreover the provinces are opposed to the extension of federal power, though the Canadian Teachers' Federation is pressing for a national Office of Education (CEA, 1973).

Institutes which assume curriculum development responsibilities, such as the Atlantic Institute in Halifax, the Institute of Research in Education in Quebec, or the Ontario Institute for Studies in Education in Toronto, are all financed through the provincial Ministries of Education and were established to serve provincial goals.

The functions of these Institutes differ greatly, but each works with a faculty of Education to provide graduate students and assistants interested in teaching, research, development and administration with experience and training in curriculum work. These graduates are in demand in schools where they may influence curriculum development. A wide range of research and development projects selected by review boards as being of interest in their province are undertaken. The Ontario Institute for Studies in Education, for example, has major curriculum projects aimed at developing thinking skills in elementary school children, bilingual education, Canadian studies, and the discussion of public issues. Smaller projects include the construction of informal mathematics textbooks, projects designed to develop and test approaches to the teaching of morality, a collection of miscellaneous materials to stimulate pupil interest in history, called 'Ten Years in a Box', and a study of teaching techniques used in regular and special classes. (Office of Co-ordinator, 1972.) Similar work is in progress in the

Universities of British Columbia and Alberta and elsewhere.

Perhaps one of the most interesting features of Canada, and one which is becoming increasingly important, is the diversity of cultural and linguistic allegiances. There are multitudes of cultural groups, recognized and to some extent, catered for. Thus, from one random page of a current programme announcement by the Canadian Broadcasting Corporation, which has both French and English television and radio stations, one sees programmes called 'Black/White Adoptions', 'Stephen Worobetz: Ukrainian-Canadian Lieutenant-General', 'Japanese Buddhists in Winnipeg . . . and Friends', 'How to plan a cosmopolitan city?' a programme about southern European immigrants and Chinese communities in Toronto, Montreal, and Vancouver—'Ethnic Games', 'Arranged Marriages'—about Arab Canadians—and programmes featuring Estonian, Jewish, Czech, and French cultural phenomena (CBC, 1973). Two of the minority groups, the Quebecois and the Canadian Indians, are increasingly determined to preserve independence as nations and can claim treaty and constitutional rights to support their positions. Some curriculum materials already exist for the Dogrib, Chippewyan, and Eskimo peoples and for a number of other groups (Robinson, 1973).

Though the settings and forces have made for diversity, there are reasons why students are not entirely lost when moving from school to school and region to region. All Canadian curricula are in the European tradition and arrived here directly or through the United States. The variations are no greater, and usually less, than those a student might meet moving from country to country. Students are all subject to those cultural influences which cross regional and national boundaries, including powerful media and the frequently overpowering Canadian and American commercial enterprises. Regardless of policy, teachers tend to use similar methods in schools across the country and often use the same or similar textbooks and curriculum materials. The situation is more difficult, of course, for students from those cultural communities which are almost totally unassimilated, such as pockets of Portuguese, Indians, Eskimos, and Orientals in various parts of the country.

Recently, efforts have been made to improve communication. The published documents from commisions and curriculum committees have become more readable and attractive and are widely circulated. The Canadian Education Association has, for many years, held annual meetings at which officials meet and exhange ideas. Lately there has been a great rise of interest in Canadian nationalism (Milbeth and Herbert, 1973). In 1967, a Council of Ministers was initiated and Education Ministers from each province now meet

annually. Curriculum is discussed at these meetings though, unfortunately, nothing is made public. The provincial curriculum
directors of some of the regions also hold joint meetings. In 1972 a
national curriculum group was formed, the Curriculum Association
of Canada, with the purpose of fostering communication and co-
operation among all interested in curriculum. The Association is
now part of the newly formed Canadian Society for the Study of
Education and has already sponsored programmes at which curriculum workers from several provinces exchanged ideas.

It is greatly to the credit of the teachers that there also are active
provincial curriculum organizations which hold annual meetings.
In some provinces classroom teachers have taken the lead in
establishing curriculum institutes (Vokey, 1973), providing in-service
training and publishing curriculum pamphlets and influential reports.
These are local initiatives, and though they do not reduce differences
between provinces, they do aid communication.

The Canadian Studies Foundation, a new national body, funds
projects proposed by local groups across the nation. It is attempting
to combine regional autonomy and local teacher initiative with a
central, national support and communication system. If they succeed
in retaining these apparently conflicting advantages in their
curriculum development projects, this foundation should become a
valuable model for similar bodies (Tomkins, 1973; Miller, 1973;
Sabey, 1971).

Diversity of context, conditions of life, in cultural style, in
aspiration, of resources, physical, human and educational all make
for the complexity with which curriculum development in Canada
must come to terms.

Curriculum development

As may be expected, definitions of curriculum vary from province
to province, from those which confine it to documents prescribing
substantive knowledge to be taught to those which include all
educative experiences in the life of the child. Curriculum development is seen by some to be the exclusive prerogative of the Ministry,
by others as the duty of the teacher. Most positions lie somewhere
between.

Structure and policies

Curriculum development is not usually regarded as the unique
responsibility of any particular group of people. Each level of the
educational system assumes some function, though roles differ. The
provincial Ministries have had the greater influence on curriculum
thus far. As the elected representatives of all the citizens of the

province, the Minister has the ultimate legal, political, and economic power over the public schools and over many other educational agencies (in the Northwest Territories and the Yukon, these responsibilities are carried by the Superintendents of Instruction under the auspices of the Federal Government).

Within each provincial jurisdiction there is a Director of Curriculum, a civil servant, with a staff which forms the Curriculum Branch. The titles and duties vary somewhat from province to province. Amongst other duties, this branch is instrumental in establishing curriculum committees whose members include trustees, school district administrators, representatives from teachers' organizations and, of course, staff members from the Ministry. These curriculum committees produce Programmes of Studies under the direction or with the assistance of the Curriculum Director's staff. Such documents are usually developed according to a linear model: the overall philosophy is identified, concept and skill objectives are defined, and suggested content and instructional strategies may be added (Naylor, 1971). First drafts are field tested, evaluated, and revised before they are submitted for authorization and dissemination throughout the province. In final form, they usually consist of statements of agreed goals, concepts, and skills. They suggest, and, at times may almost prescribe, what to teach. They are legally binding and cannot be modified or changed without the approval of the Minister. They may be accompanied by teacher's guides or handbooks containing lists of approved or recommended texts and suggested resources.

The Minister also from time to time establishes Provincial Commissions. Though these are only advisory, they sometimes are the most exciting and far-reaching instruments of curricular reform in Canada. For example, the Royal Commission of Inquiry on the Organization and Finance of Education in the Province of Quebec, established in 1961 under the leadership of the Right Reverend Alphonse-Marie Parent, P.A., provided a blueprint for a revolution in the structure and responsibility for education in that province (Parent, 1963–65). The 'Parent Commission' recommended the appointment of a Minister of Education with a seat in the Provincial Cabinet. Where the powerful Roman Catholic and Protestant committees had previously been responsible for school government and inspection each in their own school systems, these responsibilities would now be assumed by a secular curriculum service, part of the Division of Instruction.

The powerful impact of Commissions on curricular reform is further exemplified by the Provincial Commission on Aims and Objectives of Education in the Schools of Ontario, the 'Hall-Dennis

Commission' (Provincial, 1968). Their report, *Living and Learning*, located the responsibility for curriculum decision-making at the school board and individual school level. It assigned the responsibility for detailed curricular programming to the teachers in the schools. This marked a drastic change from the central Ministry control, implemented by inspectors, that was previously in force. The Worth Commission Report on Educational Planning contains far reaching recommendations for change in educational philosophy (Alberta, 1973). The Commission presents the case for granting all citizens the right to recurrent education to enable them to participate in the reshaping of their environment and society.

In addition to official influence, curriculum development activities derive input from other sources. In many provinces, from British Columbia to New Brunswick, strongly organized provincial teachers' groups have their own curriculum staff and committees or groups of teachers interested in developing and revising curricula (Church, 1966; New Brunswick, 1973). Their influence on curricula is exerted through briefs and position statements, through published documents such as curriculum units or guides, and through their respresentation on Ministry Curriculum Committees. In some provinces, such as Quebec, the powerful unions appoint their own representatives while in Prince Edward Island, the Ministry controls appointments to these committees (Murphy, 1973). Lay advisory committees may be appointed by the Ministry. Provincial pressure groups of organized parents and politically strong citizens may also affect the curricula. Administrators and supervisors influence the curriculum in their domains.

All provinces, in their official utterances, grant some curriculum functions to the individual classroom teacher. He has some freedom to define specific objectives, select content, and decide on teaching strategies and instructional materials, as long as these are consonant with provincial policy. How much teachers actually use this auto-nomy depends on the prescriptiveness with which this policy is administered by the Ministry staff, on the support teachers get from their administrators and professional associations, and on their own interpretation of the teacher's role in curriculum development (Friesen, 1973; Nason, 1971).

The provinces

How do these structures work in particular provinces? After ranging broadly across the nation we have selected two provinces for a close look, though unfortunately at the cost of neglecting equally interesting developments elsewhere.

Quebec has experienced a movement towards centralization and provincial control of education. The Minster defines the educational objectives, authorizes programmes, identifies the educational disciplines, and determines the distribution of time amongst these disciplines (Quebec Government, 1971). Though the teachers are officially responsible for determining the curriculum of their pupils, they are guided by the Plan D'Étude, or syllabus, for each subject (Index). These syllabuses contain topics and guidelines for teaching, the textbooks and materials which may be used, and other instructions to the teachers. The Plans D'Etude are developed by the Direction Générale de l'Enseignement Élémentaire et Secondaire and officials of the Ministère de l'Education working in co-operation with representatives from regional boards, teachers' unions, and other participants (Quebec Government, 1970, 1971).

School boards in Quebec tend to be divided into those for Catholic Francophone and Protestant Anglophone students though there are important exceptions, especially in Montreal. 'Protestant' is a synonym for non-Catholic and includes agnostics, Muslims and Jews. Organized religions no longer have tight control of the curriculum, though some of the teachers in Catholic schools are still clericals, and daily catechism classes are usual. The eight-year college classique with a church-determined programme with no options and compulsory religious 'metaphysics', which led to a degree from the university to which the school was affiliated, has disappeared. After elementary school the student now goes to a comprehensive high school until grade 11, then to a community collège, always referred to as 'CEGEP' (never as Collège d'Enseignement Général et Professionnel, or College of General and Vocational Education), equivalent to grades 12 and 13 in the other provinces. CEGEP curricula are now developed in ways very similar to those of high schools and include a three-year terminal technical, as well as the two-year academic preparatory programme. To facilitate curriculum development and dissemination, the Ministry has appointed Educational Development Officers to help with the implementation of new programmes and their adaptation to local conditions, and in helping to assist local school boards to develop curriculum aids and research (Official Bulletin, 1971).

There are changes still to come in Quebec, according to high Ministry officials. The Ministry is engaged in a serious examination of objectives and curriculum development procedures. For example, the behavioural objectives approach was considered and rejected as too prescriptive. Schools are to become one agency among many which serve youth and must select and limit their goals, yet their focus will be social and emotional as well as intellectual. Schools must learn to change as rapidly as society and must, perhaps, look elsewhere, outside the formal educational structure, for programmes and personnel to help.

In the province of Ontario according to official policy, curriculum includes everything educative that happens to the child. This view became firmly established after the publication of the Hall-Dennis Report. Its definition of curriculum as 'all those activities in which children are engaged under the auspices of the school' (p. 75) is broadly interpreted (Crossley, 1973; OTF, 1973). As Kelvin Crossley, the Director of the Curriculum Development Branch of the Ministry of Education, Ontario, points out, even regulations about the student's right to walk the school corridors may help or hinder him in using the library or a resource centre. Such regulations are considered as much a part of the curriculum as the subject matter topics. The Ministry's definition of curriculum therefore includes the 'hidden' curriculum both in and out of school. A force regarded with particular concern here is the impact of the mass media from both Canada and the USA, which may well suppress the effects of the formal school curriculum.

Since 1971, curriculum development in Ontario has followed a cyclical pattern. Curriculum guides are to be revised continuously in six-year cycles: one year of soliciting and collecting input, one year of preparation of materials, and four years of implementation. The new materials will represent a key change in curriculum philosophy in this province. They will no longer cater primarily to the 16–18 per cent who continue through grade 13 and enter university, but will consider the whole range of possible consumers, the gifted and the retarded, those with manual, and those with academic, aspirations.

The function of the high school is seen as transitional or preparatory. As students mature, they are to be held increasingly responsible for their educational choices, and decreasingly protected from the consequences—another key change in curriculum philosophy, and a potential source of controversy.

Increased student responsibility is accompanied by increased teacher responsibility, particularly in curriculum development. At the same time, the official policy of equal education for all results in curriculum guides for the teachers which must relate to broader areas of philosophy and subject matter and which must consider student interest and overall programme retention power. Many teachers have felt that the guides are too general but opinions are divided between those teachers who would prefer more structure and those who would prefer to construct their own curricula.

The official stance in Ontario, then, seems to be one of increasing decentralization. School boards have increasing power to establish priorities within broad provincial policies. However, since the Ministry keeps tight budgetary rein on the total expenditure, cynics have described the policy as one of decentralization of responsibility with centralization of control.

Students' perspective

While the provincial Ministry wields the official power over the curriculum, the student and his family have lately achieved much greater control. Citizens in some areas have succeeded in establishing publicly and privately financed alternative schools with curricula of their choice. Some have 'voted with their feet', by moving, or changing the student's official address, to areas where school boards have the type of programme they prefer. In some areas school attendance boundaries have been entirely abolished. A case will illustrate this development.

Anne decided to enrol in an alternative school founded by some high school students but now administered by the local school board and to leave the 'square' high school administered by the same school board. She studies English, Greek, and biology. One of the regular teachers attached to the school offers classes in English language and literature to those students who are interested. For biology Anne is working individually with a teacher, and for Greek she goes for a regular weekly tutorial with a fellow student to a 'catalyst', Dr Mac Wallace, a distinguished professor of Greek. Catalysts are people from many professions who are persuaded by interested students to supervise their work. As a result of this system, the curriculum changes from month to month, as an advertising manager offers a course in advertising, or a programmer agrees to supervise students who want to work with computers, or as one or more of the students initiate or abandon other projects.

Students in alternative schools are not usually classified into grade levels, but receive high school credit on the recommendation of their teachers and catalysts when they have completed work at a particular level. Anne is unusual in that she expects to get credits for each of her subjects: grade 12 credit in English, grades 11 and 13 credit in science, and grade 11 credit in Greek. However, her real interest is in needlework. She spends much time learning to embroider, to spin and dye yarn, and in related artistic pursuits. She hopes to go to a craft school, but has not attempted to get credit in 'art' for this work, though this might have been possible. In Ontario a high school credit is defined as 'the amount of work that would normally be done in 110 to 120 hours of scheduled time'.

Alternative schools are still rare, but are on the increase in several provinces (Directory, 1973). Most students go to more conventional schools. If Anne returned to a regular high school she would have to attend many more classes, and since she is of university-entrance calibre, she would be under pressure from teachers, guidance workers and administrators to take such subjects as English literature, mathematics, French, history, geography, science, and physical education. In most provinces she could only take subjects offered by the school. In Ontario, only two credits in music out of the 27 high school credits needed for a diploma can be taken out of school. In Alberta, however, she could take from other agencies up to 52 credits out of the 100 credits needed for graduation. The actual number and diversity of her electives and options would also depend on the size of the school, the administrative policy, her grade level, and even the beliefs of individual guidance counsellors, teachers, and principals (Sharp, 1973). In a regular high school she would certainly have much less time to work at her primary interest, though probably she would take a broader range of subjects and might have a choice of technical subjects such as typing, home economics or even 'technical literacy' courses. She would also feel under pressure to conform to the social and athletic interests of her peers. Her courses would be taught much more formally, in classes averaging 20 to 30 students in size. The curriculum would have to conform more closely to that approved by the Ministry, though this is being interpreted more liberally now.

If she went to school in Quebec, as an English-speaking 'Protestant', she would probably attend an English-speaking comprehensive high school. In all areas where there is a sufficiently large Anglophone community, there are Francophone Catholic and Anglophone Protestant Schools. She might be in grade 11, the last year of high school, or she might go to the first year of the two-year university preparatory programme of the local CEGEP. The three-year programme is a terminal programme for technical students. In either case the curriculum would have been developed under the auspices of the provincial Ministry, by the same procedures, through different committees.

In both provinces there are school districts administered by the secular school boards and 'separate' or 'confessional' schools administered by the Roman Catholic Church. The locations of these districts usually overlap, and their differences in curricula and teaching techniques might make a valuable study. To our knowledge no such information is at present available.

Trends

Five important areas of change in curriculum can be identified in today's Canada: provincial policies, organized research and develop-

ment, the cultural impetus, roles and rights of teachers and students
and changes in the communication network.

The official provincial policies are likely to remain the most
powerful determinants of trends in school curricula in Canada. There
can be no doubt of the direction these have taken over the last decade.
Incongruously, often by Ministerial edict, the trend has been towards
shared responsibility, less prescriptive curriculum guides, and towards
equal education for all in publicly financed schools. This trend has
not yet resulted in equal financial support for elementary and high
school students, though there may be some move towards such
equality. It has, however, resulted in the de-emphasizing of university-
bound streams and external examinations, the encouragement of
vocational and leisure-time options, and the authorization of courses
aimed at the needs of particular cultural and occupational groups.
Courses and curriculum materials offered for and by Indians,
Eskimos, Metis, and white cultural groups on their traditions,
customs, and skills may well increase greatly, both at elementary and
high school level (Renaud, 1971). They may in future be offered in a
number of native and minority languages in regions where there is
sufficient demand. When the alternative courses have proliferated,
this is likely to stimulate a reaction on the grounds that only a core
of work in the majority language can secure equality of opportunity
for these children.

Alternative schools, though few, are on the increase. Such schools
are likely to arise in urban areas, perhaps even here and there in
rural areas. In the cities, some alternatives may take the form of
schools within larger high schools, offering students and their parents
more choices. High school students in many regions may be expected
to take more responsibility for selecting and arranging their programmes, probably involving non-school agencies in their education.

Since Canada is a wealthy country with untapped human and
material resources, the current reductions in education budgets are
not likely to limit curricula permanently. No doubt some fluctuations
in the scope of the curriculum will take place, and school administrators will have to use their ingenuity to avoid sharp increases in
expenditure which a careless expansion of alternatives would bring.
Policy-makers will be harder pressed to balance the alternatives local
communities want against the protests of those who believe in
similar programmes for all. Much will depend on the media. Television and other mass media could magnify complaints, since they
are likely to be more newsworthy than successful diversification, and
so set off a destructive trend. In fairness to the Canadian broadcasters,
however, it should be observed that they have tended to be constructive towards the schools.

Organized research and development projects, as opposed to curriculum policy development, are much more localized and dominated by a few centres. If the historical trend runs true to form, Canadians will continue for a few years the tradition of adopting procedures developed for conditions abroad. We can expect the larger and wealthier of the provinces to support small versions of the competitive, heavily capitalized, packaged US curricula, though their success here may not be any more impressive than that reported elsewhere. Instead of the passé university discipline-oriented pattern, we may find that curricula will be based on one particular reasoning style such as inquiry, or on portions of psychological theory borrowed from Piaget, Skinner, or Ausubel. Projects with a more pupil-oriented approach may follow the United Kingdom pattern of teacher-developed curricula and the teacher centres, suitable for countries where teachers have a tradition of independence and are relatively knowledgeable about the origins and capability of their pupils.

After some early failures, it seems likely that Canadian curriculum developers will pay careful attention to the diversity of cultural, cognitive, and intellectual characteristics of their own students, and experiment on a small scale with matching curricula to particular types of students. The affective components may also get closer attention.

Provinces which are still mainly oriented towards formal curricula embodied in textbooks are likely to follow these trends thoughout the larger and wealthier ones, though at their own pace. Cultural and language diversity is likely to feature importantly in Canadian curricula. Since it is unlikely that teacher preparation institutions can produce teachers with the diversity of cultural knowledge and skills required, there may be more reliance on lay persons seconded part-time from other occupations. Teachers will then have to be prepared in the wise use of human resources in curriculum planning. Universities and colleges will prepare teachers of teachers in the new skills: the balancing of cosmopolitan and local loyalties, selection of teaching styles, the surveying of local needs and of lay personnel and student resources, and ways of incorporating these into a larger curricular framework.

Associated with these changes will be the curricular impact of the new student and teacher activism. Though this activism probably will not be as extreme in Canada as elsewhere—we expect neither Red Guards as in China, nor student revolutions as in France—there will be enough to stimulate questioning of current values and procedures. Uncomfortable as this may be, it will be helpful in reducing the impact of bureaucracies and careerism in teaching and academia and will support the decentralization of curriculum decision-making.

One of the most promising trends in Canada is the increase in communications among educators of different provinces and among teachers and university personnel. The Canadian Studies Foundation is at present the only national organization commissioning curricular research and publications. It may become the model for other interprovincial developments. Though provincial curriculum organizations have existed for some time, there is now a Curriculum Association of Canada. While Canadians have traditionally tended to look outside the country for leadership, curricula, and outlets for their articles and reports, this tendency is beginning to be moderated. The quality and quantity of publications in curriculum from Canada can be expected to increase in future, and if the new orientation does not become excessively parochial or production oriented, curriculum development in Canada and elsewhere will benefit. We hold this cheerful view, rare in recent educational writing, and are confidently expecting a lively future for curriculum development in Canada.

References

ALLABY, L. (1973). Report on Canada Studies. *Principals in Council.* The News-letter of the Principals' Council of the New Brunswick Teachers' Association, 11, (2), 4–5.

ALLESTER, W. V. (1971). 'Curriculum Planning and Implementation: A British Columbia Teachers' Federation Point of View.' An address to the B.C. Association of Supervisors of Instruction. Kelowna, B.C., November 11, 1971.

BERRY, G., FRIESEN, D., and HERSOM, N. (1971). *Curriculum development for classroom teachers.* Edmonton, Alberta: Alberta Teachers' Association.

CANADIAN BROADCASTING CORPORATION (1973). *Select.* Toronto: CBC.

CANADIAN EDUCATION ASSOCIATION (1973). 'CTF presents brief on federal office', *CEA Newsletter,* May-June, No. 265, p. 2.

CHURCH, J. S. (1966). *Curriculum Planning.* Vancouver: British Columbia Teachers' Federation.

COMMISSION ON EDUCATIONAL PLANNING (1972). *A Choice of Futures.* Edmonton: Report to the Cabinet Committee on Education.

COORDINATOR OF CYCLIC REVIEW (1967). *Curriculum Guidelines: Primary and Junior Division, PIJI.* Toronto: Ontario Department of Education.

CROSSLEY, K. (1973). Interview with J. Herbert.

DIRECTORY OF CANADIAN ALTERNATIVE AND INNOVATIVE EDUCATION (1973). Toronto: Communitas Exchange.

FLEMING, W. G. (1974). *The Pursuit of Equality of Educational Opportunity in Canada.* Toronto: Prentice-Hall of Canada, Ltd.

FRIESEN, D., and HOLDAWAY, E. A. (1973). 'The Curriculum Debate in Canadian Education', *Education Canada,* 13, (1), 30–3.

GOVERNMENT OF QUEBEC, DEPARTMENT OF EDUCATION (1971). 'Kindergarten, Elementary Education, Secondary Education: General Framework.' (Regulation No. 7).

HERBERT, J. *et al.* (1973). *Teaching and Pupiling: Classroom behaviour of Children and Teachers in Regular classes and those of Gifted and Slow Learning Children.* Toronto: The Ontario Institute for Studies in Education.

'INDEX OF OFFICIAL PROGRAMS FOR ENGLISH', *Official Bulletin, Department of Education.* Quebec: Information Service, Department of Education (series). For French schools the Bulletin is called *Bulletin Officiel du Ministère de l'Education.*

LAWRENCE, O. R. (1973). Personal communication 25 May. (Assistant Director of Instruction, Department of Education and Youth, Government of Newfoundland and Labrador).

McDIARMID, G. L. (1971). 'The meaning of curriculum and its development', *Education Canada,* 11, (2).

MILBURN, G. and HERBERT, J. (1973). 'Is Nationalism out of step in Canada?' *Nationalism and the Curriculum,* Special Issue, *Curriculum Theory Network.* Toronto: The Ontario Institute for Studies in Education.

MILLER, T. (1973). 'Project Canada West: Curricula for Canadian Studies', *Education Canada,* 13, (1), pp. 20–4.

MINISTÉRE DE L'ÉDUCATION DIRECTION GÉNERALE DE L'ENSEIGNEMENT ELÉMÉNTAIRE ET SECONDAIRE. (1971). *Programme D'Etude Des Ecoles Elémén-taires: Orientation Nouvelle Des Sciences Humaines a l'Eléméntaire Deuxième tirage.* Québec: Gouvernement du Québec.

MINISTÉRE DE L'ÉDUCATION DIRECTION GÉNERALE DE L'ENSEIGNEMENT ELÉMÉNTAIRE ET SECONDAIRE. (1970). *Plan D'Etude: Francais—Enseignement Secondaire Document Provisoire.* Québec: Gouvernement du Québec.

MURPHY, A. (1973). Personal communication. (Prince Edward Island Teachers' Federation. Charlottetown, P.E.I.) 25 April.

NASON, H. M. (1971). 'A Development System for the Educational Program of Nova Scotia Schools.' Professional Development Associates Report, *A Total Educational Program Development System for Nova Scotia Schools.*

NAYLOR, W. B. (1971). 'Curriculum Implementation.' An address to the B.C. Supervisors of Instruction Conference, Kelowna, B.C., 11 November, by the Director of Curriculum, Department of Education, British Columbia.

NEW BRUNSWICK TEACHERS' ASSOCIATION. (1973). *Professional Development Newsletter.* February.

NEWFOUNDLAND TEACHERS' ASSOCIATION. (1973). *Special Interest Councils Handbook.* (undated, circa 1973).

OFFICE OF THE COORDINATOR OF RESEARCH AND DEVELOPMENT STUDIES. (1972). *Research and Development Projects for Year 8* (1972–73). Toronto:The Ontario Institute for Studies in Education.

ONTARIO TEACHERS' FEDERATION, CURRICULUM COMMITTEE (1973). 'Curriculum Concerns for the '70's', *The OTF Reporter,* 26 (Spring) pp. 18–20.

PARENT, A. M. *Commission royale d'enquéte sur l'enseignement.* Quebec: Report, 1963–65. Vol. 1, The structure of the educational system at the provincial level. Vol. 2, The pedagogical structure of the educational system. Vol. 3A, The structures and the levels of education. Vol. 3B, The programs of study and the educational services.

PROFESSIONAL DEVELOPMENT ASSOCIATES, EDUCATIONAL CONSULTANTS (1971). *A Total Education Program Development for Novia Scotia Schools.* A Report for the Novia Scotia Department of Education. Ottawa, Ontario, November.

PROVINCE OF BRITISH COLUMBIA, DEPARTMENT OF EDUCATION, Division of Instructional Services, Curriculum Development Branch (1971). *Administrative Guide for Elementary Schools.* Victoria, B.C.

PROVINCIAL COMMITTEE ON AIMS AND OBJECTIVES OF EDUCATION IN THE SCHOOLS OF ONTARIO (1968). *Living and Learning.* Toronto: Newton Publishing Co.

RENAUD, A. (1971). *Education and the First Canadians.* Toronto: Gage Publishing Company.

ROBINSON, P. (1973). Personal communication, 23 May. (Curriculum Division, Department of Education, Government of the Northwest Territories, Yellowknife.)

SABEY, R. (1971). 'Project Canada West', *Education Canada,* 11, (2), pp. 18–23.

SASKATCHEWAN TEACHERS' FEDERATION (1972). 'Curriculum Diffusion.' A Paper for Presentation to the Minister of Education of Saskatchewan. January 29, Mimeo.

SHARP, J. (1973). 'Who decides student options varies across the country', *Edmonton Journal,* 5 June, p. 15.

TOMKINS, G. (1973). 'National Consciousness, the Curriculum, and Canadian Studies'. in *Nationalism and the Curriculum.* Special Issue, *Curriculum Theory Network.* Toronto: The Ontario Institute for Studies in Education.

VOKEY, M. (1973). Personal communication. (Director of Professional Development, Newfoundland Teachers' Association.) 30 April.

WARRAN, P. J., *et al.* (1967). *Report of the Royal Commission on Education and Youth.* Province of Newfoundland and Labrador.

WRIGHT, J. (1973). (Manitoba Department of Youth and Education.) Interviewed by N. Hersom, 4 May.

CHAPTER 4

Curriculum—its meaning and use in Denmark

Tom P. Olsen

Introduction

In an American book of comparative studies in education the author is reputed to have said, 'In Denmark, compulsory education was introduced in 1814 for all children from their seventh to their 14th year, but since that time very little has happened.' This quotation is to remind the author that very little indeed is known outside Denmark about the Danish school system, its content and organization, and how these matters have developed and are changing. The reader, whose interest might be stimulated by this quotation or who has a particular interest in the educational systems of small countries like Denmark, as part of a Scandinavian approach to education will discover that much has happened since 1814.[1, 2, 3, 4, 5.]

On the other hand, the author of the above quotation is, without perhaps knowing it, right in his conclusion. The principles underlying the curriculum and teaching are still based upon the same philosophy, one tenet of which is that *schooling* is an option for each individual member of society. It is not compulsory. Only *education* is compulsory. The main responsibility for education rests with a child's parents, who can decide whether to send the children to the Local Education Authority schools, provide teaching at home, or send them to private schools strongly supported by public funds. The concern of the State is that no child should have teaching below an officially designated standard.

The freedom and possible variety in education and schooling follow an historically deep-rooted tradition in Denmark, stemming from the 19th century, as represented by N. F. S. Grundtvig, the founder of the Folk High School, and by Kristian Kold, who initiated a movement of free, private schools. The official school system has been influenced by such schools and has not had a monopoly in the teaching of children. This means that, in Denmark, the word 'curriculum' has not one meaning, but many. What goes on in the school may take many forms so long as it is within the framework laid down by Parliament.

The State also provides the resources for schooling and for the training of teachers. Within the national framework, the Danish school curriculum has always been a matter of local decision and choice, and in this respect differs from the practice in Norway and Sweden. This principle has both advantage and weakness. The weak point is an almost inevitable difference in education which a centralized system can avoid, at least in some degree, through its regulations.

In Denmark there is *not a prescribed course of study or plan for learning* which will be the curriculum for all children to learn and all teachers to teach. The meaning of 'curriculum' has to be understood in a context where decentralized decision-making is accepted but within a national policy where one of the salient values is the idea of equal opportunities for all.

1. The meaning of curriculum

In Denmark, the government does not decide what shall be taught. It only gives *guidelines* about the content, structure and amount of teaching. The Minister of Education puts proposals before Parliament concerning the nature and purpose of education which are embodied in the Act of Parliament for primary and secondary schools. The Minister is then at liberty to state the objectives for different subjects in The Folk School, which are seen as teachable and essential for the education of children in school, and the subjects to be taught and which the school is obliged to offer e.g. Danish; English and German; physics/ chemistry; history, geography, biology, religious and social studies; handicraft, music and gymnastics. For each subject, except Danish and Mathematics, it is further stated the number of years and within which grades the teaching of the subjects should take place. For example the subjects of history, biology, geography, religious and social studies have to be offered for at least five years, and at the latest, begin at the third grade. Apart from a compulsory list of subjects the school is obliged to offer some free-choice options.

In addition the Minister regulates the weekly teaching time. It is actually stated that first and second grades should have 15 to 20 hours teaching, third and fourth grades 20 to 25 hours, and fifth to ninth grades together with the voluntary tenth grade, 25 to 30 hours.

A third point of importance is the requirement that each school sets up *a teaching plan*, which is by way of being the curriculum for a given school. Parliament, or rather the Minister of Education, offers some scope for each additional organization to plan for itself while requiring a *planned curriculum*, to use Saylor and Alexander's term,[6] which gives a detailed indication of the content of the subject to be taught, the number of lessons per subject, and the subjects to be taught at each grade.

In facilitating the design of local teaching plans (school curricula) the Minister of Education prepares a *guideline* for each subject containing both general considerations and concrete proposals as to subject matter, content, possible teaching methods and indications of how the teaching may be organized. It is meanwhile necessary to stress that the basic idea of the guideline is to guide and to help the individual school, not to have them conform to a certain norm or unify a possible variety in the country. Theoretically there could be about 2400 individual plans, but given the fact that the local community has considerable influence the number of plans tends to conform to the number of local authorities. In practice, even this possible diversity is further reduced.

At the national level we have no curriculum, only the framework and very first sketch of what might become a curriculum at school level. The general guidelines for education and teaching might be called an *advisory curriculum* which embodies recommendations but no regulations, and is not binding on the schools. If we look more closely at the local curriculum, we find the different subjects broken down into smaller parts (topics) and the distribution of these for the different grades. The teaching plan or local curriculum tells the reader which part of a given subject should become an object of his teaching. However, it is almost impossible to imagine the actual content of lessons as the topics are normally broad. There is nothing which determines the teaching programmes or the sequence of content within topics, and it is not possible to guess the distribution of teaching between conventional class instruction and more progressive and experimental methods.

In addition, our teaching plan covers the aims of the school, the objectives of the subjects, and a more detailed list of what is to be taught, but nothing about the organization within the year nor anything about the teaching methods to be employed. Thus it seems to be an exaggeration to say that the Danish advisory curriculum and teaching plan is a curriculum in the most common sense of this term. In the Danish curriculum plan, pretty much is left open and the 'what and the how' for the teachers are not prescribed.

2. The idea and use of the advisory curriculum

In the Act of 1899 for primary and lower secondary education, the Ministry of Education clarified the intentions for the publication of an advisory curriculum. This advisory curriculum appeared for the first time in Denmark on the 6th April 1900.[7]

To avoid any misunderstandings or objections the Ministry of Education expressly says 'rules for the teaching plan and the allocation of time suggested must not be perceived as decisions which one inescapably has to follow. They are guidelines for the local authorities in the planning of teaching and a possible aid for the teacher, particularly the young, inexperienced teacher, to support their initial attempts at planning their teaching'.

Until 1900 the central authorities had to only a very limited extent made regulations and given recommendations about the objectives to be served by different subjects at each grade and about the ways and means to achieve them. Up to that time decisions had been delegated to the judgement of the individual teacher.

The central authorities were aware of the dilemma in which general education for the country as a whole found itself. On the one hand there was the agreement based on tradition, 'that the school should be given room for autonomy and personal spiritual nourishment' and on the other hand 'there is the necessity for unity and order in the work of all the nation's schools'.

Professor Carl Aage Larsen, The Royal Danish School of Educational Studies, suggests the contemporary resolution of this dilemma when he says that the national advisory curriculum is not only 'a guide to the local education authorities in the design of teaching plans, but also a means to furthering equal opportunities for children all over the country, and support for the teacher in his daily work'.[8] It is this triple purpose that has been maintained during this century and is still valid for both primary, lower and higher secondary education, although some of these school forms have been regulated by standard examinations at the centre.

Primarily the user of the advisory curriculum is the teacher who is obliged to work within the objectives and topics indicated. But there is plenty of scope for the teacher and the pupil to decide on priorities among these topics and on the possible inclusion of others; that is, if they can agree, and it is convenient and feasible. The Danish teacher has, in fact, had a very high degree of autonomy and freedom in his choice of topics as well as teaching methods and the organizational setting of his teaching.

Today there is a new factor. Pupil participation and responsibility are required by act of Parliament, so that the planning and organization of teaching must be a result of co-operation between teacher and pupil. Both parties have explicitly to argue for the 'what' and 'how' of teaching in the classroom. In practice the pupils—and their parents—will now also become users of the advisory curriculum and of the local teaching plan.

But not only are pupils and parents of considerable influence—so are textbook publishers. They are interested in and use the advisory curriculum in order to bring production into line with the current thinking within subjects. The advisory curriculum updates subject content, its topics and methods, and this often results in the production of new teaching materials, textbooks and teaching aids. In fact it is often stated in the preface to textbooks that they are based on the guidelines of the advisory curriculum and so can be approved for use in schools. Even so, it is worth remembering that there is no such thing as an 'officially approved textbook' in Denmark, as for example there is in Sweden, where only approved textbooks may be used in state schools.

At this point the impression may have been gained that teaching in Denmark is almost entirely in the hands of the individual teacher based on his own thinking and choice of subject matter and teaching methods. Ideally, it could be so, and in practice it is for some teachers. However, the fact is that most teachers rely very much on the topics in the advisory curriculum and are dependent on published teaching materials. This statement is not founded on empirical research but is inferred from an inspection of publishers' catalogues and from statements made by teachers who participate in in-service teacher education.

3.   The process of curriculum development

The threefold aim of the advisory curriculum—to advise local authorities, be of help to teachers and further national interest in education—possesses reality and validity in the process of curriculum development, but the means for developing the advisory curriculum has changed during this century to include all the individuals involved in the curriculum and in giving reasons for the changes which are recommended.

The Committee which produced an advisory curriculum in 1942 had six members and was assisted by 13 persons who possessed special expertise. In 1960 there was a similar Committee of 20 members who asked for advice from more than 170 individuals and were contacted by more than 50 organizations who offered evidence. The present Committee for Curriculum of The Folk school has 23 nominated members and, with permanent subcommittees included, the membership is extended to more than 200. In addition, those in contact with professional unions and organizations are consulted. Thus, the number of Committee and subcommittee members has gradually grown and the Committee has also become more aware of, and receptive to, 'outside' opinion.

Participants from the Teachers' Union, the Inspectorate and the

Department of Education account for the majority membership of the Committee. There are also a few individuals whose function is liaison with higher education and with further teacher training. All members are from the teaching profession and many have admini- strative positions. The membership does not include representatives of parents, pupils or professional pedagogues. The Committee is characterized by its narrowness in executive, administrative and organizational expertise, whereas the subcommittees are broader both in practical experience and theoretical knowledge of the subject disciplines and of education.

The Committee with its subcommittees has the task of creating an advisory curriculum which includes the best paedagogic practices and updates the subject matter in accordance with recent develop- ments in the disciplines.

Some teachers are called on to give evidence to Committee meetings, and are encouraged to send in their evidence, present their viewpoint and draw on their experience for the benefit of the Committee.

In the preface to their report to the Minister of Education the Committee says 'these proposals and considerations for the educa- tion of pupils in the schools have profited from and build upon the developments achieved by teachers in their work'.[8] Teachers as such are only indirectly involved in the creation of the advisory curriculum, and mostly they see the Teachers' Union members of the Committee as their spokesmen. However, it is fair to say that the teachers are waiting for most of the process to be repeated at the individual school within their own educational community.

Finally, an innovation which the Minister of Education recently instigated should be noted. Before he put the proposal outlining the aims for The Folk School before Parliament he most untraditionally invited some 200 influential individuals from all walks of society to a two-day conference to sound their opinion on the characteristics of 'an educated person'.

Roles in decision making

In Denmark it is Parliament which officially makes demands on and suggests lines of development for the schools to the Government as has been the case in 1937, 1958 and 1969. One of the reasons for suggesting curriculum development is either dissatisfaction with the existing state of things or the desire for curriculum development to be geared to the present and future needs of society. Consequently, the major decisions about general education, e.g. the curriculum of the Folk School, are political and are binding at a national level. Such things as the aims, the types of subjects, the structure of schooling and of examinations are political decisions moderated by the realities of teaching.

Parliament provides the aims and lays down, as it were, the rules of the game, while the participants, in particular the teachers, provide the practical considerations which must be faced if the aims are to be implemented. It is in the process of implementation that teachers have to engage in a series of technical-didactic tasks and the quality of the solutions depends on their professional knowledge and skill. Parliament decides upon a given subject but its usefulness in education as a means to the achievement of a given objective has to be worked out. This is the job of the teacher. In short, the teacher, as the subject expert and as the pedagogue is the agent paid to find ways of realizing a political-educational utopia (or so it sometimes seems) for the good of the children and society—this after the main framework of subject matter to be taught is determined by a political decision.

Matters of change and the usefulness of the advisory curriculum

What types of problems have we been trying to tackle, what reasons have there been for changing the curriculum? In the '40s and '50s the school system had been striving to reduce two boundaries, one *physical* and one *psychological*. The first problem was to give equal opportunities, quantitative and qualitative, to children whether they lived in rural areas with village schools or lived in urban areas with town schools. All previous attempts were perceived as more or less failures when the oldest rural pupils applied for entrance to the higher secondary schools in the towns. The second problem was the two-tier secondary schools system, one a selective school providing potential 'success' because of its examinations system and the 'examination free' school without such potential. Parents and employers could not accept the latter as an alternative, equally good school, having other functions. The lack of balance in the school system, where 'success' and 'failure' establishes an insoluble conflict, had to be changed if one wanted to pursue the intention of a *general education for all children*.

More and more politicians argued that principally it was a mistake to maintain a selective school within the framework of compulsory education, though this idea did not find full support until the middle of the '60s in Denmark which is late compared with other Scandinavian countries. The obstacle seems to have been the teachers who were allowed to teach in the selective schools without having a university degree; a necessary qualification to teach in such schools in other countries.

The problem of selection or not after at least five years in school e.g. an 11-plus hurdle was not forced to a resolution by the government. The power of decision was given to the parents of each fifth-grade child and gradually during the '60s the percentage of parents electing for a non-selective system increased from a very few in 1960 to 61 per cent in 1964 and to 86 per cent in 1967. As much as anything it was the *de facto* decisions of parents that gave fulfilment to a major purpose of the advisory curriculum, namely, 'equal opportunities for all children', in so far as one accepts that selection at the age of 11 had radically different consequences for different children.

Another criterion for equality is, as Carl Aage Larsen[8] mentions in his evaluation of the existing advisory curriculum, equal transition and entrance to vocational and further education after having stayed for the same period in the school, regardless of which part of the school. In this case the obstacle was gradually eliminated by introducing voluntary examinations in the eighth to 10th grades (previously 'examination free'). More important than this formal aspect of schooling was the fact that the teachers, under the auspices of the advisory curriculum, felt committed to establishing worthwhile alternative teaching and to the provision of an optimal free choice of subjects and supporting guidance to create a purposeful transition from school to work and further education. The teaching was not specifically occupational preparation but encouraged the development of such social skills as co-operation through working in groups; self-confidence and responsibility through working with 'options,' especially general and social studies.

Evaluating the advisory curriculum

The influence and help of the advisory curriculum in both instances is difficult to evaluate, but it certainly started a debate among the teachers about the functions school was to serve. Certainly the decentralized school with its role in adapting the curriculum to its needs showed an ability to adjust teaching to the needs of society and monitor these adjustments. The curriculum has primarily to give security to the teacher in his job without taking away his initiative. However, if this is the intent, a curriculum as an instrument for teaching should perhaps concentrate more on identifying problem areas, clarifying criteria for selection of content and on specifying teaching situations than on giving topics and examples of instructions.

The third purpose of the advisory curriculum, it may be recalled, was to help local education authorities in the provision of teaching, and its success in this respect can be evaluated by a review of local plans. From these it is clear that the advisory curriculum has become more than a help, it has radically reduced the possible variety to the

degree that an official inspection of schools will come to the conclusion that 'a standard, national curriculum has been the result.'

There are several possible explanations for this:

1. too hard and difficult a task for the teachers and LEAs to
implement;
2. too short a time to create meaningful alternatives;
3. too much effort relative to the results that can be achieved
because teachers behave as individuals not as a group working for
the school;
4. the advisory curriculum is too theoretical compared with the
realities of teaching.

A tentative and speculative answer may be that the teachers, by
and large, are unprepared for and surprised by the question 'What
should be taught?'. They do not consider it a real problem. In their
schools they are unaware of the rapid changes in society and the
enormous expansion in knowledge. All they heard of at college
concerned the methodology of instruction and teaching. It is only
in recent years that courses in curriculum theory and didactics have
become generally available, and heavily subscribed to, as in-service
courses for practising teachers. They also form part of the programme of teacher training. Thus, the teachers should be in a better
position and able to analyse and eventually suggest alternatives
when the Act presents the next advisory curriculum for The Folk
School in 1975.

Development trends and an example

It is possible that the increasingly frequent changes in the legislative
basis of Danish schools (1899, 1937, 1958, 1973), accompanied by
alterations in the advisory curriculum, have led to a more guided
pattern of curriculum revision and innovation than might have been
the case, had these changes been less frequent. The advisory
curriculum in a way updates teaching, its content and methods, to
the best practice. In the interregnum between two bills the Minister
of Education, normally basing his judgement on an evaluation of the
Board of Educational Experimentation of The Folk School, can
permit deviations from LEA teaching plans and so facilitate innovation in schools and lay the groundwork for future planning. It should
be noted that the impact on curriculum development of innovations,
projects and research, has until now been very limited. In addition,
there has been only the slightest hint of a 'curriculum development
movement' where teachers, as the practitioners, have led changes.
Curriculum improvement has arisen largely from the advisory
curriculum, the demands and expectation of the relevant Act, and
from the further education of teachers. As a result, there has been

a tendency to clarify the concepts, structure and methods of subjects taught in schools. The thinking and planning of work by teachers has very definitely moved away from 'the introduction and teaching of examples, facts for reproduction' towards 'teaching of the exemplary elements for understanding and insight'.

However, all innovations and improvements in curriculum and teaching are faced with the tradition of tests and examination. An answer to the problem which this creates has tremendous pedagogical importance. It is clearly incompatible with a decentralized system. 'Centralization of curricula and standardization of assessment go hand in hand',[9] as has been observed. It is also a problem where there are conflicting interests. Examinations seem essential both to society's conception of education and to the teachers' perception of the evaluation of their teaching. The Teachers' Union says officially 'an evaluation in marks or standardized statements seems not unusable as an evaluation of teaching'. How these conflicting interests will be resolved remains an open question.

The Committee on Curriculum recommended in its report that 'there should be an examination at the end of teaching in the tenth grade'. The Minister, however, could not implement this proposal. His argument was that one can hardly imagine examinations without marks, and examination results expressed in the form of marks are a very simplified form of the evaluation of teaching. Instead he suggested a description of the fields of study, which the pupils, separately or jointly, had engaged in and from which they had acquired knowledge, skills, working methods, and modes of expression which were the objectives of teaching. The terminal certificate would carry information useful to the pupil himself and to others, as it would be related to objectives of his courses of study, not norms, and should be built on a minimum of randomness and subjectivity.

This outcome may be viewed as a clear consequence of the intention to establish a non-selective 'comprehensive' school in which an attempt is made to moderate the competitive element amongst the pupils and to reduce the academic demands associated with some subjects. The segregation of pupils into successes and failures, and of subjects into 'hard' and 'soft' should stop. The chosen means, e.g. the subjects and options, are all perceived as necessary to the achievement of the general aims of schooling and to the education of all children irrespective of ability.

The non-socialist parties expressed their anxiety about the abolition of tests and examinations at the end of schooling. Differences in arguments span from, 'we make dangerous experiments with our children', to 'the labour market will establish their own tests and examinations', and that of a 'Folkeskole' that may be very different from one municipality to another. These parties suggested that other types of tests and examinations should be developed through pedagogical research.

A pedagogical analysis of the advisory curriculum, a political invention, brings one to the conclusion that it is consistent with the aims and functions which the school in our Danish society serves and is very much in accordance with the traditional system for curriculum development in Denmark. On the other hand it gives rise to many problems amongst which the most important are (a) transition to and entrance for higher education, whether technical, vocational, or academic; (b) teacher reactions to the lack of a regulative and motivational factor in teaching; (c) the question of equal opportunities in teaching all over the country.

The future—what and how?

Future change in the curriculum has two aspects, one is concerned with sort of change, another with ways and means. The discussion of the function of the school either as an instrument to change society or as a means to strengthen existing trends is well understood in Denmark. Comments from such influential organizations as the Labour Union, the Employers' Union, Teachers' Union and Pupils' Union, together with political programmatic statements are the background for the following tentative surmises as to the way things may go.

No longer a state within a state, the school will cease to be isolated from society, and consequently people from outside the schools will ask questions and want to know what goes on in the school and why. The teachers will in time have to argue with these people, justify what they teach and negotiate the objectives to be served.

This openness and orientation towards the world outside the school will probably have its counterpart inside the school where open planning and co-operation amongst the staff will be the rule, not the exception. Division into subjects and the traditional academic domains as the overwhelming basis for general education from the first to the 12th grade will undergo some change. There will be more integration and co-ordination between the subjects. The curriculum will cover problems which can be seen in the context of society as it is, rather than (as at present) only in relation to an idealistic application of the arts and sciences. The humanistic and societal standpoint will be more in evidence than a technological and academic approach. The structure, concepts and methods from the disciplines, theoretical and practical, will still be essential in education, but they will be valued for their actual application and usefulness as tools for understanding and action in a democratic society.

A greater flexibility and less rigidity in the choice of curriculum subjects, socio-problem centred teaching will come to the fore and require new views of who should be the teachers. It seems probable, although the Teachers' Union is now issuing warnings and has started a defensive fight, that people other than teachers from Teacher Training Colleges will contribute to the staff of the schools in the future. This issue is very closely related to the recognized social problem of 'a shrewd recruitment' to higher education. The school of today does not suit children who have very different or incongruent social, economical or sexual cultural backgrounds, and as Denmark wants to give equal opportunities to all, the cultural pluralism of society has to be taken into account. Of importance in making such an adjustment are (a) staff of schools with wide and different experiences; (b) a balance between theoretical and practical areas of the curriculum; (c) comprehensive schools for all children, probably for the first 12 years of schooling. Such issues as are raised by these matters will need to be dealt with in the future, are not only matters of teaching, but are questions of both political and social relevance and importance.

So far as the process of curriculum development goes, the accelerating trend to a decentralized approach will continue. Nevertheless, the decision about the functions and the purposes of the Folk School will still be taken by Parliament, as they have always been. This principle does not in Danish eyes conflict with the trend towards a more active involvement in both national and local decisions of parents, pupils and teachers. The former narrowness of the Curriculum Committee will be replaced by a greater openness and the participation of many more members of society.

Finally, an Advisory Curriculum in the form known today will become outmoded, as its character of making proposals and giving suggestions will no longer be of help in a rapidly changing society. What will be needed and hopefully available, are several alternative advisory curricula, so that there can be eventually participant users, not merely consumers, of a curriculum.

Bibliography—some available in English:

1. BRICKMAN, W. W. (1967). *Denmark's Educational System and Problems.* Washington US Office of Education.
2. DIXON, W. (1959). *Education in Denmark.* London: Harrap.
3. THOMSEN, O. B. (1967). *Some Aspects of Education in Denmark.* Toronto: University of Toronto Press.
4. UNESCO (1961). *World Survey of Education,* Vol. III.
5. THE DANISH INSTITUTE (1972). *Schools and Education in Denmark.* Copenhagen:
6. SAYLOR, J. G. and ALEXANDER, W. M. (1966). *Curriculum Planning for Modern Schools.* New York: Holt, Rinehart and Winston.
7. MINISTERIALTIDENDE (1900). *Bafalinger af almindeligere Karakter.* Copenhagen:
8. THE MINISTRY OF EDUCATION (1971). *En reform af de grundlaeggende skoleuddannelser.* Copenhagen:
9. HOLLEY, B. J. and REID, W. A. (1972). *The Organization of Curricula and Examinations in Sweden.* Mimeo, Teaching Research Unit, Birmingham Univ.
10. THE MINISTRY OF EDUCATION (1972). *Forslag til Lov om foleskolen.* Copenhagen:

CHAPTER 5

Curriculum Development in England*

J. G. Owen

History lends depth to any description of the process, purposes and problems of curriculum development. The longer the time-scale, the clearer is the picture of differing influences which move the work of schools in specific directions from age to age.

In England, those influences on curriculum which can be identified are a mixture of certain kinds of thinking by individual philosophers, of good practices by particular teachers and of the regulations of central government.

Not all the forces which have had weight are visible; immeasurable and virtually unverifiable effects such as those of parental expectation or the requirements of employers or the even vaguer needs of particular communities and of the larger entity of society—these, too, have left their mark.

Each influence has in one way or another contributed to the meaning which is attached to curriculum in England at the present time. This amounts to saying that a hidden ideology is at work. Within this are included the effects of a long culture of education, of a broad range of definitions of human happiness and a readiness to accept the private nature of life—or at least to accept modes of living which do not have to conform to explicitly defined norms or to highly specific requirements laid down within regulations of state.

The ideology, whether hidden or not, is indefinable but all-permeating. It allows deviance within recognizable limits; it helps to produce, in the end, a near uniform sense of Englishness. Yet in England the idea that curriculum might be totalitarian is something to shudder at. How can you, after all, have sameness, or even random comparability in the curriculum of schools in which the constant boast is that teachers are autonomous?

* I am indebted to the Cambridge University Press for permission to draw extensively on my book 'The Management of Curriculum Development' (CUP, 1973).

The answer lies in the probability that behind the English illusion the facts are rather different. Reality is most clearly seen when one looks at the way in which teachers receive their professional education. For instance, those who train teachers can never give completely free rein to their own ideas. They are limited by the things that English society expects a school—and a teacher—to achieve. Teachers have to prepare children to pass examinations, to become good citizens, to become employees who work hard and who become part of a social scene where honour and truthfulness, loyalty and love, trustworthiness and reliability are qualities of value.

Teachers have also to try to ensure that children are helped to become—or are not hindered from becoming—adults who have sensitivity, political balance, sound ethical judgment, wit, courtesy and honesty.

At the same time schools are expected to promote children's respect for the spiritual and religious values of their society as a whole as well as of individual members of that society; they are expected to affect their pupils in a manner which diminishes bigotry and prejudice, which promotes tolerance while not encouraging excessive permissiveness and which continually requires children to learn how to test the limits of their experience and their feeling. Teachers, in short, must help children in a great variety of ways to grow—socially, spiritually and intellectually.

Although it must try to take account of each of these needs, the process of professional preparation also has to recognize the importance of the personality and intellect of individual teachers, their maturity and their capacity to interpret their experiences. But at the same time these factors belong to the realm of human nature and are influenced less by training than by the mere passage of years.

In England the emphasis on the personal nature of a teacher's contribution to his job affects the definition which is given to curriculum. Because official requirements are not codified there is a natural temptation to assume that the teacher's own choice of what to teach and how to teach is all-important.

But teachers change from generation to generation; yet the curriculum of English schools is something which is considered to be highly stable. From this we have to assume at the very beginning of any definition that autonomy, freedom of choice and the muted nature of official voices do not have the dominance which is sometimes claimed.

Go back, then, to history. The official voice was first heard in the 1830s, in matters affecting central government grants to denominational schools. Grants were made on specific conditions. In the 1860s, these were spelled out more clearly. In the 1870s the requirements, although they were less explicitly stated, had a broader effect; it was from that time that the major effort dated to devise a system of compulsory education.

In the first decade of this century, the official definition of what schools were expected to do extended from elementary schooling to the beginnings of secondary education. By 1920, the influence of officialdom—although not stated in that way—was stronger because it had begun to express itself through the medium of syllabuses for public examinations. Then, until the 1940s secondary school curriculum ran the risk of having life choked out of it as syllabuses became more refined, more demanding and less open to individual interpretation. At the same time primary schools, too, were subjected to tight demands of examinations for the purpose of supporting the selection of pupils for one or other of three classes of secondary school.

When the major English statute was enacted which governs present-day education (the Education Act of 1944), educational thinking had nearly succumbed to the idea that three types of secondary school meant that there were three intrinsically different types of child—and that there were not only three types of intelligence but also a category of curriculum to match each one.

From 1950 until the present day, movements of change in secondary education have produced the idea of a comprehensive secondary education which matches the comprehensive (that is, undifferentiated) nature of English primary schools. As the programme of switching to comprehensive secondary education has gained ground, so has the meaning of curriculum changed.

It has not changed in a way which is altogether radical. Rather, it has transformed itself in the education of children aged eight to 16 years into something which is comparable to the curriculum which has, since the 1920s, applied without challenge to the education of children aged five to seven years. It has, in brief, reverted to a pattern which above all attempts to recognize potentials and differing stages of readiness for the next phase of learning.

Like any swing in fashion, the movement of curriculum towards a largely child-centred view of the school world has, in some definitions, gone too far. It has gone far enough, for instance, to ignore (or forget) that education until mid-adolescence or late adolescence is a matter of initiation. Adults in their own way know what their world will require of those who are growing up. Unavoidably, that part of compulsory education which is concerned with initiation into the adult world has to be adult-centred. An all-encompassing attempt at child-centredness in the curriculum is therefore likely to be illusory.

The make-up of curriculum in English schools in the present day is, then, a matter of history, of fashion, of inherited attitudes and of changing social demands—and social demands are particularly dominant within the present vogue of curricular purposes.

By now a conventional distinction is drawn between that part of curriculum which tries to meet social need and that which pays more obvious attention to academic education. In some ways this raises issues which are comparable to those which matter in, for instance, better known distinctions between teaching and instructing, between specific subjects and broad curriculum, between syllabuses which other people determine and those potentials of individual pupils which might have a claim to be carefully nurtured.

In brief the distinction between social and academic curriculum represents an attempt to educate the child as someone who must live with other people and as someone who must prove himself (through examinations) to be capable of matching other people's expectations. The pupils in both contexts is being educated for his own sake. But in one definition it is his own adjustments with others, his own satisfactions and his own style of life which are supremely important. In the alternative, he is to be educated in order to fit into a pattern which is not essentially that of his own desires.

Curriculum in England can (as in other countries) have several meanings. One set of British definitions in the recent past covered a range such as this:

All the learning which is planned or guided by the school, whether it is carried on in groups or individually, inside or outside the school. (Kerr, J. F., 1966)

That the curriculum consists of content, teaching methods and purpose may in its rough and ready way be a sufficient definition with which to start. These three dimensions interacting are the operational curriculum. (Taylor, P. H., 1966)

A programme of activities designed so that pupils will attain, as far as possible, certain educational ends or objectives. (Hirst, P., 1968)

The contrived activity and experience—organized, focused, systematic—that life, unaided would not provide. . . . It is properly artificial, selecting, organizing, elaborating and speeding up the processes of real life. (Musgrove, F., 1968)

Each definition says something important. And it does not have to be argued that curriculum itself *is* important and that the changes through which it passes, in the judgment or in the assumption of theorists, interested laymen, parents, employers, teachers and students, have to be kept under unceasing review.

These four examples point to those differences which make curriculum in England partly a matter for self-determination by schools, partly a matter of what teachers are trained (and accustomed) to teach and partly a matter of what the public expects.

Not surprisingly this mixture of purposes and expectancy has led, over the years, to a blurring of certainties about what curriculum consists of. It is a matter of intellectual attainment and of social training. It aims at helping pupils to learn to think clearly and to be confidently sensitive in the realm of feelings. And all the time the purpose of the curriculum is to produce a student who has skills in the world of activity and work, and sympathy, kindliness, concern and a degree of self-abnegation in his private and familial relationships.

This variety of views represents the state of thinking towards which teachers in both secondary and primary schools nowadays work. Anything as large and nebulous as society is only seldom involved. More often, but not always, the purposes of a curriculum are concerned with self-regard.

II

If a country lacks an explicit ideology for its social life and if as a consequence it does not demand a specific product of its educational system, it is inevitable that private aspirations will become more important than public need. It is not the state which is intended to benefit from the educational system but, instead, the individual citizen.

Here again there is the risk of lurching into semantic fantasies. The state, it can be claimed, is made up of the contributions of individual citizens: if they are content and if they have lived up to their own expectations, then the state itself should be in a condition of health or, at least, of self-fulfilment. But a satisfied or self-satisfied citizen is not inarguably the prerequisite of an efficient, industrous, or productive state. In turn, the aim of satisfying the individual student *may* be an acceptable purpose for one style of curricular design—but it need not go far towards satisfying the needs of either state or society.

In England, the purposes which lie behind contemporary exercises in curriculum design are generally not connected with the needs of the state. They are not, that is, concerned with targets of trained manpower or with a political product. The curriculum of schools enables those who have the ability and the will, to go on to universities or to polytechnic education or to a teacher's professional education—or to other vocational aspects of further education.

Due to the self-determining nature of post-school education England passes through recurrent crises (or so they seem at the time) of not having enough scientists or engineers or technologists with highly particularized skills. Too many arts graduates, too many people with a qualification (but no job prospect) in social sciences—these are recurrent themes in the connected story of school education and higher education.

The crises of shortage or over-supply are from time to time identified, researched and analysed. Reports and recommendations are made. But schools continue to pay first heed to the capacities of their pupils and then to their aspirations. Colleges of further education, polytechnics, colleges of education, and universities have no alternative to taking the product of the schools. Thus, the system of satisfying oneself continues; but the pupil in school (and the student in a college) is often barely capable of deciding what he himself needs. Other people—notably parents, older siblings and teachers—have a weighty influence. These influences are, however, mixed and their effects are unclear. This in turn adds a further measure of confusion to any view which is taken of the purposes of curriculum.

III

Differences in the approach to an activity create distinctions of style. Style in itself is a label which carries a load of vagueness. Admittedly what is vague can be refined if a number of more specific questions can be answered. Who are the people who bring about *any* development within the curriculum? What kind of decisions do they make? How do they implement their decisions? What might prevent certain decisions from being put into effect?

These four questions in themselves deserve several large studies to be devoted to them. But more brief answers must be attempted: who, first, are the people who bring about any development of curriculum?

The answer, in England, starts in a deceptively simple way. The teacher is the major figure. But the way in which he changes what he does day by day (which amounts to a crude and simple but perhaps accurate definition of curriculum development) depends on his own experience and on what other people will expect of him. Like any other professional whose training is bound (in the process of teaching him to work with people rather than with things) to overlook, leave out or simply not think of certain human situations, he will sometimes feel that his training was incomplete. He will seek models of what to do. The most reasonable model lies within his own experience. His own teachers and tutors, the methods by which he learned or by which he was instructed—these will be the paradigms to which he will first turn.

If the teacher looks for models or for guidance in the present day rather than in his past experience he will pay attention to what others expect of him. What others expect can be expressed in a number of ways—by the head of a school, by the head of a subject department or by parents.

Parents are only slowly becoming respectable in the sense of being allowed to ask questions about curriculum. But they have, of course, been arbiters for a long time of the repute of a school and of particular teachers. And whether or not they are openly acknowledged, parents are certainly visible out of the corner of the eye of the average teacher in England.

Less openly acknowledged is the influence of the employer; perhaps the acknowledgement is less open because it is less readily recognized. For if education after all lacks a specific purpose in training for a job or for filling a niche in society or for fulfilling a particular role in the state's pattern of manpower demand, it is excusable that the employer should be regarded as an outsider. But this is, of course, precisely what the employer is not—at least once the formal business of education is over. He himself can be open to the pressing demands and recriminations of commercial customers, trade unions and government boards. But in turn he wields a predominant influence over individual lives. And he casts his shadow before: in anticipation of the employer's actual demands children will (through what has been said to them largely by their families) expect their work to need certain qualities, skills and attitudes.

As formative as the demands of employers are those of whatever happens to be the next stage of education. If the pupil stays at school beyond the minimum leaving age in England, he usually enters the Sixth Form, that is the sixth and seventh years of secondary schooling. He stays on in school either in order to gain an examination qualification of the elementary type (Certificate of Secondary Education or General Certificate of Education at Ordinary Level which he failed at the age of 15 years) or to push his qualifications further in order that he might qualify for entry to a university, or to a course of teacher education, or to certain courses for a higher accreditation in polytechnic colleges or colleges of further education.

These latter qualifications are, at school, usually enshrined in syllabuses for the General Certificate of Education at Advanced Level. The syllabuses (in the same way as those at the younger and more elementary stage) make up the curriculum of pupils at school. In addition to a collection of syllabuses their education does, of course, include more. But the core of expectations which teachers have to satisfy at these stages is made up of syllabus demands which are imposed by other people.

Part, then, of the answer to the question of who are the people who bring about development within the curriculum lies amongst parents, amongst those who themselves taught the teachers in an earlier generation, those who are employers and those who make up the examination boards which define syllabuses for differing stages of qualification.

Qualifications and examinations are inseparable in any attempt to define the style (and the style-makers) of curriculum in England. An élitist, sharply differentiated society which survived beyond the second world war has gradually given way to a supposedly broader development of popular democracy, of mass information and of pretensions to mass participation in matters which affect government, public expressions of taste and broad-ranging expectations of social behaviour. But behind the popular image of present-day English society it is noticeable how well-guarded are the doors to positions of power, influence and cleanly-earned money.

The history of academic examinations in England—as a procedure of administration and as a means of producing a series of graduated hurdles—is well documented (Wiseman, 1961). At this point all that needs to be said is that the teacher as a participant in curriculum development is much affected in the secondary school by those requirements which are laid on him in the name of examinations.

Are there other, less obvious requirements imposed on the major participant in curriculum development? Yes, and in the name once more of external influence.

In addition to public examinations, the range of constraints laid on teachers in secondary schools includes the influence of central government in matters which, at first sight, do not bear on curriculum. For instance, the physical state of a school—its area and juxtaposition of classrooms, workshops and other teaching spaces—can have a significant effect on curriculum construction. Another influence, which can sometimes act as a constraint but at other times be totally constructive, is that of the number of teachers who can be employed.

Both the physical dimensions of schools and the number of teachers who work within them (and hence the size of pupil-groups) are matters which markedly affect how a curriculum is constructed.

The effect is certainly indirect since government policies which control school building programmes and teacher supply are affected by economic as well as by political considerations: these factors are seldom regarded as directly relevant to education in a broad sense or to particularities of curriculum.

What else is affected by central government? Most obviously the items of schooling which can be quickly changed are those which are amenable to alteration by regulation. If the government of the day wishes to alter the shape, colouring or emphasis of schooling it issues official guidance, usually in the form of a document which is circulated to all local education authorities. Such circulars carry high potency. Thus, when in 1965 one government asked local education authorities to produce schemes of comprehensive secondary education, a sharp change of policy in terms of curriculum as well as of school organization was the consequence. A *volte face* by another government—in 1970—reversed this process and placed yet another influence on curriculum.

In 1973 one circular asked local education authorities to produce schemes for a large-scale provision of nursery education. This means that primary education needed to change its centre of gravity: instead of a six year curriculum, schools now had to re-jig their programmes of early learning—and particularly of reading and of early maths—in order to take account of the flying start which the majority of children would have by entering nursery education on a part-time basis at the age of $3\frac{1}{2}$ years.

Equally important in effect on curriculum was another circular of guidance in 1973 which defined methods for implementing another central government policy, this time for the expansion of educational opportunities into the university sector beyond the age of 18 years. Here again, by retaining certain minimum qualifications of entry into post-school courses at the same time as it broadened the range of non-degree work which would be available to 18-year-olds and 19-year-olds, the government of the day placed new curricular responsibilities on schools. And the teacher as a participant in the process of development again became the servant of other people's policies.

To change the organization of schooling and to alter the type of accreditation course which might, at the college stage, follow schooling has a more or less direct effect on what is taught. But methods of teaching can also be touched by policies of central government: to teach in a capacious, well-equipped school of modern design is sometimes thought to be more conducive to experiment and novelty in the curriculum than the task of teaching in a physical setting which is older and less blessed with the presence of modern aids.

This argument can be over-played but there is still much truth in it. If a new curriculum calls for something other than the rigid timetabling of teachers to fit classrooms which in turn are to fit fixed sizes of pupil-group, difficult and compartmentalized buildings will be a hinderance. Thus the physical envelope of teaching, within which many factors of time, light, space and noise matter almost as much as the question of whether there is simply enough room, can affect a school's curricular energy.

The same can be said of the teaching ratio. Although the sorting out of pupils and teachers is ultimately a matter for the Head of a school, the possibility of running a system in which small groups, mass lectures, seminars, individualized learning and large group work came together within one school day depends on how many teachers are available overall to individual schools. If the supply of teachers is not adequate to allow flexibility in deciding the size of pupil-groups (or if there is not enough accommodation to fit a variety of methods of teacher deployment), experiment in curriculum can be held up. To delay experiment might, in the longer view, be beneficial. But in short-term and medium-term policies of trial and error, limitations of space and of the number of trained teachers can be a considerable impediment. Again, the teacher cannot be entirely free from central government policies—however indirectly they might touch the daily task of teaching.

Equally indirect in its effect on curriculum change in England is the shift which can be seen from decade to decade in policies of teacher-training. These policies are by tradition better known to colleges of education, university institutes and departments of education than to schools and schoolteachers. Nevertheless, decisions, for instance, to concentrate effort on the training of teachers of junior pupils (eight to 11 years) and secondary pupils (11 to 16) can react unfavourably on the supply of teachers of infants (five to seven years) if the concentration of resources starves other training courses. Too few teachers might be trained or their training might be less than adequate.

Again, to try to concentrate resources of teacher training in such a way as to counteract a professional shortfall amongst teachers, for instance, of mathematics or of religious studies creates another type of distortion in teacher supply. The effects are, once more, indirect but the position of the teacher as a controller of curriculum development might clearly be altered by shifts in large-scale training policies.

The participants in change go, then, well beyond the teacher himself. Curriculum in England is indirectly affected by tradition, public expectation, government policy and government economics. But curriculum is also affected by such ready-made teaching materials as are available to the teacher. That which is commercially published, its cost and its manner of presentation matters a great deal. Thus, publishers and their textbooks, writers and their experimental materials, school suppliers and their own policies of selection also matter. Indirectly they, too, become participants in the process of change. They are free from official strictures; their choices of what to make available to teachers are governed by the market.

In contrast to these random, sometimes unplanned and often inconsequential activities, the teacher occasionally hears the voice of the speaker of supposedly pure truth from the research field. In England that voice is seldom loud. Research is not broadly commended and it is perhaps even more a matter of surprise that it does not often advocate its own credibility. But it exists and it is generally well written-up. That it lacks influence may lie less in its self-commendatory nature than in the difficulty which teachers find in having access to it.

IV

The nature of decisions which are taken about curriculum development has five aspects: the political, state-originated alteration which swings curriculum in the direction of favouring younger children or of expanding higher education speaks for itself. The nature of decision-making is part-political, part-economic, part-social and part-pedagogic. The nature of the decision could, presumably, be more exactly described in light of the advice or influence which led to the first formulation of the policy. This, however, is generally concealed.

Secondly, decisions about curriculum which indirectly stem from policies about teacher supply or about the economics of university-based as against non-university expansion of post-18 education—these could be claimed to be political but more obviously economic in their origin. Economics here would be brought into play on a large, national scale.

Third, there are social decisions. To raise the school leaving age might be an economic or a political decision (to take young workers out of the labour market, to reduce competition for jobs and to allow national statistics of unemployment to appear less grim), but it could also affect the degree to which future generations of parents would be better educated—and hence better capable, one would hope, of giving their own children fuller support in the process of being schooled. To create a new curriculum for those who might, in the first years after the compulsory raising of the school leaving age, be reluctant to stay in school, presents a fresh challenge to re-awaken interest, to provoke the involvement of pupils and to reveal the significance which schooling might have for a child's later life.

A fourth range of decision is connected with this same idea that curriculum development might re-awaken an interest in learning. But instead of reluctance, here we might see curriculum development as harnessing itself to the enlargement of educational opportunities for those who, either in themselves or through their parents' eyes, *wish* educational opportunity to be enlarged. To provide a new curriculum for those in the sixth and seventh years of secondary schooling in England (that is, in the Sixth Form) calls less for inventiveness or fresh interest than for a capacity to lead a larger number of young people through to the lucrative opportunities which lie before them in institutions of higher education.

Fifth and last come those decisions about curriculum development which have their roots not in politics or economics, not in social improvement and in the enlargement of opportunities but, instead, in the pedagogic ingenuity and insight of teachers. In contrast to those large scale decisions which fall into the first four categories, the attempt to develop an improved curriculum at the teacher's own level is a matter of individual decision. The nature of decisions in this domain is coloured by the needs and capacities of individual pupils, by the situation of (and support locally given to) particular schools. At this level, the nature of decisions about curriculum change depends above all on the quality both of the leadership which a Head can give to an individual school and on the quality of individual teachers.

Within these five broad categories of decision, those nuances of curriculum development which, perhaps, matter most in England are more firmly connected with the means by which improvements are implemented than with their points of origin.

V

The implementation of any plan for curriculum development is a process which is often described as clean and orderly, with aims which are clearly delineated and results which are accurately verified.

Not surprisingly this type of description is sometimes too clinical. It misses the confusion, irresolution, uncertainty and carelessness of human activity. It also misses what has come to be known as style—and the differing styles which belong to the personalities of people who are involved in the job of development. Because differences of style make an inevitable impression it is fallacious to presume much for the perfection of models or to pretend that the people who are involved in development can ever be less than predominant in their influence—whether for success or for failure.

Plans nevertheless have to be laid; they have to assume that those who put them into practice are rational and well-intentioned, that they understand what plans are for and that they have the intelligence and will-power to ensure that things do not go too wrong. On this basis are laid the variety of strategies, programmes and schemes which are made by those agencies which are involved in reform.

The major distinction which is drawn in the implementation of reform lies between national and local effort. On a national scale, the impact of improvement stems from several sources. It can come from advisory publications of the Department of Education and Science (aimed at schools) or from stronger directives of guidance from the same source (aimed at Local Education Authorities). It can emerge from surveys of current practice in schools—conducted by national inspectors of schools and again published by the central ministry. Or, again, it can result from social surveys of the practices of school and of the expectations of parents, teachers and children— surveys which although they are conducted by a central agency which is not controlled by the Department of Education and Science nevertheless carry, in integrity and forcefulness, considerable persuasiveness.

In national terms, too, centrally-initiated projects of the Nuffield Foundation or of The Schools Council have a broad effect, directly on schools. Here the force of persuasion is not that of official *fiat* but of well produced, heavily researched and widely tested materials and teacher guides. No commercial interest is involved other than that of the publishers of the materials. Another form of influence comes from the British Broadcasting Corporation through schools broadcasts (television as well as radio). In these there is a distinctive element of helping, and perhaps of retraining, the teacher. There are also series of combined radio-television programmes which are aimed directly at teachers, for the purpose of in-service training. The Independent Broadcasting Authority and the commercial companies also transmit child-aimed school programmes.

The BBC in particular clearly combines the job of publishing with that of devising new approaches and materials which can have a substantial effect on curriculum.

This is roughly the same position as the Department of Education and Science holds. The Department surveys certain parts of the curriculum field and issues survey reports which are formative as well as informative. It also makes regulations and publishes circulars of guidance to local education authorities about school building programmes, about the number of teachers to be employed, about

the pay of teachers and about large innovations such as the introduction of broad-scale nursery education. Each of these can create
alteration in curriculum and can act as a force in the process of
development.

A different position is held by commercial publishers: they may
indeed publish for Nuffield and for The Schools Council. More often
they will publish the work of private people—in the form of textbooks, non-book teaching materials, guides for teachers. They will
act within the process of implementing improvement because they
hold England's longest tradition as diffusers and because they are
acknowledged and trusted by schools for the materials which they
market.

The means of implementing change lies partly, then, within
nationally handled schemes of research and publication; points of
origin may be ministerial, reform-orientated (Nuffield) or commercial.
Also on a national scale, the work of certain voluntary associations
of teachers is important in implementing change. The National
Association for the Teaching of English, the Association for Science
Education, one or two powerful groups in the maths world—these
too have an admittedly less formal but still deeply felt effect on the
thinking and on the practices of teachers.

Associations are not likely to attempt large-scale strategic change
but their own surveys, courses, and publications will be devised in
such a way as to shape a programme. And programmes or packages
of new work which have clear purposes and a step-by-step approach
to the teacher now stand a better chance of being taken up than the
isolated textbook. Thus, the commercial publisher is involved in
putting out material which is programmed rather than random and
concerned as much with a worked-out educational purpose as with
commercial speculation.

But to implement an improvement depends on needs more than on
publication. Teachers will alter, develop and change their practices
more readily and efficiently only if they believe in what they are
doing and if they have been given the chance to become involved in
bringing about that stage of change which lies within their own
schools and their own classrooms. This requires schemes of training—
and of retraining—in new materials. It also means that teachers
should be given the chance to think about what they are doing and
what they might do as a new alternative.

If a new approach to moral education is put forward by, for
instance, The Schools Council, teachers who are involved in those
subjects which bear on religion and social education, on history and
on literature need to satisfy themselves on the judgments and
assumptions about values which a new project will entail.

But questions of value enter less obviously into a project for the improvement of, for instance, technical studies or of elementary engineering in schools—or at least *moral* values are not so heavily involved. Other values have still to be weighed: the teacher has to balance known benefits against potential gains before he alters his teaching. Values have to be assessed which are connected with the purposes of learning. A judgment once more has to be made—based on factors which relate directly to the job of teaching and less directly to the personal beliefs and personal style of thinking of the teacher himself. But whichever kind of judgment has to be re-assessed, whatever stimulus or purpose is involved in the judgment, a course of in-service training assists the teacher by reducing his isolation and by letting him learn from the mistakes as well as the successes of other people.

Implementation of curriculum development in England relies heavily, then, on retraining. This takes many forms—arranged by national inspectors, by local inspectors or advisers, by university schools of education, by colleges of education, by local teachers' centres, by the professional associations of teachers, and by project teams within the large development programmes of The Schools Council. Courses vary in length and in method. They employ differing types of experts and tutors. They involve teachers to differing degrees in their own training. And, of course, they differ very much in the way they are regarded by teachers; there are few common criteria for assessing the usefulness or success of courses. But there is much more agreement about the forces which help curriculum development to flourish or to go forward only slowly. The good influences and unwanted constraints are, in the English picture, easy to spot.

VI

The resister, the phoney, the man with but a single idea, the excessive cynic, the proceduralist, the universalist—each of these acts in constraint on development. Those things which amount to blank resistance or well-mannered apathy, fake enthusiasm, obessiveness or continuously corrosive lack of belief in the *possibility* of benefit in the process of development, each of these most obviously checks improvement at the level of the individual school.

Outside the school and within the local education authority what used principally to impede development was an unwillingness to take a chance in helping groups of teachers or individual schools to venture on experimental work. If additional money was needed for materials or for visiting, for an extra part-time teacher or for access to other schools, even a rich Authority found it difficult to find the right rules within which to give the type of encouragement that was needed.

Gradually, new rules have been made. Most local education authorities now set aside funds specifically for the purpose of fostering curriculum improvement. Advisers have been appointed whose job this is; teachers' centres and their wardens have come into being.

Had new rules not been made then aids to development would not have been forthcoming. The desire to stick to old procedures would have held things up—as indeed they still do in certain areas of England. At national level, a comparable alteration in procedures has allowed for a great growth in government-sponsored in-service training and, in particular, in the development of continued in-service training schemes between the Department of Education and Science and universities. Money, expertness, repute and good sense can come together—and exercise a demanding but benign influence on development work at large.

The good influences are as easy to identify, then, as the bad. They have their points of origin in many places. Changing approaches to the initial training of teachers, different modes of handling teaching practice and the induction of new teachers into their first full job, changes in the methods by which curriculum and teaching are organized within schools as well as changes in the outward organization of schools (by introducing nursery education or by setting up middle schools or comprehensive secondary schools), all these make it easier for the review and renewal of what is offered to and learned by the child.

A more detailed picture of the checks and spurs on curriculum development has been drawn elsewhere—and has already been drawn many times and in different ways. Because there is already a comparatively large literature about curriculum development in England—when it had barely begun in 1964—there is the risk that those who are responsible for development may become too self-regarding. This, in turn, can lead to complacency, to fatigue through the over-use of particular ideas or to the kind of nausea which descends on one when the repetition of ideas reveals only their pallor and inadequacy.

But while the history of curriculum development is still young it is perhaps easier to pick out the good and the bad. It is easy, still, to look back to the originators of reform—to Brian Young and Tony Becher at the Nuffield Foundation and Derek Morrell, Philip Taylor, John Banks and Jack Wrigley at The Schools Council. It is remarkable to see, too, how quickly the cast-list grew and changed in the early years, to trace the influences which people have carried with them into the basic fabric of English education after some direct (and usually national) involvement in curriculum reform.

Constraint on improvement always has to be regarded as something to be rid of: occasionally, while curriculum development moves fast and far in its early years in England, it is possible to sense that mere fashionableness and the vogue for change may do more harm than good.

But behind this fear there is considerable achievement too in an education system which had been largely static in terms of curriculum change for many years. That achievement lies in the creation of a climate of thought which is interested in but not bemused by novelty. This in turn has made government, at both central and local level, more ready to find those resources which planned changes need. From this practitioners have been given the confidence of seeing curriculum development taken seriously. And given that confidence, the major influence of benefit in implementing reform is the readiness of teachers to devote time and energy to the job of professional improvement.

VII

The appraisal of development projects is central to any attempt to work out why teachers should co-operate willingly in the process of review and of improvement. At the root of it lie quite ordinary differences between willingness and reluctance in the way in which any of us will immerse himself in work which requires extra effort: I will be more likely to work with zest in what seems good. I will probably be apathetic or hostile towards what seems mediocre or to be over-sold.

How are judgments about quality and mediocrity reached? They do not always emerge from a rigourous process of evaluation: they are matters of hunch and of feeling, they depend on opinions which are passed around informally within a kind of curriculum underworld. Reputations are made and destroyed for projects and schemes in an informal but decisive manner.

Much of the favour which teachers feel for what they think are worthwhile projects of reform depends on practicalities. This means that if new teaching materials are involved, they must be pedagogically sound, comprehensive in what they aim at, well-produced, logical in their order of use and clearly explained. But how does all this emerge?

As a first example, a large series of sub-projects was launched under the overall title of *Linguistics and English Teaching* by the

Schools Council with the co-operation of the Nuffield Foundation and the Communications Research Centre at the Department of General Linguistics in University College, London in 1967.

Until that year a programme funded by the Nuffield Foundation had made it possible to enquire into the relevance of linguistics to the teaching of English as a first language. When the Schools Council became involved, it developed two projects of practical aid to schools: one, less well known, has the title of the 'Language in Use Project' and is concerned with pupils of secondary school age. It aims to help children to understand the nature and function of language and, at the same time, to develop the ability to handle spoken and written English. Another project which is aimed at younger pupils (ages five to seven years) is by now thoroughly well-known and much used. With the title of the *'Initial Literacy Project'* the purpose has been to examine the ways in which children are taught to read and to write and then to establish, as far as possible, why some methods are more successful than others.

The materials of the Initial Literacy Project have been published under the title *Breakthrough to Literacy*: these have consisted of short books which, after large-scale school trials, have tried to relate reading materials closely to the spoken language and first-hand experiences of children themselves (Mackay, *et al.*, 1970). The materials have also included a simple apparatus for sentence-making and for children's own collection of words. Guidance papers have been published with them; these emphasize the necessity for teachers to be constantly and deeply involved in the process of helping children to speak and to write and to share those experiences on which early language work is based. The message to teachers has also stressed the importance of 'patterning' and the need for as clear as possible an adult understanding of the influences which create variety amongst children's language patterns.

The shape of this particular project shows how a so-called pure research interest in (and knowledge about) what was a fairly recondite area of theory can be translated into usable, practical classroom materials. No claim is made for there being an ideal time or an ideal stage of development amongst children when the material can best be used: nor is it assumed that the materials are either revolutionary or that, in some respects, they go beyond what good infants' classes already do. But because it had to find out how far clear thinking could in fact aid the practising teacher if theory and practical work were to confront each other with understanding, the project was both necessary and (as it turns out) beneficial.

The benefits have, of course, yet to be proved: no formal evaluation of the project's effectiveness has yet been published and in the natural evolution of teaching methods it may take many generations of children to give us enough evidence to say firmly whether the project has major importance or simply an incidental effect. In terms of a single decade, however, there has been a helpful coincidence of this project with an increased sense on the part of teachers that activity and knowledge about language was growing.

A growing use of the terminology of oracy and of elaborated codes coincided with public criticisms about literacy in schools. Were reading standards high or low? Were all slow learners basically poor readers? Could a reluctance to learn on the part of some pupils in secondary schools be traced to early failures in reading? Uncertainties were cleared by the assistance which could be given to teachers by the straightforward popularization of theory.

The director of the Initial Literacy Project, Professor M. A. K. Halliday, has expressed the aim of his work as being not to provide all the answers but to provide teachers with a basis from which to give children good guidance (1964). This he has contrasted with earlier approaches to language, when the teacher either filled holes of ignorance in the child's knowledge or, through benevolent inertia, relied on the hope that it would be enough if each child could soak in an atmosphere in which language was used constantly in a variety of ways.

The aim of the director has been translated into action by the project organizer, D. Mackay. And action has followed not only on the preparation, testing, and amendment of materials but also on assiduous in-service training and explanation of the project's purpose and methods.

A second example of the genesis and growth of a project for curriculum improvement can be drawn from an area of work where there are far fewer certainties than exist even about the early acquisition of language. Here, the subject-matter is that of moral education.

In England, the origins of education included both schools supported by denominational interests and slightly later developments in state education where teaching was assumed to inculcate qualities such as industriousness, respect for the law, and humility in the face of eternal truths. Although early ideas about curriculum explicitly centred on reading, writing and arithmetic, the moral care of children was also assumed to be part of a school's job. The task was, of course, to be shared with the home and somewhat unequally shared, too. Parents were expected to provide a good home. Schools acted in reinforcement of the efforts of good homes and in compensation for homes (and parents) who were less good.

The language of moral education started in a simple way.

Gradually concerns about delinquency, broken homes and about the more subtle connection between parental interest in education and a child's attainment at school combined to alter the balance of responsibility. Since the last war a louder voice has been heard in official reports on education about the ethos of schools, about the ways in which school organization affects the ways in which children learn and, in turn, about the ways in which teacher-pupil relationships (as well as between pupils themselves) affect both the moral nature of learning and the *process* of learning.

In 1963 it was the Newsom Report on early leaving (*Half Our Future*, 1963) which highlighted the disparities of opportunity and of treatment which pupils might receive in English secondary schools. The Schools Council in 1965 published its *Working Paper 2: Raising the School Leaving Age.* Within it was laid out the type of programme of curriculum improvement which could give new meaning to secondary school work for pupils who had lost interest.

It was also hoped that the shape of the secondary school curriculum could change: instead of allocating two or three years to the preparation of some pupils for a public examination at 16 years and using the initial year or two of secondary education as a pre-preparatory stage (again for a minority of pupils) there was some optimism that it would be possible to design a continuous five-year curriculum, from 11 years to 16 years, and that distinctions might be eliminated (or sharply diminished) between the needs of pupils who would sit for public examinations and those who would be rejected.

Working Paper 2 acknowledged that the climate of learning had changed in English schools. Britain's empire had virtually disappeared and the balance between permissiveness and authoritarianism was changing. Values which had been assumed to be unchangeably established were now open to question.

When the Schools Council came to devise a programme to match the aspirations of Working Paper 2, the broader question of changing values was cast in more particular terms, particular to schools, to teachers and to pupils. Moral education became the label which was attached to several of these particularized concerns: if schools were to have responsibility for ethical or moral education (and this in the late 1960s was not quesioned), how were pupils to be taken to the point where they could make judgments, assess priorities, choose appropriate actions, justify them and defend them? Could moral choice be regarded as something towards which a person could be educated? Or was the whole field of moral perception a matter of genetics, of subconscious choices in child-rearing, of social psychology and of the immeasurable pressure of society's expectations?

If the education system was to grasp the problem of moral education, it had to assume that it was reducible to school treatment. Moral choice had, therefore, to be regarded as a human skill and one which could be acquired without unavoidable regard for matters of family upbringing, parental belief or environmental deficit. Further, if the process of acquiring skills of moral decision were to be promoted at school, it would be necessary for children to face real moral questions but to be able to answer them in a manner which would not produce the direct and sometimes disturbing consequences of moral choice in real life. But could situations of such choice be simulated?

At the time when those questions were before the Schools Council, the Farmington Trust was at work on something very comparable. The Trust, based on private philanthropy, had a working base at Oxford in a small team led by John Wilson. In publications before 1966 (Wilson, J. *et al.*) (when the Schools Council began its negotiations for the setting up of a project in moral education) John Wilson had set about de-mystifying ethics and social morality. He had aimed some of his publications specifically at schools: he was a moral philosopher, clear thinker and, most important, someone with good experience of school teaching.

Two projects emerged from early negotiations with John Wilson and the Farmington Trust. Both officially emerged as independent projects located at the Department of Educational Studies at the University of Oxford. But the influence and guidance of Wilson and the Trust became and remained strong.

The project which first had the main effect had been directed at the age range of 13 to 16 years. The title of the project was straightforward, simply *Moral Education* 13–16 (1967). The director, Peter McPhail, concentrated on questions which were posed in *Working Paper* 2 (Schools Council, 1965). The formulation of the problem changed during the life time of the original project; the formulation of possible answers was also altered. But the defined aims remained close to the central question: could curriculum, methods and teaching materials be devised which would help children in secondary schools to adopt a more considerate style of life? Could these children adopt patterns of behaviour which would take into account the needs, interests and feelings of other people as well as their own? Was it possible to aim at both changes of attitudes and changes of behaviour?

A project which attempted to answer conundrums such as these could only remain attached to reality if it enlisted the direct advice of schools. This was done and much of the project's work was carried out with the considerable involvement of working parties of teachers:

'As a result of considering . . . . teachers' views on how children
should be educated morally, the project decided

i not to think of moral education as a separate school subject

**ii to devise materials which could be used in a variety of subject
situations**

**iii to investigate those moral activities which were most frequently
mentioned as having moral value**

**iv to concentrate a considerable proportion of . . . . energy on
encouraging the introduction of a morality of communication at both
interpersonal and organizational levels.'**

From this official Schools Council description of the project it
can be seen how varied the overall approaches were to be. Materials
were built up from the suggestions and reactions of secondary school
pupils, secondary teachers monitored the production, trial and
evaluation of material and the connection between the project team
and the world of schools was very strong.

A considerable number of first publications appeared in 1972.
Among these was an introduction to the project itself (and by now the
title of the Project was *Lifeline*), a teacher's guide to the first part of
the project which also covered the purposes of the three other
parts, work materials for pupils themselves and a 'handbook on
the practice of democracy by secondary school pupils' (entitled
Our School, 1970).

The method of work has its own interest. The first part of the
project (*In other people's shoes*) was concerned to heighten the
sensitivity of children towards the needs of other people. The main
emphasis was on caring. The first series of materials asked practical
questions: they posed certain simple types of moral situation and
asked pupils what they would do. Each dilemma in this series was
concerned with two people. Hence it was unavoidable for the child
to think about other people's feelings and interests.

Next came materials which asked pupils to suggest what would
happen when certain kinds of hypothetical moral choice were made.
The purpose was to give children practice in working out the
consequences of an action. In these exercises, of which there were
many and which stemmed from a broad variety of origins, the aim
was to strengthen a child's awareness and imagination about the
possible or probable effects of specific actions.

The third part of this series centred on pupils' points of view. They
were, in effect, asked to reason, to exercise imagination and to
identify themselves with others in a way which would enable them
to combine their knowledge and their own first-hand experiences in
such a way as to produce what was hoped to be more considerate
behaviour.

The second major part of the project (*Proving the rule?*) went beyond the individual pupil. It admittedly started by exploring the effect of rules on individual people but the principal concern was with helping adolescent pupils to resolve the conflict of demands in behaviour when pressures were created ,by groups whose work lay outside the individual person's own experience.

The third and most sophisticated stage in the project's materials attempted to take the pupil beyond the present day and his native society. The aim this time was to help pupils to find and to adopt considerate answers in unfamiliar situations.

Throughout the project's efforts stress has been placed on the development of considerateness. Thus, of the third stage, it is said (and this comes from Peter McPhail's guide for teachers, *In other people's shoes*) that 'a boy or girl who can produce solutions considerate to others in response to this material and is motivated to do so is a sophisticated mobile social and moral performer'.

The outline to this project is simple and its demands, too, are simple. None of the situations which are posed for pupils is too absurd nor does it appear excessively artificial. Realism and credibility combine to win the attention of children as well as the support of teachers. Nevertheless one difficulty may mean much to the project as a whole: it is essential that the samples and case studies should as far as possible be devised to meet the situations and need of particular schools. It is also necessary that the teacher should not adopt an authoritarian approach to the way in which children handle the materials.

This last point had emerged at a slightly earlier date as an important one for the success of another project aimed at secondary school pupils and again taking its origins from the Newsom Report and *Working Paper* 2. This, the Humanities Curriculum Project, first concentrated attention on the production of materials but rapidly discovered the need to be more concerned with the organization and methods of teaching.

The Humanities Project was launched in 1967 jointly between the Nuffield Foundation and The Schools Council (Stenhouse, L., 1968). Its principal task was to enable growth to take place in the understanding discrimination and judgment which pupils could exercise in the human field. It was not so much a matter of personal conduct but, rather, of understanding the dilemmas of society. And since, as the director of the project (Lawrence Stenhouse) expressed it, dilemmas mainly arise around controversial issues which divide society, any consideration of major dilemmas could be expected to divide pupils, parents and teachers. What was needed was a 'dialogue between informed views' rather than a consensus. The views of teachers diverge, so do the views of children and their families. Hence, to analyse and understand the nature of such dilemmas as arise in questions about poverty, relations between the sexes, war, law and order and race relations what was needed was not formal instruction but disciplined discussion. In terms of effect upon pupils, too, what should be fostered was seen as personal responsibility and accountability for one's views and one's own actions rather than skill in searching for authority or for the legitimation which could be derived from other people's approval.

In brief, the Humanities Curriculum Project required that a teacher should remain impartial. Instead of acting as someone who formed the opinion of pupils he had instead to help them to weigh the evidence which was available. This causes difficulty because many teachers expect to act (and indeed were originally trained to act) as professionals who have to put a view forward, to argue for values and rationally to persuade pupils towards a certain view. Impartiality is in some ways awkward because it is alien to the idea of school-mastering.

This issue has been examined extensively and deeply in the materials which the project has published in and since 1971. Because it has taken the effects of its requirements on teachers very seriously it has opened to debate matters of significance and value to the present day view of professional teaching. And the difference in the way in which the question has been worked on between the Moral Education Project and the Humanities Curriculum Project points to some of the differences between one programme of curriculum development which accepts the need to scrutinize the implications of its own work ever more deeply and another which limits its role to demonstrating for teachers how a particular range of examples, materials and methods can be handled in pursuit of one well-defined end.

In contrast to the three projects which have been described as products of the Nuffield Foundation and The Schools Council jointly or of The Schools Council alone, a fourth represents another type of curriculum development in England.

This one—the Primary Extension Programme—was mounted by the National Council for Educational Technology in 1970 and was intended to run for three years. Under its director, Frank Blackwell, and with the aid of an independent source of funding (the Bernard Van Leer Foundation), the project is aimed at giving additional help to socially disadvantaged children between the ages of three and eight years.

One major aim has been to acquire the confidence of teachers quickly: teachers are given, too, examples of how they might develop their own materials and methods. The production of a complete course of materials is not the purpose. Rather, it is felt that teachers can be helped by being given a start, a confidence from the beginning which can take them further and deeper into finding new ways of giving direct help to children in talking, inquiring, making up their own ideas, writing about them and using them as a base from which to explore activities which lie within their own experience.

As the project's own description of its aims puts it:

'The programme uses simple apparatus for teacher and child and exploits filmstrips, audio cassettes and specially prepared printed booklets as its principal means of communication. The variety of media explored includes teazel-board materials, pictures, overlay illustrations, posters and books, work with "Instamatic" cameras and machines such as the Language Master and the Audio-Page. Audio-visual media are used not only to assist children to learn, but also to illustrate to teachers the use of some of the materials in action. A busy teacher can not only be given more information in this way, but also an opportunity to share other teachers' experiences.'

Because it is essentially a project in which it is hoped that teachers can take a new view of their own and their pupils' way of handling materials and equipment, of using time within school and in local expeditions, and of arranging the contributions of children to their own learning as a sensible base for a diversity of approaches to each next stage, the training of experienced teachers through short courses and the dissemination and sharing of ideas about new methods at Teachers' Centres have been activities of major importance. Approaches which were at first incredulous have changed into enthusiastic commitment. And the simplicity of the project's ideas command the respect of teachers: here, after all, is something straightforward and workable without any major revolution in previous practices. It is after all an *extension* of primary education. And although the search for new ideas here is not explicitly concerned with curriculum, methods and content, purposes and value are closely meshed. The larger (and usual) questions about curriculum are bound to arise.

VIII

Some of the problems and issues to which four fairly typical projects of development give rise at the present time in England have already been touched on.

Behind the particular opportunities and problems of separate pieces of planned change lie long-standing questions. These relate to the creation of a sense of trust for what is new and to the desire to sustain a constructively critical view of innovation among teachers. But the questions which arise also bear on the time, resources and energy which schools and teachers can be expected to devote to the review of what they do. Above all, one major question is posed: what might schools take on instead of those established approaches which may have lost repute or may have ceased to be attractive (to either pupils or their teachers) or may simply have become stale?

Sometimes this range of questions—and many more—are bunched together under the labels of resistance or rejection. But the further the process of curriculum development unfolds, the more obvious it becomes that separate projects have specific problems. Not all the difficulties arise from questions about values or about the role of teacher. Innovations of method and approach pose equally difficult problems: is retraining to aim at breaking down disbelief, at *selling* what is new? If not, can any attempt succeed which tries simply to put novelties in front of teachers, for them to pick and choose from an unprejudiced way?

To be too random or unstructured in managing what is offered to teachers risks confusion, disregard and boredom. The alternative is to thin out the many projects which are alive at any given moment (about 200 at any one time) and to concentrate on what is proved to be sound.

But what is proved sound depends on evaluation. This is built in to Nuffield Foundation and Schools Council developments but even then the evaluation is often late—necessarily so because proofs require results and these only fall into discernible patterns after the first four or five years of a project's work. There are, however, many other developments, particularly those which emanate from new outputs from educational publishers, which need not fall into any official, objective or lengthy pattern of assessment. What is more likely to carry weight is the set of opinions which teachers form and share with each other about each new thing which they experience. Hence, rigour and formality of evaluation is unlikely to be a good enough basis for a process of thinning out.

A second alternative is that a school should create its own structure of curriculum and should try out and then either reject or include within it, any project which carries particular weight. The assessment here is made by the school. If the structure of curriculum is faulty in its logic or imperfect in its definition of what the school wishes to achieve, judgments which are made about particular projects can be imprecise or distorted. And this process places a heavy weight of responsibility on the Heads and those senior members of staff in schools who are often untrained in curriculum management, who are directly concerned only with one subject or

with one small group of subjects, and who by experience and tradition
have relied on the separate judgments of individual heads of subject
departments.

The patterns of influence which affect the judgments and decisions
of Heads (and indeed of all those who make choices about curriculum
design at a local level) are as yet uncharted. Studies of power and
influence in the primary school, carried out by Taylor at the
University of Birmingham (Taylor, P. H. *et al.*, 1974), have started
to reveal a surprising picture and one which does not altogether
support the ideal of zealous teachers, clear minded planning and the
sharing of aspirations. In another way but with comparably unfore-
seeable results, Elizabeth Richardson at the University of Bristol
has started to reveal, in a study based on comprehensive secondary
education, how groups of teachers can influence—and react to—
each other in the process of planning new policies of curriculum,
new social structures and new teaching roles to replace the traditional
organization of schools (Richardson, 1973).

What is at present known in England represents only a shadowy
and half-made picture of the forces which operate on the side of
curriculum development.

IX

Curriculum development is meant to produce change. It can be
planned and some of its outcomes can be foreseen. But it differs from
other kinds of development in rather obvious ways. Changes on the
whole are not a matter of design, are not activities to which a known
end can be hoped for, nor are they matters of startling and radical
discovery which are likely to change men's view of the world at large.

Education changes slowly, shapelessly and in a way which is more
or less uncontrolled. The management of it is not a matter of dealing
with hard fact, clear aim, established policies, brilliant scientific
rivalry, nor is it something which often receives acclamation within
the public domain at large.

If education in England improves, develops, changes or differs in
any way from decade to decade, it is because particular people in
particular fields have had the patience, good fortune, insight and
good experience which is necessary to make them credible when they
wish to commend something new to other people.

The Education Acts which govern England and Wales affect the
curriculum of children from below the age of five to young people of
about the age of 18. There are definable segments within this age
range and teachers have loyalties, experiences and preferred ideas
in each sub-division.

Curriculum development at its most practical is concerned with an education service which offers schooling to a carefully defined range of pupils. The definition of the age and type of student makes things workable. It also means that when those who manage curriculum development wish to appeal to teachers who are responsible for providing education in its most direct form in classrooms, they have to be aware of the particular audience to whom they speak. Teachers are part of a publicly controlled system: their loyalty, when change is mooted, is to principles of professionalism rather than simply to ideals of better learning.

Thus, in the context of England's statutory service the development of curriculum is a matter of manageable and definable things or persons. The persons are parents, teachers and children. Curriculum development will not work unless those who are parents of children in schools present sufficient support and understanding at home for the work of schools to have some bite. Curriculum development will not work if teachers are not trained to expect that their role will change, that their task will need overhauling every five years or so, or that their outlook on what is meant by professionalism will be subject to both informed and unenlightened influences during the entire period of their working life.

Children matter because curriculum in the end is intended to ensure that they become better people than those who were educated before them. If curriculum is simply meant to provide a repetition, generation by generation, of comparable attitudes, similar expectations and identical capacities to fulfil roles within the industrial or social world, then the idea of development need not be raised in any way. But the larger system of social and economic expectation in which the education service is placed is further away from the teacher in the classroom. His relationship to the bigger system is indirect.

Apart from people, the manageable parts of the curriculum deals also with resources. Money matters because it can provide better education both initially and in terms of in-service training for teachers. Money matters, too, because it can provide better buildings in which children may carry out their learning and, also, that essential part of the process of curriculum development, namely the provision of a physically identifiable teachers' centre. Money also matters because it can buy materials which directly affect children's ways of learning. But the financial system behind education is something to which the teacher is only indirectly connected.

Conclusion

If the future of curriculum development is confined to quite simple definitions of practical matters affecting people and resources, the outlook may appear fairly bleak. People can be changed (even if we could skilfully use the ill-judged idea of social engineering) only slowly. Resources, too, can be increased year by year only in a very marginal way. There is little room for manoeuvre. There is little that can be quickly added to the repertoire of the developer. And there is not much that he can expect by way of greater direct assistance from those who can change the professional preparation of teachers. If, therefore, he is to manage anything it has to be confined to matters of attitude. Yet we know that it is illusory to speak about attitude-change as though it were something which in itself was concise, definable, or capable of being planned.

The education service provides the bare bones around which to create the body of curriculum. There is ample room for despair about the speed of change, about the depth of its effect and about the measure to which it is possible to avoid abuse of that which is new. Yet, as in all public activities, it is unreal to expect that things can be neat and tidy. Curriculum is dependent upon so many variable factors and upon so many differences of experience, training and attitude that the process of development faces an almost impossible task.

Those who are responsible for development have to be aware not only of the various ways in which people can do things systematically within their own field but, also, they have to remember the weight of human experience. They have to have sense, maturity, an awareness of the history of educational change, and above all to have patience and a faith in people. They have to know that it is unreal to expect rapid change or to assume that people will take on fresh attitudes of value overnight. And they will also know that to stand back—aghast, apathetic and lethargic—will achieve nothing. They have to balance enthusiasm with commonsense, knowledge with zeal, experience with hope.

If local government reorganization in England places rich and poor local education authorities together, money will have to be spent for a decade in reducing disparities and in trying to equalize basic items such as capitation allowances, grants to pupils and expenditure on school apparatus, equipment and books. If the spending of money has to be made consistent in the process of creating uniformity where it previously did not exist, the expansion, improvement and development of education services cannot be afforded.

In the immediate future the system of education in England will, then, not radically change nor is curriculum development likely, in the next 10 years, to flourish.

As a background to development we need constantly to be aware that there is no inevitability about the progress of curriculum development. Equally, there is no inevitability about the way in which teachers may be expected to alter what they do. Teaching is a profession in which much depends, as in other professions, on the integrity and energy of the individual member.

If a teacher knows that there are new ideas afoot, if he realizes that the method, content, purpose and style of teaching is under review, he will act unprofessionally if he does not take his own steps to find out and think about what is new and then act—and whether he acts in acceptance or rejection matters less than that he should have devoted honest thought to the problem. Hence, the basis of curriculum development has to be trust that the teacher knows where he needs help. He may only need slight stimulus or some added confidence; he may need only a little fresh information before setting off on his own quest.

Curriculum development, educational reform and the overall improvement of schooling can eat up any amount of energy, skill and money. If, however, the *statement of problems* is sufficient, if teachers can be trained and expected to see a continuing responsibility to monitor their professional performance and the efficiency of their professional equipment, they will find their own method of self-renewal. Resources would then cease to go in one direction. And the emphasis on retraining which starts from sources outside the teacher himself would diminish. The traditional resources of education could be used to stimulate and to interest teachers, to provide a variety of non-training aids and to provide a milieu in which the person's own sense of responsibility would be a paramount force. Instead of the continual repetition of one type of answer (that of formalized in-service training) to the question of how best to promote improvements of curriculum, the creation could begin of what has sometimes been called a learning community.

The shape and focus of such a community would change from time to time. The most essential part would shift from being sometimes within a school to a college of education, to a teachers' centre, to a research unit, to a library—or to discussion and to private reading on the part of the teacher himself. The provision of money for the organization of development and training would pay less attention to fixed systems than to the possibility of catching needs, teachers' readiness, inclinations, time and energy at the moment when these could best be directed to one purpose.

If a future pattern of development could reflect more of the sense of change by which we usually learn, review and reform any part of our professional way of life, there would be no need to look ahead to steadily mounting costs and to the steady exhaustion of sources of leadership. Leadership would matter less than stimulus and inspiration—and these could come from a number of different directions.

At the same time curriculum development has to be something which means a great deal to the teacher. It has to offer hope to those who have faith in the total effects of education and it also has to be something which does not pose questions about extremes of unreality. Those who have a responsibility for curriculum development have to know the limits of change. They have to see what it is that change requires of people.

Time may show that curriculum and the extension of reform within it is likely to be a permanent concern for those in English education. At present we can only assume that this will be so. But the assumption is as yet too tenuous to support a heavy structure of planning and rationalization.

Books and Sources: England

BELL, R. (Ed.) (1971). *Thinking About the Curriculum*. Milton Keynes: Open University Press.

BISHOP, A. S. (1971). *The Rise of a Central Authority for English Education*. London: Cambridge University Press.

CANE, B. (1969). *In-service Training*. Slough: NFER.

CAVE, R. G. (1971). *An Introduction to Curriculum Development*. London: Ward Lock Educational.

CORBETT, A. (1971). *Innovation in Education: England*. Paris: OECD.

DEPARTMENT OF EDUCATION AND SCIENCE (1970). Statistics of Education, special series no. 2. *Survey of In-service Training for Teachers, 1967*. London: HMSO.

DEPARTMENT OF EDUCATION AND SCIENCE (1972). *Education, a Framework for Expansion*. Cmnd 5174 (1972 White Paper). London: HMSO.

GLATTER, R. (1972). *Management Development for the Education Profession*. London: Harrap.

HOOPER, R. (1971). *The Curriculum Context, Design and Development*. Edinburgh: Oliver and Boyd.

HOYLE, E. (1969). 'How does the curriculum change?' *J. Curric. Studs.*, 1, 1 and 2 (Published by Collins.)

JENKINS, D., PRING, R. and HARRIS, A. (Eds.) (1972). *Curriculum Philosophy and Design*. Milton Keynes: Open University Press.

KERR, J. F. (1968). *Changing the Curriculum*. London: ULP.

MACLURE, J. S. (1969). *Educational Documents: England and Wales 1816–1968*.

MERRITT, J. and HARRIS, A. (Eds.) (1972). *Curriculum Design and Implementation*. Milton Keynes: Open University Press.

MONTGOMERY, R. J. (1965). *Examinations: an Account of their Evolution as Administrative Devices in England*. London: Longmans.

MORRELL, D. H. (1966). *Education and Change*. (Joseph Payne Memorial Lecture.) London: College of Preceptors.

MUSGROVE, R. and TAYLOR, P. H. (1969). *Society and the Teacher's Role*. London: Routledge and Kegan Paul.

OWEN, J. G. (1969). 'Administration of Social Change'. In: BARON and TAYLOR (Eds.) *Educational Administration and the Social Sciences*. London: Athlone Press.

OWEN, J. G. (1972). 'Curriculum and teachers' centres: a progress report', *Trends in Education*, Autumn. (DES).

OWEN, J. G. (1973). *The Management of Curriculum Development*. London: Cambridge University Press.

RAYNOR, J. and GRANT, N. (Eds.) (1972). *Patterns of Curriculum*. Milton Keynes: Open University Press.

RICHMOND, W. K. (1970). *The School Curriculum*. London: Methuen.

SCHOOLS COUNCIL (1967). *Working Paper no. 10: Curriculum Development: Groups and Centres*. London: HMSO.

TAYLOR, G. (Ed.) (1970). *The Teacher as Manager*. London: Councils and Education Press.

TAYLOR, P. H. (1970). *How Teachers Plan their Courses*. Slough: NFER.

WILSON, J. B. (1972). *Philosophy and Educational Research*. Slough: NFER.

Books and Sources: other countries

BENNIS, W., BENNE, K. and CHIN, R. (Eds.) (1969). *The Planning of Change*. New York: Holt, Rinehart and Winston.

BRUNER, J. S. (1972). *The Relevance of Education*. London: Allen and Unwin.

CENTRE FOR EDUCATIONAL RESEARCH AND INNOVATION (1972). *The Nature of the Curriculum for the Eighties and Onwards*. Paris: OECD.

GARDNER, J. W. (1963). *Self-renewal: the Individual and the Innovation Society*. New York: Harper and Row.

GROBMAN, H. (1970). *Developmental Curriculum Projects: Decision Points and Processes*. New York: F. E. Peacock.

GROSS, N., GIACQUINTA, J. B. and BERNSTEIN, M. (1971). *Implementing Organizational Innovations*. New York: Harper and Row.

MCLURE, R. M. (Ed.) (1971). *The Curriculum: Retrospect and Prospect*. Chicago: University of Chicago Press.

MARTIN, W. T. (Ed.) (1966). *Curriculum Improvement and Innovative: a Partnership of Students, School Teachers and Research Scholars*. Cambridge, Mass: Robert Bentley Inc.

NATIONAL EDUCATION ASSOCIATION (1967). *National Planning in Curriculum and Instruction*. Washington, DC: NEA.

ONTARIO INSTITUTE FOR STUDIES IN EDUCATION (1966). *Emerging Strategies and Structures for Educational Change*. Ontario: ISE.

PAYNE, A. (1969). *The Study of Curriculum Plans*. Washington, DC: NEA.

RICH, J. M. (1972). *Conflict and Decision: Analysing Educational Issues*. New York: Harper and Row.

RUBIN, L. (1970). *A Study in the Continuing Education of Teachers*. Santa Barbara, California: Centre for Coordinated Education, University of California.

SCHEFFLER, I. (1973). *Reason and Teaching*. London: Routledge and Kegan Paul.

SCHWAB, J. J. (1970). *The Practical: a Language for Curriculum*. Washington, DC: NEA.

SMITH, L. M. and KEITH, P. M. (1971). *Anatomy of Educational Innovation*. New York: Wiley.

SUSSMANN, L. (1971). *Innovation in Education: United States*. Paris: OECD, Centre for Educational Research and Innovation.

TYLER, L. L. (1970). *A Selected Guide to Curriculum Literature: An Annotated Bibliography*. Washington, DC: NEA.

TYLER, R. W. (1950). *Basic Principles of Curriculum and Instruction*. Chicago: University of Chicago Press.

WISEMAN, S. and PIDGEON, D. (1970). *Curriculum Evaluation*. Slough: NFER.

References

BLACKWELL, F. (1970). *Primary Extension Programme*. London: Council for Educational Technology.

CENTRAL ADVISORY COUNCIL (ENGLAND) (1963). *Half Our Future*. London: HMSO.

HALLIDAY, M. K. (1964). *Linguistics and English Teaching*. London: Nuffield Foundation.

HIRST, P. (1968). 'The Contribution of Philosophy to the Study of the Curriculum'. In: KERR, J. F. (Ed.) (1968). *Changing the Curriculum*. London: University of London Press.

KERR, J. F. (Ed.) (1968). *Changing the Curriculum*. London: University of London Press.

MACKAY, D., THOMPSON, B. and SCHAUB, P. (1970). *Breakthrough to Literacy*. London: Longmans.

MUSGROVE, F. (1968). 'The Contribution of Sociology to the Study of Curriculum'. In: KERR, J. F. (Ed.) Op. cit.

RICHARDSON, E. (1973). *The Teacher, the School and the Task of Management*. London: Heinemann.

SCHOOLS COUNCIL (1965). *Raising the School Leaving Age*. Working Paper no. 2. London: HMSO.

SCHOOLS COUNCIL (1967). *Moral Education* 13–16. Curriculum Development Project. London:

STENHOUSE, L. (1968). 'The humanities curriculum project', *J. Curric. Studs.* 1, 1, 26–33.

TAYLOR, P. H. (1968). 'The Contribution of Psychology to the Study of the Curriculum'. In: KERR, J. F. (Ed.) Op. cit.

TAYLOR, P. H., REID, W. A. *et al.* (1974). *Purpose, Power and Constraint in the Primary School Curriculum*. London: Macmillan/Schools Council.

WILSON, J. (1961). *Reason and Morals*. London: Cambridge University Press.

WISEMAN, S. (Ed.) (1961). *Examinations and English Education*. Manchester: Manchester University Press.

CHAPTER 6

Curriculum Development in the Federal Republic of Germany

Frank Achtenhagen

The importance of ideologies for curriculum selection has been emphasized by Mauritz Johnson: 'A given society may demand that curriculum be selected in conformity with a specified set of political, social, economic, or moral values' (Achtenhagen and Meyer, 1973). This question of the normative power of the bearers of social ideologies has always been central in German discussions of curriculum problems. It has been supplemented with a continuing controversy over what would be the 'objective,' 'scientific' way of working in the social sciences, and especially in educational theory. Always present, in addition to the prevailing social powers, are certain historically rooted intentions, which give rise to various 'counterideologies', which in turn exercise an influence on the field of policy. The resulting conflict finds expression in highly controversial publications on the *methology* of curriculum development.

Historical context of German curriculum development

Some historical review is necessary as a basis for understanding why it is that the German education literature is full of methodological commentary and advice, but short on concrete elaboration of specific projects. Such a review must focus on the endeavours of the *Geisteswissenschaftliche Pädagogik*, the demise of which has been formally declared (Dahmer and Klafki, 1968), but which nevertheless endures in the fields of educational theory and teacher training. Only through an examination of this theoretical position is it possible to interpret adequately various features of the German discussions of curriculum (cf. also Klafki, 1971).

Didactics aand lehrplantheorie

The starting point of the *Geisteswissenshaftliche Pädagogik*[1],

[1] Roughly translated, a humanistic pedagogy, one based on the human sciences. But some terms cannot be translated: 'Lehrplantheorie' may be construed as a theory of instructional courses, but it is not identical with 'curriculum theory' in the Anglo-American sense. Therefore, the German 'Lehrplantheorie' and 'Lehrplan' will be used throughout.

which dominated German pedagogics until the mid-1960s, was the break with those normative systems of education which try, through an appeal to final and highest norms (of a theological or philosophical nature), to align particular educational practices with these norms. Such normative systems assert that the aims and goals codified in the curriculum should (1) be deduced from the highest moral values, (2) be an expression of 'true' educational intention, and (3) be consonant with the divergent interests of children and youth. These normative systems were reflected in the field of educational policy by the ecclesiastical school board and by the prohibition against training elementary teachers in the universities.

Pedagogics was established as a separate discipline within the classical faculties of philosophy of the German universities in connection with the formulation of the methods and insights of hermeneutical philosophy by Wilhelm Dithey and others. Among the distinguished exponents of this *Geisteswissenschaftliche Pädagogik* were Friedrich Paulsen, Eduard Spranger, Max Frischeisen-Köhler, Herman Nohl, Wilhelm Flitner, and Erich Weniger.

The didactics of this 'school' were grounded in the belief that it is impossible to deduce curricula and instructional prescriptions in an unequivocal and conclusive manner from normative systems. Attention shifted, therefore, to the questions of how the Lehrplan currently regulating the everyday life of the school had been arrived at and what forces were instrumental in forming the curriculum. In 1930 Erich Weniger (1965) formulated the generally accepted answer: the *Lehrplän* are the results of a power struggle among different political groups, and even after their codification, the state, church, scientific community, and other groups would continue to try to exercise an influence on the aims and goals of the schools. Consequently, the new *Pädagogik* accepted as its central premise that the identification of aims, goals, and content for translation into concrete curriculum elements for a given period of schooling was neither a purely pedagog affair nor a matter of absolute mandate. It was necessary, therefore, to reject, on the one hand, the conception that educational theory could determine aims, goals, and objectives on its own authority and, on the other, that the teacher was obliged to accept uncritically every curricular demand put to him. Thus, the *Geisteswissenschaftliche Pädagogik* tried to specify how much freedom there should be in the instructional process, both for the teacher, who must decide the organization and development of each training period and therefore needs some freedom of action, and for the student, who should not be caught in a struggle for power between political forces seeking to win over the new generation.

The crucial role of curriculum construction was assigned to the political government which was responsible for educational planning; as a 'regulating factor' the government would give the various political groups an opportunity to influence youth. The legal justification for such influence was the fiction of a minimal consensus among all political groups. Weniger found two basic factors serving to justify this model in 1930: the government had replaced the rigid plans of instruction with more 'global' plans (*Richtlinien*) and it had instituted training for *all* teachers on an academic level.

Further justification for the theoretical position was the fact that the government took charge of the supervision of schools at the level of a ministerial department. This supra-regional agency, rather than local school boards, decided on the textbooks and syllabuses. Therefore, on the grounds that educational authority had been removed from the locally oriented, direct influence of separate political groups (especially the church), the *Geisteswissenschaftliche Pädagogik* achieved a greater degree of generality, centering its theoretical interest less on the construction of media and textbooks and more on the broader problems of general education (*Allgemein-bildung*).

The primary didactical problem was how to reconcile, in a pedagogically responsible way, the political and social tasks of the school and the development of the pupil. A typical formulation was, for example, 'What content is most appropriate for the fullest development of sensitivity and objectivity in young people now and for their own future lives?'[2] The central problem of didactics, therefore, was the application of pedagogical theory to educational practice, i.e. in support of the rights of youth and the autonomy of the individual. Thus, this pedagogical theory interpreted its function as providing an idealistic counter-position to the demands and claims to supremacy of the political groups.

This position, which leads to the identification of general human aims, goals, and content, persisted and even intensified after World War II, as the representatives of the *Geisteswissenschaftliche Pädagogik* returned to their professorial chairs, from which the majority had been driven away. The moral catastrophe of National-socialism gave rise to intensified efforts to specify general human objectives. Consequently, the *geisteswissenschaftliche* style of working underwent a period of revival.

The teaching programme, which was also called *Bildungstheo-retische Didaktik*, was consistently concentrated upon a search for

2

'Welche Gehalte sind für die Erschliessung der Sinn—und Sachwirklichkeit des jungen Menschen in unserer Zeit und des jungen Menschen für diese seine Zeit wesentlich?'

content which would foster the 'process of cultural development' (*Bildungsprozess*). Practice was guided by four principles:

1. The starting point of all considerations and efforts is the 'reality of education'(*Erziehungswirklichkeit*). The theory must both clarify and share responsiblity for this reality, with its limitations and difficulties.
2. Concepts are to be defined in terms of educational practice and intentions.
3. All manifestations of education are considered as historically given. All propositions which expound and prescribe timeless rules of education are rejected, and efforts are concentrated upon the interpretation of previously codified propositions.
4. The 'reality of education' is to be respected in its complexity, precluding the formulation of simplistic connections as a scientific basis. Initially, this principle was directed against normative concepts of a theological, philosophical, or political nature, but later it also became instrumental in combatting the empirical character of statements which had to be formulated restrictively in order to be testable.

Critique of the geisteswissenschaftliche pädagogik

The importance of this 'school' of pedagogy lies in the fact that the majority of German professors of education are influenced by it. The problems, methodological conceptions, and style of argument associated with it persist to the present day. Indeed, it can be averred that this persistence is one of the most important reasons why German curriculum development needs improvement.

In broad terms this system of pedagogical thought is subject to two main criticisms:

1. It lacks an efficient constructional theory. Some manuals for instructional practice exist, but the aims, goals, and recommendations have been formulated too vaguely. Only with luck is there any possibility of their being applied successfully.
2. A traditional procedure which concentrates on the interpretation of existing instructional structures neglects the possibilities of change. The primary impetus for school reform has not come from educational theory.

Both of these critical points can be demonstrated by the didactic proposals for school subjects made by this educational theory. When these proposals were translated into workable instructional plans, they did not result in school reform, even though there was a very strong political and theoretical interest in more constructive and operationalized methods of instruction and learning, as evidenced by the enthusiastic adoption of instructional technology and programmed instruction.

Various factors may have accounted for this interest in change:

1. After 1945, all fields of life in Germany needed to undergo a phase of reconstruction.

2. The extent of backwardness in the social sciences, particularly in relation to the United States, became evident not only with respect to research but also in the applied fields.

3. Comparable to the American 'Sputnik-shock', the slogan of '*Bildungsnotstand*' (national educational emergency) had currency in Germany. Primarily, the question was whether a sufficient number of graduate students would be produced.

4. The '*Strukturplan für das Bildungswesen*' (structural plan for the school system), which had been passed in 1969 by the first German *Bildungsrat* (National Council of Education), questioned the classical tripartite school system with its *Gymnasium, Realschule, Hauptschule,* and vocational education.

5. Around 1965, large scale school experiments began. These *Gesamtschulversuche* (comprehensive school experiments) were deliberately planned as contrasts to the traditional school system.

The *Geisteswissenschaftliche Pädagogik* succeeded in countering these experimental efforts for two principal reasons. Against the background of the discussions of the *general* aims and goals of education, the limited horizon of instructional technology and programmed instruction became manifest, especially since statements regarding the desirability of aims and content were lacking. Furthermore, the German prophets of these modern methods were not well versed in the tradition of educational theory. The obvious inconsistency between the scientific precision of technical methods and the naivete of accompanying theoretical arguments made for easy criticism. It also became apparent that sufficient evidence of successful results could not be provided.

Secondly, it was easy to show the limitations of the outlines of didactics based on behaviouristic or cybernetic arguments. Additional difficulties existed with respect to the related empirical methodology. In particular, the re-translation of Karl R. Popper's *The Logic of Scientific Discovery* evoked a passionate discussion among German educational theorists. The controversy over didactics concentrated on methodological problems, i.e., those pertaining to the 'right scientific' approach. Not the results, but the reasons for the method and terminology, dominated the discussion.

This reformulation of problems was reinforced by the entry of the social sciences into educational theory. When this happened, the *Positivismusstreit*, as Adorno called the controversy over positivism, found its way into the educational discussion, which it has now dominated for many years. Representative of the two contending parties are the names of Popper, Rudolph Carnap, Carl G. Hempel, and Hans Albert on the one side and of Theodor W. Adorno, Max Horkheimer, Herbert Marcuse, and Jürgen Habermas on the other. Empirical methods were resisted by degrading them through brilliant interpretations which succeeded in demonstrating the compatibility of the *geisteswissenschaftliche* method with the new dialectic critique of ideologies and of society.

But, while the *Geisteswissenschaftliche Pädagogik* was upheld by the *Positivismusstreit* in its scepticism toward empirical research, it was assailed from the other side by the dialectic critique, which maintained that its premises were too idealistic and its critical potential had been insufficiently realized. Its premises regarding the role of the state in curriculum development and the 'minimal consensus' between political groups, it was charged, overlooked the conservative or stabilizing function of the schools. Thus, the new questions raised by the critique of ideology precipitated a radical discussion of education that went beyond the question of the status and use of empirical methods. In short, with the onset of the methodological discussion, the *Geisteswissenschaftliche Pädagogik* neglected the theoretical aspects of a constructive foundation for curriculum development.

Origins of the curriculum discussion
In view of the situation in educational theory, it is not particularly surprising that foreign (especially Anglo-American and Swedish) models of curriculum development were received with enthusiasm. These models were introduced to Germany primarily by Klaus Huhse's review (1968) and by Saul B. Robinsohn's more systematic book, *Bildungsreform als Revision des Curriculum* (1967). The accentuation of the constructive aspect, the criticism of the traditional schools, and the suggestion of a solution struck a responsive chord in both the theoretical discussion and public opinion. For a number of years, almost every educational proposition was related to curriculum problems, and politicians campaigned for election on curricular slogans. This euphoria has since given way to more sober considerations, however, and the theoretical difficulties of the *Geisteswissenschaftliche Pädagogik* have reappeared, albeit redecorated with a new terminology. Again there is the preoccupation with methodological discussions and a corresponding neglect of the reality of practices in the schools, regard for empirical methods in

both research and instruction, the corresponding permanent extension and complication of curriculum development, and the propaganda of action research in lieu of traditional research, of 'open curriculum' and 'teachers' centres' in place of traditional organizational forms, and of new methods of teacher training. These phenomena are best understood by reference to actual projects, as well as to the general theoretical discussion.

Actual problems of curriculum development

Along with the adaption of curriculum development procedures, a new terminology was introduced, especially to replace *Lehrplan* and its combinations. Consistent with the heated debate, many different definitions of 'curriculum' and 'curriculum development' can be found.

The meaning given to curriculum

The prevailing tenor of the German curriculum discussion is reflected by the definitions given in *Strukturplan für das Bildungs-wesen* (Structural plan for the conduct of education) of the *Deutscher Bildungsrat*. These definitions differentiate *Lehrplän* and 'curriculum' (pp. 62–63), the former referring to a framework of differently accentuated learning programmes (the curricula) for the students. Besides this differentiation of offerings in one and the same school (which is unusual in German schools), the curriculum 'determines not only objectives and contents, but also the necessary sequences and learning steps and the corresponding methods, materials, and technologies'. In addition, there is the evaluation of objectives, which necessarily has two aspects: How good is a curriculum? and How well does the curriculum succeed in achieving its goals?

Another common element in German discussion of curriculum development is the identification of decision processes, of which five types can be discerned in the various projects (Achtenhagen and Meyer, 1973). There are decisions (1) to collect information, after reflection upon scientific research and its social application; (2) to select and classify scientific hypotheses; (3) to order a specific segment of information and assign it to learning sequences or curricula; (4) to use a curriculum instructionally; and (5) to evaluate the curriculum. A number of projects have been designed at various decision levels since Robinsohn's booklet first appeared (cf. examples in Achten-hagen and Meyer, 1973; Hesse and Manz, 1972; Meyer, 1972).

State of research activities

The thesis which has been advanced above is that the theoretical difficulties of the *geisteswissenschaftliche Didaktik* can be found at present in the activities of curriculum development (even if they are obscured by a new terminology). This problem will now be considered under three headings: the first refers to the observed research activities, the second to the contemporary literature, and the third to promising directions.

The practice of curriculum development. After the initiation of the curriculum discussion, a number of projects were formulated and presented to the pedagogic public. Initially the differences of opinion among these projects was stressed, but upon sober reconsideration it became quite apparent that they resembled each other greatly (Achtenhagen and Meyer, 1973; Hesse and Manz, 1972). Nor is this surprising, since all of the projects tried to substantiate the conclusions of the *geisteswissenschaftliche Didaktik* by means of the instruments of empirical social research. The adaptation of foreign curriculum literature served for the most part to reformulate the problems in a new way. It should be noted that the field of evaluation was underdeveloped in Germany, and the term 'evaluation' has never really been understood as a subsequent theoretization of curricular practice.

For various reasons, less and less is heard from these research projects. Some are killed by the refusal of controlling political bodies to supply the necessary financial and personal resources. Much controversy has surrounded attempts to recall responsibilities of the politically competent curriculum development into the central divisions of the ministerial bureaucracy and to accommodate the curriculum reform to the modest budget for education. Other projects have been wrecked or redefined. Aside from the naive overestimation of the attainability of research goals, the reasons why projects were ruined can only be surmised to involve methodological, financial, personal, temporal, and political difficulties. Unfortunately, no firm knowledge is available as to the real reasons, the revelation of which would presumably provide essential understanding for further curriculum development.

Some projects are, of course, still in progress. They have been surveyed by Haller (1972), who found it possible to classify 119 of the 130 projects investigated into five idealized types:

1. Innovative curriculum development—63 projects characterized by a scientific orientation (analogous to Grobman's 'developmental curriculum' projects), the construction of learning materials for an extended period, and the additional production of teachers' handbooks, films, tests, and the like;

2. projects of teacher's teams—15 such efforts to promote curriculum development without cooperation with universities or other institutions;

3. modified *Lehrplankommissionen*—nine new-style commissions for instructional plans currently sponsoring 16 projects which go beyond the usual goal-codification function of German commissions to the operationalization of goals through the development of learning materials (cf. Mager, Bloom, or Krathwohl);

4. thematically limited projects—13 groups which only wanted to plan certain lessons, e.g., a controlled experiment for programmed instruction;

5. basic research-orientated projects—12 projects which aim not only to develop concrete curricula but also to conduct more theoretical and basically orientated research, mostly involving ability grouping or test construction.

Haller's study was limited to those projects which had been announced by institutions, ministries, and associations. Nevertheless, the classification gives an idea of the spectrum of activities subsumed by the term 'curriculum development'. It is also interesting to note the distribution of subject fields with which the projects dealt:

Natural sciences—22 projects, which at the time of the study had developed 400 lessons, with ten times that many needed;

Mathematics—16 projects, mostly working on mathematics for younger students, e.g., introduction to set theory;

Social science—24 projects on social learning, history, local government, and related fields;

Geography—seven projects;

Language and literature—nine projects in the field of German (especially language promotion programmes), one in Latin and Greek, eight in modern foreign languages;

Religion and philosophy—seven projects;

Arts, music, and sports—five projects;

Vocational education—seven projects;

Multiple subjects—19 projects, not, however, dealing with the integration of the subjects.

It should be noted, in summary, that many of these projects are still in progress and that only a few have been completed. Significantly, very few are in the design stage, a symptom, perhaps, of declining interest in curriculum development on the part of theoreticians, teachers, and politicians. In other words, the German discussion of curriculum development took place on a very high theoretical level in the context of considerable political urgency—before the first practical trials had been carried out.

The results of interviews conducted by Haller with researchers in 23 selected projects indicate some of the difficulties in German curriculum development. Conspicuously, a relatively high number of project collaborators (about 33 per cent) had only been associated with a university and had no practical school experience. In addition, the results revealed a great lack of prior theoretical and practical knowledge of curriculum development. About 53 per cent of those interviewed claimed to have had adequate knowledge of curriculum development when they began working on their projects, but about 46 per cent had had no experience in such activities. No doubt, participating in a concrete project establishes the necessary curricular competency. Some 43 per cent of the staff members were seeking to qualify themselves scientifically through research work in a project. The high levels of training demanded by the project groups imply that these curriculum activities are dependent upon the universities.

The isolation of the various curriculum projects in the Federal Republic is remarkable. One of the improvements most desired by the interviewed staff members is better communication about other projects' experiences and about practical school situations; only 25 per cent expressed satisfaction with their opportunities for external scientific communication.

Another interesting finding of this pilot study was that curriculum development appears to be an activity *sui generiss* having little connection with practice in the schools. Apart from the differentiation of theory and practice, it appears possible to distinguish also between more theoretically and more pragmatically oriented theoreticians.

The state of the curriculum literature. A new kind of literature is proliferating which is relatively independent of this practical research and development activity and which at least is referred to as *curricular*. It specializes in the discussion of the published petitions or proposals for curriculum projects. The focus of interest is not instruction itself, but the proposals as to how it should be organized. At another level, with other terminology, the methodological aspects of project petitions are discussed. The motivation for this discussion is not primarily educational, but rather sociological and economic (cf. Huisken, 1972; Becker and Jungblut, 1972; Hesse and Manz, 1972). The politically motivated theoretical cant which is directed at curriculum petitions is very interesting and certainly necessary, but since it lacks empirical equivalents which might serve as a basis for corroboration, the inferences made regarding the consequences of proposed projects cannot be refuted because the curriculum elements to be elaborated by the projects do not yet exist. The most important argument in this new literature reveals a general suspicion of technocracy, coupled with hints at political henchmanship. The writers try to evaluate speculatively whether the goal of individual emancipation can be promoted and definitely attained by a specific project and whether the results of curriculum development generally are unequivocally liberating.

Thus, the critique is couched in such a way that any curriculum research undertaking which does not involve political activism in a desired direction would automatically be obsolete. For, in view of the many unsolved social and political problems, this type of research would not be capable of changing the quality of instruction; learning and teacher training might be improved, but the aims of the educational system would remain untouched.

This suspicion of technocracy with respect to empirical research is not new. Bahrdt (1970) interpreted the conflict over the 'right' methods of social research as symptomatic of a low 'degree of maturity' in a discipline. Barhdt's thesis concerned sociology, but it applies equally to the actual state of German curriculum theory. He pointed out that discussions are being resumed on questions that were regarded as essentially having been settled. To suspect all kinds of empiricism or technocracy is anachronistic. There was once agreement among the experts that 'blind' empiricism may not only be misused politically, but also can merely lead to the production of a 'graveyard of numbers'. But they also agreed that purely speculative theorizing which avoids the risks of falsification would be scientifically inadmissible.

Unchecked speculation is today passing through a renaissance, as if we lived in the era of Schelling and Fichte. One consequence follows almost inevitably: 'In the meantime, the cornered so-called "positivists" (who often are not positivists in the rigorous sense) refine their tools for model building to a level of generality that is simply irrevocable because it is meaningless, since the tools are never devoted to the explanation of social reality. Some persist in the outmoded thesis that science *per se* could be non-political' (Bahrdt, 1970).

Hand in hand with this relatively undifferentiated suspicion of technocracy is another argument which is also remote from practices in the schools. In this discussion of curriculum *research*, school and instruction appear as only two among a variety of variables representing social reality. The casual variables, determining the entire educational system, are economic in nature. 'Educational economics, curriculum theory, and didactics seem to contain the pattern of concepts for capitalistic strategies for rationalizing the whole educational system' (Becker and Jungblut, 1972). Not *curriculum* research itself, but 'curriculum *research* research' stands at the focus of interest. Here the hidden danger lies in neglecting Robinsohn's proposal, which provided a basis for finding a connection with school practice.

Although this critique of curriculum development is necessary and completely legitimate, it must not lead to a neglect of urgent, practical school problems, an obvious tendency which is revealed indirectly in Haller's pilot study. The efforts within the new literature of sociology and educational economics to solve the problems of curriculum development can be characterized as strategies of losing the problems by making complexity more complex. This sophistication is inevitable because any simplification within this literature would naturally come under the suspicion of technocracy.

The significant point is that this literature took Robinsohn's book seriously in its advocacy of a total revision of curriculum preceded by the necessary analysis of life situations. It is to *that* analytical task that the social sciences as a whole must address themselves. If educational consequences, and especially prescriptions for action, are to be deduced from this analysis of social life, then the task is too important to entrust to the educationists alone. Interdisciplinarity, with reference to political-economic and sociological experience, would be a necessary consequence for research.

This demand is not new for educational theory, but according to this newer literature, it has never satisfactorily been met. Under the burden of the *geisteswissenschaftliche* tradition, nearly every curriculum project would have been too analytical and not sufficiently radical or daring in design. This charge may well be justified, and it is directed at what is probably the central problem of curriculum research, namely, how the highest political norms to which a state feels bound, or should feel bound, are supported by a particular learning sequence. The German didactics use the term 'deduction' to denote this problem. Meyer (1972) identified the difficulties attending a deduction of objectives from general norms and aims: The more precisely authors express the results of deductions, the more arbitrary the deductions themselves seem to become; the broader the deductive hypotheses are formulated, the more difficult it seems to be to specify the procedure of deduction.

The earlier excursion into the *geisteswissenschaftliche Didaktik* sought to point out that the reflection on normative theoretical systems cannot solve the problem of defining objectives. Unequivocal positive deduction of norms as aims for social action is impossible. The concept of 'autonomy' itself, as it has evolved following Horkheimer, Adorno, or Habermas, is a negatively limiting category. But the newer sociologically and economically oriented literature is especially critical of the lack of deductive coherence between political norms and instructional objectives. The difficulty is apparent, for if coherent deductions cannot be unequivocally formulated, then the question arises as to how this central problem of curriculum development shall be solved, i.e., how this newer literature can resolve the dilemma without unmasking itself.

The solution that is offered may be reduced to a simple common denominator: It is necessary to look for theories which are so all-embracing that they are able to classify and solve every problem of social reality. (Here again arises the figure of 'normative didactics', which was also supported by theological and normative-philosophical dogmas.) But the general explanatory power of such a theory must obviously be proved, and the infinite regress is evident. It is no wonder, then, considering the educational discussion, that all attempts to refer the deductive coherence between political norms and instruction to sociological or political-economic foundations fail. Nor do hints at the necessity of formulating such metatheories represent the solution.

This reduction does not impugn the necessity and competence of the sociological and economic critique. The theoretically based explications of economically motivated political influences upon the educational system have fostered more perceptive observation and evaluation of pedagogical phenomena and have opened the possibilities of further analysis.

It would be incorrect to suggest that the critics of curriculum projects would not have recognized the deductive problems, for references to practices in the schools, cannot be avoided in discussions of curriculum research. Moreover, a methodology must reflect the further strategic procedure. But this new literature does not purport to set up explicit decision rules.

Proposals for future curriculum work. The current state of curriculum development in the German Federal Republic may be summarized as follows:

1. In the literature there are numerous methodological treatises dealing with practice but never arriving at it. Responses appearing in the journals of teachers' associations bluntly reveal satiation with those expositions; educational practitioners do not make use of this type of literature.

2. The Ministries of Education of the German states try to keep curriculum development on a short lead. A number have established their own central institutes, e.g., *Staatsinstitut für Schulpädagogik, München; Institut für Staatsbürgerliche Bildung in Rheinland-Pfalz; Institut für die Pädagogik der Naturwissenschaften an der Universität Kiel.*[3] In some states, e.g., Hessen, Niedersachsen, Nordrhein-

---

[3] The State Institute for School Pedagogy, Munich; The Institute for Citizenship Education in the Rhineland-Palatinate; The Institute for Science Education at the University of Kiel.

Westfalen, there are political struggles regarding the new instructional guidelines (Rahmenrichtlinien), which are formulated in accordance with some results arising from curriculum theorizing.

Alternative recommendations tend to favour dispersing curriculum development to the 'grass roots'. There is a hope that 'open curricula' and 'institutions for school-centred curriculum development' (*Institutionen schulnaher Curriculumentwicklung; Regionale Pädagogische Zentren*—comparable to 'teachers' centres') will help to resolve some of the difficulties by means of action research. These alternatives are logical responses to the theorizing literature. By revising didactic theories to deal with practical problems, it is thought possible both to preserve the political dimension of curriculum decision-making and to persuade teachers, students, and parents that they have a responsibility to help solve the problems of curriculum. The principal arguments for introducing the missing practical relevance cite such factors as teachers impatient of theory; the conflicts with the ministerial bureaucracy which, as noted earlier, often accompany the introduction of curricular reforms; the neglect of problems of educational practice; and the danger of manipulation and indoctrination in the uncritical acceptance of curricula which approach the status of 'doctrines of salvation' (Heipcke and Messner, 1973).

In preparing lessons the individual teacher acts under a double constraint in having to justify the aims and objectives to the students and to himself. Therefore, the question is whether it is possible to reconcile the potential conflicts between the teachers' objectives and the students' functional goals. One answer is that action research may be an adequate methodological procedure. As expectations of behaviour and as things to be achieved in the instructional processes, objectives may frequently be contrary to the functional goals of students (and also of teachers), which are founded in subjective needs, intentions, and interests. Usually, these functional goals are only brought to bear as starting points and motivations for the realization of the objectives. Only the formulation of a common interest by means of action research—this is the central thesis—can solve these problems. 'Open curricula', instead of 'teacher-proof curricula', must be developed.

The proponents of this thesis are not blind to its dangers. They point out that this proposal should not be a rigid model, but rather, a kind of 'leading principle', and they recognize the possibility that instruction might become the scene of permanent conflicts. They also realize that the implementation of their recommendations might place the teacher under excessive strain, unless the form of teacher training were also changed. The danger of a lowered standard of instruction is also seen. While the model of 'open curricula' justifiably criticizes a mode of instruction in which students are expected to suspend their subjective horizon of experiences and which concerns itself only with behaviour that is subjectively neutral, easily measurable, and comparable, it is essential to protect from chaotic exaggeration those curricula which tend to approach each student in terms of his own individual style of life (Rumpf, 1973). Only valid methods of evaluation can help to assess the extent of success, the quality of experience, and the desirability of particular instructional processes.

These proposals were also reflected in the recommendations of the second *Deutscher Bildungsrat* entitled, '*Förderung praxisnäher Curriculumentwicklung*' (Promotion of Practice-related Curriculum Development). This council recommended the establishment of regional centres of curriculum development for the purpose of promoting 'open curricula' comparable to those appearing in England and the United States. Through the centres, cooperation is to be fostered among researchers and teachers, employed both on a full-time and part-time basis. At the same time, the semi-official council called attention to the mishandling of the current curriculum projects, criticizing most severely the discrepancy between their high expectations and their actual results. Nevertheless, it was conceded that the projects had made it possible to diagnose actual school problems better.

The council offered some criteria for four aspects of school-related curriculum development:

1. *Development and legitimation of goals and objectives*
Availability of a general didactic frame of reference
Attention to the non-educational disciplines
Transformation of the general aims into concrete instructional concepts
Extent of potential controversy stemming from divergent interests
Relative undistortedness of decision situations
Clarity of the development and legitimation

2. *Designing and structuring*
Regard for different competencies and interests (disciplines, administration, teachers, students, parents)
Attention to a wide spectrum of non-educational disciplines
Experimental attitude of the developers
Undistortedness of the development processes (due to lack of time, external influences, conflicts, lack of organization, etc.)
Interpretation of results
Amount of innovation (what is really new?)

3. *Implementation and elaboration under practice-related conditions*
Extent of variation of instructional conditions
Extent of corroboration of expectations
Extent of secondary effects
Diagnosis of interferences with instructional processes
Working up and using the results for subsequent development
Quality of feed-back
Potential stimulation

4. *Implementation in actual practice*
Possible reconstruction of instructional actions (also under unfavourable conditions)
Loss of curricular flexibility or neglect of intentionalities
Learning success of students
Increasing competence of teachers

The close analogy between these proposals and the concept of the *Geisteswissenschaftliche Pädagogik* is fascinating. With the enumeration of these criteria, curriculum development starts all over again at the beginning, for almost every criterion listed represents a problem which should have been solved by curriculum theory. The problem of curriculum content cannot be solved by organizational designs alone. These recommendations explicitly point to the necessity of basic research. It is debatable whether such a separation of 'basic' and 'applied' research is advisable. But a concluding look to the future underscores the necessity of research, quite apart from the proposals for practice-related development.

The Future
Still awaited are not only the results of the trials of 'open curricula' under the auspices of regional curriculum centres, but also those of current projects. Among the latter, the following projects are expecially noteworthy:
1. analyses of present and future life situations, pointing out the students' competence and autonomy (cf. Zimmer, in Robinsohn, 1972);
2. projects which apply lists of educational criteria to present subjects (*didaktische Strukturgitter*—didactic frameworks; cf. Blankertz, 1971, 1973);
3. workshop projects which seek models of cooperation between university and school (von Hentig, 1971);
4. projects which probe new ways of determining objectives (Aregger and Isenegger, 1972);

5. interdisciplinary investigations of the possibilities of co-operation between educational theory and other disciplines (e.g., for educational theory and linguistics: Achtenhagen and Wienold, in Achtenhagen and Meyer, 1973).

Besides these selected current projects, we must wait for the findings of the public institutes (especially the one at Kiel) and for the effects of the new *Rahmenrichtlinien*.

Additionally, there are attempts to emphasize the relationship between instruction and learning. This field has been neglected by German curriculum researchers in favour of more theoretical and organizational considerations. Some of the factors which have hindered the adaptation of psychological research are the brevity of most learning experiments and their neglect of the curricular context with its implication that prior learning processes are basic to subsequent ones. Also the influence of learning materials has not sufficiently been taken into consideration in experimental designs and, throughout, an undifferentiated learning capacity has been assumed, overlooking individual differences.

A priority task of curriculum development in the Federal Republic of Germany, therefore, is long-term research on instruction and learning processes. This would be a very ambitious research undertaking. There is a great need for research about the interdependence (*Implikationszusammenhang*) of instructional and learning goals and objectives, of instructional and learning strategies, of media, and of personality variables.

The nesting of these questions into a curricular context seems necessary in order to assure the applicability and testability of the research. Certain limitations must, of course, be imposed on such a programme. The reference system should show precisely the theoretical amount of cognitive and affective behaviour, the theories should be school-centred, i.e., indicate the range of application in schools, and problems of individualization and ability grouping should be considered.

The enumeration of these tasks for the future closes the circle inside which German curriculum development goes forward: too many projects, too many methodological controversies, and too few concrete results.

In the Federal Republic of Germany

105

References

ACHTENHAGEN, F. (1972). 'Lehrplan-Theorie', in FROMMBERGER, H., ROLFF, H-G., and SPIES, W. (Eds.) *Die Kollegstufe als Gesamtoberstufe*. Braunschweig: Georg Westermann.
ACHTENHAGEN, F. (1973a). *Didaktik des fremdsprachlichen Unterrichts. Grundlagen und Probleme einer Fachdidaktik*. Weinheim and Basle: Julius Beltz.
ACHTENHAGEN, F. (1973b). 'Methodologische Probleme empirischer Begleituntersuchungen zu pädagogischen, Innovationsversuchen unter statistischem Aspekt,' in *Zeitschrift fur Pädagogik* p. 43 ff. Weinheim: Julius Beltz.
ACHTENHAGEN, F. and MEYER, L. (Eds. 1973). *Curriculumrevision—Moglichkeiten und Grenzen*. 3rd Ed., Munich: Kosel.
AREGGER, K. and ISENEGGER, U. (Eds., 1972). *Curriculumprozeß: Beiträge zur Curriculumkonstruktion und—implementation*. EBAC-Projekt, Bericht 8/9. Freiburg, Switzerland: Pädagogisches Institut der Universität.
AREGGER, K. (1973). *Interaktion im lehrerzentrierten Curriculumprozeß*. Basle: Beltz.
BAHRDT, P. (1970). Foreword to KERN, H. and SCHUMANN, M. *Industriearbeit and Arbeiterbewußtsein*. Frankfurt am Main: Europäische Verlagsanstalt.
BECKER, E. and JUNGBLUT, G. (1972). *Strategien der Bildungsproduktion*. Frankfurt am Main: Suhrkamp.
BLANKERTZ, H. (1970/2). 'Lehrplantheorie and Curriculum-Forschung', in: *Der Deutschunterricht*, 1970/2, p. 7 ff. Stuttgart: Klett.
BLANKERTZ, H. (1971). *Curriculumforschung—Strategien, Strukturierung, Konstruktion*. Essen: Neue Deutsche Schule.
BLANKERTZ, H. (1973a). *Fachdidaktische Curriculumforschung—Strukturansätze für Geschichte, Deutsch, Biologie*. Essen: Neue Deutache Schule.
BLANKERTZ, H. (1973b). *Theorien and Modelle der Didaktik*, (7th Ed.). Munich: Juventa.
Curriculum Research and Development. (1973). Report of a workshop for German and Dutch participants held under the auspices of the Netherlands Foundation for Educational Research (Stichting voor Onderzoek van het Onderwijs). December 7th-10th, 1970 in Vierhouten, the Netherlands. The Hague 1973.
DAHMER, I. and KLAFKI, W. (Eds.): (1968). *Geisteswissenschaftliche Pädagogik am Ausgang ihrer Epoche—Erich Weniger*. Weinheim and Berlin: Beltz.
DEUTSCHER, B. (1970). *Strukturplan für das Bildungswesen*. Bonn: Empfehlungen der Bilgungskommission.
FLECHSIG, K-H. (1969). *Die technologische Wendung in der Didaktik*. Konstanz Universitätsverlag.
FREY, K. (1971). *Theorien des Curriculums*. Weinheim, Berlin, Basel: Beltz.
HALLER, H-D. (1972). 'Verfahrensbedingungen in der Curriculumentwicklung in der Bundesrepublik Deutschland.' Gutachten für die Bildungskommission des Deutschen Bildungsrates, Bonn.
HEIPCKE, K. and MESSNER, R. (1973). 'Curriculumentwicklung unter dem Anspruch praktischer Theorie', in *Zeitschrift für Pädagogik* 1973/3, p. 351 ff. Weinheim: Beltz.
HENTIG, H. von *et al*. (1971). *Das Bielefelder Oberstufen-Kolleg*. Suttgart: Klett.
HESSE, H. A. and MANZ, W. (1972). *Einführüng in die Curriculumforschung*. Stuttgart, Berlin, Cologne, Mainz: Kohlhammer.
HUHSE, K. (1968). *Theorie und Praxis der Curriculum-Entwicklung*. Berlin: Max-Planck-Institut für Bildungsforschung.
HUISKEN, F. (1972). *Zur Kritik bürgerlicher Didaktik und Bildungsökonomie*. Munich: List.

KLAFKI, W. (1971). 'Erziehungswissenschaft als kritisch-konstruktive Theorie: Hermeneutik, Empirie, Ideologiekritik', in *Zeitschrift für Pädagogik* 1971/3, p. 351 ff. Weinheim: Julius Beltz.

KLAFKI, W. (1973). 'Handlungsforschung im Schulfeld', in *Zeitschrift für Pädagogik* 1973/4, p. 487 ff. Weinheim: Julius Beltz.

KNAB, D. (1971). 'Ansätze zur Curriculumreform in der BRD', in betrifft: erziehung 1971/2, p. 15 ff. Weinheim: Beltz.

KOLLEGSTUFE, N. W. (1972). *Strukturförderung im Bildungswesen des Landes Nordrhain-Westfalen,* Chapter 17. Ratingen, Kastellaun, Dusseldorf: Aloys Henn.

MEYER, H. L. (1972). *Einführung in die Curriculum-Methodologie,* Munich: Kösel.

MOLLENHAUER, K. (1972). *Theorien zum Erziehungsprozess.* Munich: Juventa.

REFORM VON BILDUNGSPLÄNEN (1969). *Sonderheft 5 zu Rungespräch.* Frankfurt/ Main, Berlin, Bonn, Munich: Moritz Diesterweg.

ROBINSOHN, S. B. (1971). *Bildungsreform als Revision des Curriculum und Ein Strukturkonzept für Curriculumetwicklung,* 3rd Ed., Neuwied and Berlin: Luchterhand.

ROBINSOHN, S. B. (Ed.) (1972). *Curriculumentwicklung in der Diskussion.* Stuttgart: Klett; and Dusseldorf: Schwann.

RUMPF, H. (1973). 'Divergierende Unterrichtsmuster in der Curriculumentwicklung', in *Zeitschrift für Pädagogik* 1973/3, p. 391 ff. Weinheim: Julius Beltz.

WENIGER, E. (1962, 1965). *Didaktik als Bildungslehre.* Volume I: 'Theorie der Bildungsinhalte und ded Lehrplans,' (6./8. ed.) Volume II: 'Didaktische Voraussetzungen der Methode in der Schule' (2nd ed.) Weinheim: Julius Beltz.

CHAPTER 7

Curriculum Development in the Netherlands

K. Doornbos

Preface

This contribution to the comparative study of curriculum development is based on a discussion paper that has been used for an
introductory chapter of an official report on the organization and
coordination of curriculum development in the Netherlands (1973).
Very recently, as a result of the work of the State Committee for the
Organization of Curriculum Development (COLO) the Minister of
Education, Dr J. A. van Kemenade, has taken a far-reaching
initiative directed towards the coordination of the many different
and divergent activities in the area of curriculum by announcing
the establishment of a Foundation for Curriculum Development.
This new national institute can be seen as the Dutch equivalent of the
Schools Council for England and Wales. It is expected to begin its
work in 1974.

At this stage of transition in the approach to developmental work
on curriculum and on school organization in the Netherlands, an
approach deeply influenced by studies of a more theoretical kind of
American and German origin, one hesitates to present too crystalized
a view of the events of the past decade, especially in the light of the
rather critical statements made about the fragmentary nature of the
initiatives taken and the evident inefficiency of an outdated *laissez
faire* policy that essentially left the real power in education to the
personal and professional alertness of the educators in the schools
and the innovative attitude and commercial astuteness of the
publishers. The future may well provide grounds not for criticism
but congratulation in the renewal of the curricula of schools.

Introduction

There is considerable activity in the field of curriculum development and course construction in the Netherlands. Numerous
agencies, committees, research and development teams are busily
at work, frequently independently of each other. The activities range

from the formulation of general aims for education, and the description of its content to the construction of course materials for specific fields of teaching and the preparation of examinations. All this activity is not, however, guided by a clear general plan or strategy.

Much of the curriculum development work is carried out by heads and teachers at elementary and secondary school level. The construction of a curriculum for a school, or for courses in different subjects and the specification of the objectives of instruction, usually in the form of examination requirements, serve to provide a means for ordering events in schools.

The results of this concern with immediate requirements of schools and of teaching is such that the activities of curriculum committees and course development teams are almost always related to specific branches of teaching. Curricula are developed for certain subjects, levels of teaching or types of school, or to meet examination requirements which aim to provide terminal qualifications. Until now there has been no agency responsible for the co-ordination and integration of these many activities; it is left very largely to those who are directly concerned with work in the schools. The reason for this is that, in the Netherlands, responsibility for the curriculum is to be found at the level of the local school board or the individual school. There is thus a marked decentralization of responsibility for course construction and a consequent variation of courses, textbooks used and kinds of teaching employed: a matter often the subject of criticism.

However, this variation in courses of study is limited by a number of factors which operate to induce conformity. The law, for example, regulates the subjects which are to be taught at different levels, and the examination system considerably influences the educational aims of the system. Moreover, teaching materials for courses commercially produced have a great deal in common, and give rise to the use of the same teaching methods and the same ways of motivating pupils. The relative similarity of courses is also promoted by prevailing organizational patterns which encourage traditional forms of learning (Freudenthal-Lutter, 1968).

In the field of education, gaps and imperfections in curriculum development have become increasingly apparent. Changes in society and spectacular developments in science and technology have to a great extent contributed to an awareness of these shortcomings. Also, the conviction is growing that curriculum development in the widest sense can form an instrument of educational policy, both on a national level and with regard to individual schools or groups of schools. Co-ordination of efforts to modernize school instruction is not only considered desirable from the point of view of efficiency, but also as a condition for a harmonious development of the school system. An increased awareness of what is happening has come about *inter alia* by progress made in the field of school legislation,[1] by a revival of interest in the theoretical aspect of curriculum development (Bijl, 1966; Gelder, 1967), and by the incentives which scientific research (Jaarverslagen, 1968) in this sector has obtained. Contacts on an international level such as those within the OECD (1966; CERI, 1969, 1970), have also contributed to increased realization of the inadequacy of present structures and institutions. They constitute an insufficient guarantee of aid to schools in such a degree that they may continue to meet the ever increasing demands made upon them.

By way of further introduction to the problems involved, this paper will first give a brief survey of the present state of affairs in the field of curriculum development in the Netherlands. Secondly, some requirements of the school system will be inferred from the developments which have been growing in and around the school system during recent decades. At the same time, consideration will be given to difficulties in achieving the aims of educational policy (COLO, 1971).

The analysis of the situation will be concluded by a *resumé* of the main results of this survey. For an outline of the situation at the level of educational theory and of the development of research methods relating to curriculum development the reader is referred to the contributions of J. Bijl and W. Meuwese (1973), *Curriculum Research and Development*.

Initiatives in curriculum development (1930–1973)

Steps in curriculum development and curriculum revision are taken by different agencies. Sometimes these are institutions such as school boards, which are legitimate authorities or agencies closely related to the schools. In other cases the activities originate from centres of scientific studies from such organizations as universities, learned and professional societies, as well as from schools or from private individuals.

Elementary Education

The original version of the 'Leidraad' (Manual) of the third Chief Inspectorate of Elementary Education dates from before the last World War and offers a summary of the almost generally accepted

---

[1] Most important are the implications of our new Education Act for Secondary Education ('Mammoet-vet'), but it seems that the announced renewal of the legislation for Primary Education ('Voorontwerp van een wet op het Basisonderwizs', 1970) will show the same effects.

situation 30 years ago. It contains aims and objectives, descriptions of course material and teaching instructions for each school subject belonging to the elementary school programme. The 'Manual' has been revised several times (the eighth edition dates from 1963) and has often been used for the planning of curricula and for the composition of courses in certain subjects.

In circles of specific Roman Catholic and Protestant education instructional literature was also available. In 1946 Van Hulst published a 'Manual for a curriculum for the Christian school', followed in 1952 by the 'Manual for a curriculum for Christian Education' (Van Hulst, Wielenga and Van der Zweep, 1952). Development in Roman Catholic elementary education has been strongly influenced by Rombouts, with books such as 'Naar een betere school, I' (Towards a better school, 1938) and 'Naar een betere methodiek, 1, II, III' (Towards better teaching methods, 1941).

Of more recent date is the 'Proeve van een leerplan voor het basisonderwijs' (Example of a curriculum for elementary education by the 'Nutsseminarium voor Pedagogiek' at the University of Amsterdam (1968). The 'Proeve' differs from the 'Leidraad' in the manner in which it explicitly takes into account the difference in ability and work tempo between children in the elementary school. Variations in learning situations and differentiation according to range and contents of the courses are indicated. The 'Proeve' is a largely empirical specimen of curriculum development undertaken by an institution without direct relationship to the school boards.

In the period between the 'Manual' and the 'Example' a number of movements towards the renewal of content and teaching methods of elementary education have originated from centres of scientific study (Kohnstamm, Waterink, Rombouts), from supporters of modern educational systems, united in the Dutch branch of the New Education Fellowship, the so-called 'Werkgemeenschap voor Vernieuwing van Opvoeding en Onderwijs', and from circles promoting art education and 'free expression' for schoolchildren.

The dissemination of the ideas was first through the publication of paperbacks such as (Naar een nieuwe didactiek' (Towards a new educational movement), 'Moderne onderwijssystemen' (Modern teaching systems), 'Opvoedkundige brochurenreeks' (Educational pamphlets series), 'Mededelingen van het Nutsseminarium voor Pedagogiek' (Studies in the 'Nutsseminarium voor Pedagogiek'), etc. Also, the renewal of teaching programmes has been promoted through the cooperation achievements of the progressive educational movement in teaching and other educational material, through classes given by the Pedagogic Centres on new ways of teaching and through the influence exercised on teacher-training through textbooks for intending teachers and the influence on the ideas of those training teachers. Because of these initiatives, teaching practices have unquestionably changed in many ways, even if there are still great differences between individual schools in this respect depending on how far the influence to change has penetrated.

Secondary education

At the level of secondary education the activities of the Government should be noted. Sometimes these are also related to the curriculum development for a certain type of school, such as the study of the Faber Committee (1949–1956) on the benefits of elementary technical education. In this connection a report on overloaded school programmes (1957) from yet another committee should be mentioned.

In other cases steps were directed towards specific subject areas. This is true for the larger part of the work of the 'Commissie tot bestudering van onderwijs-methoden voor het algemeen vormend nijverheidsonderwijs voor misjes' (Committee for the study of teaching methods in the vocational education of girls). The same applies to curriculum development work for agricultural education, even if there is a clear difference in its development (Schopel, 1973).

In general secondary education and in preliminary scientific education, work is also mainly subject-oriented. The creation of the 'Committee for Modernizing the Mathematics Curriculum' dates from 1961. Since then similar committees have been established for physics, chemistry, modern foreign languages and classical languages. The work of the 'Committee for Modernizing the Mathematics Curriculum' even covers elementary education and it is likely that other committees will follow this example. The Foundation for Curriculum Development, mentioned in the Introduction, is intended to function as an umbrella for all these many committees and as a catalyst for more cooperation between these specialist activities.

In secondary education the inspectorate plays an active part in the establishment of final examination programmes and the construction of examinations and thus have great influence. There is, however, a trend towards performing this work in closer consultation with the schools. In addition many more organizations, institutions, societies and commissions are studying the curriculum and making more recommendations than ever before. The National Pedagogic Centres and groups of subject teachers from different types of school are also very active in the curriculum development field, in the area of vocational and technical training of boys from 12 to 16 years, and in experiments on a new type of comprehensive education in so-called middle schools.

The revised concept of curriculum

Over the years the character of these activities has changed. Until recently the accent fell on description of subject matter, if possible in relation to general and specialized teaching aims and with regard to principles which are important in the choice of subject matter. In the last few years a clear trend has been apparent towards a more general conception of the nature and function of the curriculum and plans of work for individual schools. The relationship between general and specific teaching objectives, choice of subject matter, teaching methods and aspects of (internal) school organization is becoming increasingly recognized and occupies a central position in the work of curriculum development.

This development has been aided by work from different directions. In the educational world the work by the pioneers of progressive education should be mentioned. They created Montessori schools, Dalton schools, Jenaplan schools, Werkplaats Boeke, Roncalli College and the like.

In the Netherlands Bijl and Van Gelder in particular have made important contributions to scientific thinking on fundamental problems in the curriculum field. Bijl analyzed (1966) the life task of adults and distinguished between a number of task components considered as objectives in the establishment of the aims and content of education. Van Gelder (1958–1967) underlined the connection between the nature of the subject matter and the choice of teaching methods and suggested an analysis of the didactic process as the model for research and development work in the curriculum field.

The new way of conceptualizing the curriculum is also revealed in publications from different agencies. A case in point is 'Nieuwe onderwijsvormen voor 5- tot 13- a 14-jarigen' (New educational systems for five- to 13- and 14-year-olds') by one of the three teachers' unions in our country as also the series of articles by the Committee for Elementary Education of the Roman Catholic Educational Centre, the consideration given to the association between kindergarten and elementary schools in discussions at the Protestant Educational Centre and the plea for a comprehensive curriculum for the Dutch educational system, given in 'Opstaan tegen het zittenblijven' (Raising up Against Levelling down, Doornbos 1969).

In the spring of 1970, J. H. Grosheide, formerly Deputy Minister for Education and Sciences published a Draft for a Bill on Elementary Education. The wording of the second and third paragraphs of article nine in the draft shows that some of the recent developments and insights have been taken into account. The text of article nine is as follows.

1. The curriculum and time-table are drawn up by the school heads after consultation with the teachers and, in this or a revised form, confirmed by the authorities.

2. The curriculum shows the concrete objectives for which the teaching in the school strives. It also shows how these objectives should be reached.

3. The curriculum also reviews the organization of the teaching process, the subject matter and the books and other teaching aids to be used.

4. The time-table is drawn up within the framework of the curriculum. It also mentions holidays and vacations.

It may be expected that the changed accent with regard to the nature and functions of curricula will in the long run greatly influence the actual form taken by schoolwork—at least at the kindergarten and elementary school level. However, the road ahead is long. Preparations have been made in a modest way in the form of a few long term research projects carried out by three university research institutes. (cf. papers by Van den Berg en Postma, Sixma, and Teunissen (1973), Curriculum Research and Development) and also the annual reports of the Foundation for Educational Research. An initiative for a nationally co-ordinated study of curriculum development for elementary education will subsequently be necessary.

At the level of secondary education attention is usually directed to activities within separate subject areas. The time-table puts together the different component-activities, the traditional grade system as the predominant organizational pattern provides the framework. The revised concept and function of curriculum may therefore be harder to realize for the new insights to which it leads relate especially to the form given to work in schools as a whole. In secondary education complications almost always arise as soon as the school as a whole becomes an issue. The system of subject-teaching just has to be used in some form or other even if team teaching might sometimes be a solution. Another factor is that the training of teachers for secondary education is still very much attuned to the traditional system of class teaching.

Even so, there are developments both in general and vocational secondary education which are encouraging. An example is the report of an experiment called ' The Four Year Elementary Technical School' (Nutsseminarium voor Pedagogiek) and within specific subjects attention is being directed not only towards renewal of subject matter but also towards the introduction of new teaching methods. The course of development of the work of the 'Committee for Modernizing the Mathematics Curriculum' shows these directions. The development in the teaching of modern foreign languages should also be mentioned where fundamental changes have taken place through the use of audio-visual aids such as the language laboratory. Renewal of the content of the teaching programme has direct consequences for the planning of teaching. Emphasis is placed upon independent work and discovery methods. This implies of necessity the wider approach to curriculum development already indicated.

Function of the curriculum and courses at the school level

We should not overlook the fact that what is taught is highly dependent on commercial teaching materials; courses in specific subjects which are privately produced through a collaboration between publishers and production teams of often highly gifted teachers. Along with research and other educational factors, economic considerations play an important part in the content and dissemination of such courses. Catalogues of publishers and exhibitions of course materials such as the yearly National Educational Exhibition in Utrecht show that such courses have great range and variety.

The development work of foundations such as the Netherlands Institute of Audio-Visual Media and the Netherlands Educational Television should also be mentioned, and the production of materials from projects and centres or of some special interest which have grown over the years at national, regional or local level. The courses and materials developed are taken up and used by schools on their own initiative. In fact these materials play a larger part in determining what is taught in the schools than the curriculum as such.

Under the influence of present educational legislation and commercial teaching materials the school frequently makes do with a minimal conception of the curriculum confining itself to the announcement of the time-table, free days and vacations, and of the courses which are to be used for teaching the various subjects. It is this type of curriculum which leads to the assertion that one does not have to be qualified in order to teach.

Failure to mention the occurrence of entirely different situations would, however, not do justice to the educational system as a whole. In many schools an attempt is made—with or without reference to curricula produced elsewhere—to give a detailed description of the contents and organizational aspects of the teaching in the school in question. The teaching programmes of these schools often contain much that is creative, particularly when they are based on activities of the school staff working as a team. In most areas of our country schools are now supported by Regional School Advisory Centres.

The external support is focused on the improvement of curricula and teaching methods as well as on the welfare of individual children, especially children with learning difficulties.

Examination requirements and test development

The inspectorate has a coordinating and executive function in the establishment of examinations for secondary education. The activities of inspectors and teachers on the examination committees for the different subjects are laid down in the official examinations decrees. The examination requirements, both generally and at the level of the specific examination questions greatly influence teaching in the schools. The general requirements are expressed in the syllabuses for different subjects and the influence of question papers is conveyed by the teachers themselves. It is clear that the present system of examinations does not create a desire for a curriculum which is largely no more than a collection of mainly subject-directed activities. This applies in particular to types of schools which work directly for examinations, such as vocational schools and, up till recently, secondary modern schools.

An attempt to attain greater objectivity in judging student achievement within the framework of examinations has led to the foundation of the Central Institute for Test Development and it is becoming increasingly clear that the development of these activities needs to be coordinated with both current and future provisions in the field of curriculum development.

Summary of impressions

The brief summary so far given of the present situation provides a picture of energetic but fragmentary activities. On such co-ordination the efficiency of curriculum development depends and presently this lack of coordination is not only evident in relation to the work of the schools, but is also manifest in activities which are closely linked with curriculum development, for instance, in external support to educational innovation and the choice of methods of examining.

Moreover, it already is evident that recent theoretical work on the nature and function of the curriculum and of curriculum development cannot be put into practice because the necessary institutions and structural relationships are not present. An institution for systematic work in this direction (towards, for example, the construction and dissemination of integrated curricula) did not exist in this country until very recently and it will take several years before the first concrete results will be available for the teachers in the schools. One of the hopes is that this institution, the Foundation

for Curriculum Development, will open the curricula of the schools
to the cultural and social changes taking place in society.

Recent developments in education

Great changes have taken place in Dutch education within a period
of a few decades. Many of these changes have consequences for the
field of curriculum development.

Seven trends

The following changes and developmental trends can be seen:

1. the lengthening of school attendance by an extension of kindergarten education and increased participation in secondary and higher education;

2. innovation in and the extension of the school programmes by the replacement of obsolete subject matter and introduction of new school subjects and types of school, by changes of emphasis in the school programmes (such as extension of general education within vocational training) and also by changing teaching methods and aids (including the use of educational technology);

3. the recognition of the right to adequate education by means of variation of pace and content in educational programmes, until now mainly by creating or maintaining different types of schools, e.g. for the normal and the handicapped (so-called common and special schools) and for children of different ability at the level of secondary education by replacing the traditional tripartite system by a comprehensive system;

4. by improvements in teacher training for elementary and secondary school teachers, by the activities of the three national pedagogic centres and by the creation of about 40 regional and local institutions for educational innovation;

5. the establishment of more continuous progress of students through the school system by changes in the way in which advice on the choice of schools is arrived at and by postponement of the moment when a specific field of study or professional training has to be chosen;

6. the intensification of the relationship between the participants in education, both in the form of better communication and of teamwork between school and local authorities, and in the form of internal democratization of school life as such by giving opportunity to voice opinions and share responsibility for the affairs in schools;

7. a tendency towards participation of parents in school work, towards parental influence on school programmes and towards giving more coverage of educational problems through the mass media.

This summary of trends could (wrongly) give the impression that it already forms the basis of a programme for the future improvement of education—a programme which is, moreover, far from complete. The development of *education permanente* for instance has not been mentioned nor have developments in higher education, the increased interest of the electorate in educational policy and so on. Nevertheless, the above survey may serve as a basis for an analysis of the principal needs in the field of curriculum development.

Consequences for curriculum development

Since pupils at present follow a system of consecutive schooling there is a demand for the sequential planning of subject matter. However, the effectiveness of education might be greatly improved if the teaching of the different subjects were co-ordinated to serve better the aims of school work as a whole rather than the aims of particular subjects.

Today elementary education is no longer the only education for almost all pupils as it was in the 19th century, there is also secondary education for all. This opens up the possibility of effecting a certain redistribution of learning tasks and a rearrangement of subject matter over school types at the different educational levels.

A coherent provision for general and vocationally orientated secondary education (as provided for in the 'Mammoth' Act) requires the curricula of the schools, consecutive or co-ordinated, to be attuned to each other. This makes heavy demands on curriculum development in each of the subjects, especially with regard to the individualization of the teaching process. Coherence and co-ordination of the various educational programmes is also of prime importance when new organizational patterns, such as the system of differentiated subject levels, or such new educational institutions as the so-called 'middle school' (i.e. a comprehensive school for all children aged 12 to 15 years) are introduced. Of prime importance also from the point of view of the interests of the individual pupil are the attempts to facilitate and improve the movement of pupils through the educational system as a whole.

Changes in the school programme increasingly relate nowadays to the educational system as a whole. Examples are the activities in elementary schools to engage not only in arithmetic but also in the new maths and the plans to introduce the teaching of a foreign language—English. Because of the importance of these activities in subsequent secondary education, an increasing need is felt for a nationally co-ordinated policy concerning the introduction of these changes in curricula.

In the process of curriculum development the changing interpretations of the meaning of 'adequate education', 'internal democratization', 'relevance to society', etc. will continually have to be taken into account. So far as efficiency of curriculum development is concerned, experience and research show that the schools are best served by the supply of concrete, well-tried and well-founded teaching materials provided that (a) their place in the totality of the work of the school has been clearly indicated and (b) teachers have learned to work with them adequately. This implies an enlargement of the advisory service for schools and in this enlargement issues concerning the curriculum will need to be central.

The still rather unsatisfactory state of affairs concerning the further education of the teaching staff is caused not only by a lack of relevant regulations and organizational provisions but also by the inadequate relationship between what is being done in the school on the one hand and developments in the educational system on the other. As regards the relationship with curriculum development the dilemma can only be overcome by ensuring that the further education of teachers concentrates on learning how to handle the concrete products of curriculum development which have proved satisfactory in practice, satisfactory in the sense of fulfilling such aims of educational policy as compensating for social deprivation, eliminating the practice of repeating classes, and reducing in school the kind of failure which leads to 'dropping out'.

These consequences imply the systematic study of the aims of education. The relationship between these aims, and the concrete work in the field of curriculum development and course construction can then be drawn up in a comprehensive educational curriculum for the entire school system (Doornbos 1969, 1971).

Need for overall planning

The entire pattern of activities as indicated in the above two paragraphs, will have to be studied if organizational measures to co-ordinate curriculum development are to be achieved. The co-ordination of separate activities seems to be impossible so long as the main lines of a comprehensive curriculum for the school system as a whole are not drawn.

This does not only apply to component activities within the field of curriculum development, such as the description of subject matter, course construction and test development but also to those in the sector of more fundamental research and in the direction of innovation within teaching. The effectiveness of efforts in the widest sense is involved in this. Many factors have contributed to a school system in which there are elaborately detailed courses for the different subjects at each educational level but no coherent teaching strategy whereby the relative significance of the process of teaching and learning in the different subject areas is identified and related to the general aims of education. In consequence, it is also impossible to speak of a responsible educational policy with respect to the production of teaching materials and courses for the day to day work of the schools. In the final analysis schools are almost always dependent on the product of such private initiative as that of publishers.

A step towards the development of a coherent curriculum for the school system might also help to solve several strictly practical problems which occur when pupils change schools for one reason or another. The present situation is striking for its considerable freedom in the choice of teaching materials, methods and aids. For each subject, dozens of 'teaching systems' are available. A certain measure of plurality is doubtless desirable but at present the situation is chaotic.

Curriculum development and educational policy

Planning of activities in the field of curriculum development, however, is not only desirable from the point of view of stimulating better teaching. It is also a necessary condition for the realization of aims which are basic to educational policy. These aims are nationally published in ministerial memoranda, become apparent in legislative reform and are further elaborated in the explanatory statements accompanying the Government's budget each year.

One of the most important aims of educational policy during recent years was to promote progress in levels of achievement and prevent student drop-out. Earlier, by means of differentiation between school types at the level of secondary education and more recently (1968) through the introduction of a more comprehensive type of secondary education, an effort has been made to meet the desire for an education better attuned to the talents and interests of pupils. It was at the same time assumed that the results of educational efforts would be favourably influenced by the creation of a coherence of educational provisions at this level, supported by a coherent curriculum for the educational system as a whole.

Practical educators must obviously try to realize the aims of policy makers through their work. The means at their disposal for this purpose have largely been developed, however, outside the sphere of educational policy-making. Moreover, they work in an organizational context which is not attuned to the new situation. Despite the need to realize a national policy teachers and schools still work pretty much in isolation. This even applies to quite elementary functions due to the almost total lack of evaluation of the media employed in teaching. Consequently, a situation has developed in which even the most expert teachers have little to go on in making their choice from available courses, subject matter units, teaching aids and the like. Few of them are able to decide what is best on the one hand in relation to the aims of their own school and, on the other in relation to the pupil's education as he moves through the system.

Little is known about the degree to which the aims of educational policy is realized. This also applies to the aims of education itself. Penetrating analysis of the present state of affairs is a prerequisite for increasing insight into this difficult matter although not in itself sufficient. Research specifically directed to this point is required to supply a strong foundation of facts.

Another prerequisite concerns the establishment of channels of communication necessary to convey the results of reflection and research to their proper destination. This in turn applies both to the aims of educational policy and educational objectives. Work in this direction is only meaningful when there is some certainty that the results will be of influence upon the further development of educational policy and educational practice. Only the combined initiative of the various educational groupings will suffice to break through this deadlock. An initiative which—taking into account the aims of educational policy—is directed towards the development of a comprehensive curriculum for the school system as a whole. This alone will provide a framework in which the significance of the separate activities for the functioning of the educational system as a whole may be assessed and the role which curriculum development should play become clear.

References

FREUDENTHAL-LUTTER, S. J. C. (1968). *Naar de school van morgen*. Alphen a/d Rijn, 1968.

DOORNBOS, K. (1969). *Opstaan tegen het zittenblijven*. Nota van de Stichting voor Onzerdoek van het Onderwijs (SVO). The Hague: Staatsuitgeverij.

BIJL, J. (1966). *Over leerplanonderzoek*. Groningen.

GELDER, L. van (1969). 'Leerplanontwikkeling en de analyse van het didactisch proces', *Paed. Stud.*, 44, 258.

Jaarverslagen 1968 en 1969 (Annual Reports 1968 and 1969) of the Stichting voor Onderzoek van het Onderwijs (SVO), The Hague.

Curriculum improvement and educational development. Paris: OECD. 1966. *The management of innovation in education; report of a workshop at Cambridge*. CERI, 1969. *The nature of the curriculum for the Eighties and Onwards; report of a workshop at Kassel*. CERI, 1970.

COLO (1971). *Discussienota van de Commissie Organisatie Leerplanontwikkeling* The Hague: COLO, 1971.

SCHEPEL, C. J. (1973). *Curriculum Research and Development*. Report of a workshop for German and Dutch participants held under the auspices of the Netherlands Foundation for Educational Research, December 7th–10th, 1970, in Vierhouten, the Netherlands. The Hague: Staatsuitgevery.

DOORNBOS, K. (1971). *Geboortemaand en schoolsucces* (Date of birth and scholastic performance). With a summary in English. Groningen.

CHAPTER 8

Curriculum Development in Israel

Shevach Eden

Introduction

A curriculum expresses to a certain degree the cultural, social, and political developments of a society. It summarizes experiences and innovations put into practice by large numbers of teachers, and it initiates activities which are influenced by new ideas about life, society, and the school as an agency of change.

Among many curriculum theorists a distinction prevails between two types of curricula: the *conservative* one which is based mainly on heritage and tradition and views the school as the main agent for transmitting heritage to the new generation and the *progressive* type, the main goal of which is to prepare the youngster to become adjusted to a changing society. The first is mostly past-oriented, while the second is mostly future-oriented. This apposition may imply different starting points, assumptions, and aims of a school system but is meaningless in the Israeli context. Israeli society on the whole sees its main life style as the fusion of ancient cultural elements derived from the past of the old-new country with changing elements of a modern society. The curriculum of Israeli schools is characterized by a search for an equilibrium between the old and stable and the contemporary and changing elements in their culture. It is against such a backdrop that curriculum development should be considered.

Concepts of curriculum

The translation of the Hebrew expression used for curriculum is simply 'plan of studies' and this conception is still used in Israel as can be seen from curricula published in the years 1954–6 though those published more recently (since 1969) have more and more departed from the earlier prescription of content, and are dealing with the rationale of courses of study, their aims and objectives.

The curriculum of the earlier type was mainly an inventory of subject matter, a list of topics to be studied, shared among the respective classes in the school. In the preface to each subject objectives were stated only in a vague and general way. There were also didactic suggestions about the ways of teaching the topics. On the basis of this 'plan of studies' or syllabus, the writers, mostly inspectors and experienced teachers and a few university professors, prepared textbooks for students. They had to be approved by the 'Unit for Approval of Textbooks' in order to be used by the schools.

The 'plan of studies' of the earlier kind was prepared centrally, was *uniform* and *obligatory*. Textbooks on every subject were published. The author of a textbook had to include in his contents the list of topics in the 'plan' but was free to select materials and the manner of their organization, and to suggest various ways of teaching. A teacher could select from the approved textbooks the one which he considered suitable to the needs of his students and met his personal preferences.

The new concept of curriculum is different. It consists of: (a) the rationale of a course of study, its objectives and its contents: this is, as before, the 'plan of studies' but made more explicit; (b) various learning materials for the student, teacher's guide, and teaching aids; and (c) the evaluation instruments to be employed in assessing the course.

The new curriculum is prepared centrally in the sense that it is prepared for the entire school system by trained curriculum specialists working in various centres including the Curriculum Centre of the Ministry of Education and the Israeli Centre for Science Teaching.

Materials of a regional character, such as community and environmental studies, geography and nature study, the history of the region, local archeological sites etc. are prepared by regional teams with the advice and help of the Centre. Teachers are also encouraged to prepare materials for their schools, but this trend is as yet only in its initial stages.

The *uniformity* of the curriculum of the old type is in a process of change. For some subjects in the new curriculum there are alternative programmes, and there are various versions for different levels of students, especially for disadvantaged ones. Teachers may select topics and units according to their needs.

The *obligatory* character of the curriculum is losing ground: it is becoming more flexible. In some subjects, the core of the official programme must be implemented. In others, units can be selected by the teacher. The emerging trend toward more flexibility in curriculum implementation is marked by the desire for autonomy by the teacher. Such autonomy is at present an aspiration and a goal rather than a reality. This is especially true in a country where the enormous growth of the school population demands the rapid training of teachers, and even the recruitment of unqualified teachers. In such situations structured materials and teachers' guides are inevitable. The degree of structuring of materials varies but there is always sufficient scope to allow the teacher to prepare part of the material needed by his students.

Organization for curriculum development

Permanent centre versus ad hoc committees

The use of *ad hoc* committees with a 'completed assignment' was once the typical approach to curriculum development in Israel. This procedure has been replaced in the past six years by the 'continuous assignment' approach in which curriculum development is considered as a comprehensive, never-ending process of programme preparation, piloting and improvement.

Even after the completion of a final version of the specifications which guide text-book authors, and even after the curriculum centre has published learning materials which have passed through many trial versions, the work of the planners is not completed. The planning and writing team go on to other aspects of the same project such as preparation of background material for the teachers and the modification of the materials to meet special needs. They also continue to observe the implementation of the programme and to follow up any new developments in the subjects, as well as to note changes in curricula in other countries.

This approach to planning and the tasks outlined demand the existence of a permanent Centre, which will have available experts in various subjects and in teaching them.

Cooperation between all groups concerned

The curriculum in Israel, as in other countries, was usually prepared by school inspectors and teachers. Post-Sputnik, after 1957, saw in many countries the involvement in curriculum development of scientists, mathematicians and experts in fields, as well as the great public foundations. These newcomers to the field ignored the educators who had up till then been responsible for curriculum planning.

While the old-type curricula were criticised for not keeping abreast of development in the sciences and for not placing sufficient stress on the development of higher mental processes, the new programmes dealt mainly with the subject and its structure, but did not deal sufficiently with the developmental aspects of the student and his needs, nor the conclusions drawn from research on learning.

From a realization of the weaknesses of both approaches, it became obvious that what was needed in successful curriculum planning was the cooperation of all groups—subject matter specialists, experts in curriculum planning, school inspectors, active, experienced teachers, and educational psychologists. All these could offer many and varied contributions and thus possibly avoid the mistakes of the past.

The organization of a project

A project group in the Curriculum Centre prepares a curriculum for a specific subject for a particular educational stage. It consists of a Working Team and a Planning Committee.

The team is responsible to a Project Director and usually has four or five members, most of whom continue with their teaching. Their work is to prepare material for discussion at the Planning Committee, on the basis of suggestions originating from the Planning Committee and appearing in the relevant literature.

The Planning Committee meets frequently during the first stage of the work when the basic aims, principles, general framework, and chapter outlines are dealt with. During this stage the team members are beginning to develop the learning materials and to experiment in classrooms.

The sequence of activities is as follows:

The writing of the material. The actual writing of the material is generally done by the teacher members of the team. On the basis of feed-back they rewrite the material and produce the final version.

Follow-up. This is undertaken again by the writers of the material, while the material is being used in classrooms. They do not evaluate the teacher, *only the material*, in order to secure first-hand information for its improvement. In many cases the team member undertaking this work will consult with teachers on their reactions to various sections, and make observations on the time taken to teach the material.

Preparation of material testing. This is the specialized work of another member of the team. He must be well versed in the content and aims of the material taught and capable of formulating suitable questions and constructing reliable tests. He will use the services of the evaluation unit in the Centre to analyse results, formulate conclusions, and suggest improvements.

Teaching aids and equipment. The identification of these must be handled by someone who is familiar with all possible sources and is able to oversee the production of new audio-visual and other teaching materials.

Coordination of the project with instructional television and radio. In the first years of the Curriculum Centre, curricular materials were submitted for preparation as telecasts and in order to ensure that the correct presentation was achieved members of the curriculum team worked closely with staff of the Instructional Television and Radio Centre. In current projects a teacher working in the Instructional Television Centre takes part from the very beginning in the curriculum project. In this way the television perspective is present right from the start.

The coordinator and curriculum planning expert. Curriculum planning may be looked upon as a specialized capability calling for appropriate University training, extensive reading, and a professional vocational attitude.

The Project Coordinator or Director is responsible for all the work carried out by the team. He leads and directs it and in effect, trains the team members during their work. The Coordinator must be academically trained in the subject matter he deals with, as well as in education, and should have had a successful teaching career.

The planning committee, its composition and function. An expert, usually a university professor, is appointed as Chairman of the Planning Committee. Such an appointment gives more independence to the Committee in its work and is of help when the proposed curriculum is submitted for approval to the Ministry. The Committee's main function is to create conditions which facilitate the introduction of new subject matter into the curriculum, and the modification of existing content.

Each Committee will have an expert adviser to serve it. He will act for the Committee in two roles—as adviser and as an influential citizen. The expert acts as an adviser when he is presenting information, analysing alternatives, and pointing out the consequences of adopting any alternative in the particular field in which he is highly qualified, as an influential citizen when he expresses his opinion on matters which are of general concern though not specifically within his field of expertise. The distinction between the two roles of the expert is hard to make. Clearly, defined expectations may help in using experts in curriculum planning. These expectations are likely to be best expressed by the kind of questions put to him.

Most experts working in the Curriculum Centre are subject-matter specialists. Some are experts with a highly specialized knowledge, others have a broad intellectual background. The former are consulted by members of the team or by the Coordinator, whereas the latter are invited to participate in the Committee's deliberations. Philosophers and sociologists are consulted in the initial stages when objectives and principles are determined. The advice of psychologists is used mostly in the planning of the learning activities. Experts in the field are not expected to have ready answers to all the problems

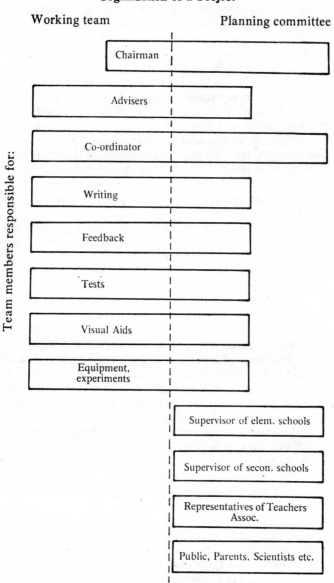

Organization of a Project

encountered, though it is usual for the Coordinator to be aware of relevant research findings.

In most of the Committees the subject matter specialist acts as chairman. The Coordinator of the team is the curriculum specialist. The success of the Chairman depends not only on his ability to provide leadership and reach consensus but on his understanding of the limits of his expertise and his modesty over issues in which he is not expert. Sound activity on the part of a Planning Committee depends also on the strength of the curriculum specialist, who is usually a teacher or a part-time lecturer in a School of Education, though not in all cases has this division of responsibilities between the two key persons been favourable to innovation in curriculum. To have a subject matter specialist as Chairman of a project may have been necessary in the early days of curriculum development but it is an open question whether this practice should continue.

School Inspectors provide the links between the curriculum development team and the schools and in addition make a contribution to the work of the Committee. Their main task is to aid in the implementation of the programme. It is their responsibility to supply the necessary background information and to be a source of feed-back once the new programmes are introduced; and since the Curriculum Centre's main objective is the planning of a comprehensive and overall curriculum from kindergarten up to and including the 12th grade, the Committees include school inspectors for different levels of the school system.

Stages in curriculum development

The organization of a project is only one aspect of curriculum development. Another is the decisions and choices which have to be made, and to these we shall now turn, first to policy decisions which may be concerned with general education issues or with proposals for developments in specific subjects.

General decisions are concerned with such things as the interpretation of the aims of education as a whole, and Knesseth (the Israeli Parliament) following the practice of other countries, formulated in 1953 the basic educational aims which were incorporated in an Education Act. In addition such matters as the place of vocational training, its extent and character; the kind of pupil grouping to be employed in schools, and the curricula to be adopted for various schools are matters of general policy.

Specific subject decisions relate to such matters as the allocation of time for each subject; the extent to which various subjects will be taught at different age levels forms the basis of directives issued to the Curriculum Centre which are then used as guidelines by the committees and teams appointed to prepare the curricula for the various subjects, or the introduction of new subjects or topics.

The Curriculum Division of the Centre makes the administrative decisions concerning which group—the Curriculum Centre or other curriculum groups active at the Universities—will be asked to prepare the required curricula. This is followed by the setting up of a Planning Committee for each subject and the appointment of the Project team in cooperation with the interested Ministry departments.

It is at this stage that curriculum decisions concerning the objectives for teaching each subject are defined and the basic principles for each curriculum outlined. The Planning Committee for the subject constructs the basic outline of the curriculum and the general teaching framework for that subject, from kindergarten age through to the 12th grade. This framework lists subject content and its allocation to the various classes.

The proposed curriculum (in almost all cases in its final shape together with samples of material for the students and teacher) is then submitted to a Subject Committee for its approval. Should there be any disagreement between the Subject Committee and the Planning Committee, the matter is referred to the Minister of Education for final decision. During the six years of the activity of the Curriculum Centre there was only one such case of disagreement and then the Minister agreed with the curriculum planners. After the approval is obtained, the proposed curriculum is published in the form of a trial edition.

The trial edition is submitted to scientists, educators, and interested public figures and their comments are sought partly by means of questionnaires and partly through discussions at meetings of teachers and inspectors. Curricular materials may be submitted to the members of the Planning Committee for such changes and improvements as seem justified and prudent. As soon as the curriculum receives the final approval it is published and becomes the programme for teaching.

A great deal of time is needed to change the trial edition of a programme into a final one and textbook writers hesitate to prepare a textbook related to a programme which has to be changed after a short period. And last but not least, there remains reservations about the final character of a programme as suitable for its purpose even for a limited period. There is a growing tendency to make it possible for developers of materials to introduce changes continuously.

At the same time as the basic outline of the curriculum is being prepared, the team starts with the preparation of all relevant teaching materials including students' text-and work-books, teachers'

Stages in Curriculum Construction

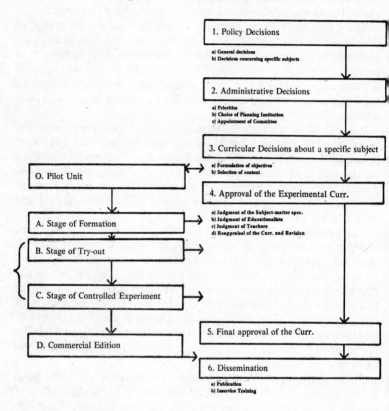

guides, background teaching material, teaching aids and equipment and the preparation of tests.

Three stages in the development of the teaching material can be distinguished: the 'formative' stage, the 'try-out' stage, and the 'controlled experiment' stage. The formative stage includes all activities before the programme reaches the 'try-out' stage. The objectives are clearly stated and the central ideas, concepts, and topics are identified.

As the material is being developed, it is submitted to subject matter specialists, an educational psychologist, and an expert in teaching methods for comment. Some projects have a subject matter specialist participating in all its sessions: others arrange for discussions between the expert and the writer of the material. In many subjects, particularly the sciences and in agriculture, suitable experiments, equipment and teaching aids have to be prepared and are often invented.

The trial stage is usually carried out by teaching the material in six classes. These are chosen to include pupils with different mental levels and social backgrounds in different schools. Successful and experienced teachers are chosen for this stage as it is materials prepared for the student and teacher which are being tested and not the influence of the teacher's ability. These teachers receive training and instruction both before and during the trials.

At this stage of controlled experiment—the 'running in', as it were —the material is taught in 24–30 classes representative of the country as a whole. In some subjects, particularly in physics, the number of classes is usually limited to about 16 (in 16 different schools) because of the expense involved in supplying the necessary apparatus and equipment. About six of these classes are placed under intensive observation, while progress in the others is followed through teachers' reports obtained verbally or in writing and in test results. Using this information, a third edition is written and is finally published commercially.

Recent developments

The beginning of the seventh year of the Centre is marked by a change in the process of curriculum development due mainly to the needs and stresses to which the educational system is subjected, but also to the growing experience and skill of the Centre's workers. It has been decided to change from a three-stage to a two-stage process: a formative stage for which an additional task will be the try-out of duplicated materials in one or two classes, and an experimental stage which will combine the former second and third stages. The material will then be taught in 20 to 30 classes. All teachers of these classes will be trained for the experiment. Tests will be given to all classes, but follow-up observation will be undertaken in only half a dozen classes.

In exceptional cases—a new project, a complicated topic, or after failure of the experiment—an additional experimental stage may be introduced.

The curriculum planners' responsibility is to prepare the material in a form which can be disseminated and implemented in the school system by others in the educational system. A variety of agencies are involved in this process in Israel.

The Pedagogical Directorate which is responsible for the inspection and supervision of schools and for deciding how educational problems are to be tackled is one such agency. Within the Directorate subject supervisors are responsible for the introduction of new curricula in their subjects but, due to their wide responsibilities, the supervisors' role in the introduction of a specific curriculum, though important, is limited.

Other agents in the dissemination process are the teachers' training colleges. They familiarize the next generation of teachers with the new curriculum. Also making a contribution is the Department for In-Service Training which is responsible for courses held during the school year and in vacations. It makes use of experts in subject matter and the people directly involved in curriculum planning. Its work is still in the initial stages. The programmes which it mounts for dissemination are discussed and approved in consultation with supervisors and the Project Coordinator from the Curriculum Centre.

In addition 26 regional Pedagogical Centres which provide guidance in the use of teaching aids, equipment and textbooks and hold permanent and temporary exhibitions have become involved in the diffusion of new curricula. Recently these Centres have employed educational advisers on their staffs. The adviser is usually an experienced and successful teacher from the district, who takes charge of group training as well as advising individual teachers who consult him. Advisers in a subject from all over the country meet at times in order to discuss both developments in the curriculum of their subject with Project Coordinators and training in their implementation.

Certain projects such as mathematics and science have 'guides' associated with them who receive special training and are, in turn, responsible for giving continuous advice to teachers during their work. Currently, a group of guides in language arts is being trained. No general plan for this kind of work has yet been drawn up the function of the special curriculum guides is still to be clarified and their production organized.

Plans and preparation have also been completed for training Coordinators of Subjects in the schools. These are teachers specially trained in the new curricula, and will have the responsibility of instructing other teachers in using the new materials.

The logistics of curriculum renewal remains a considerable problem: one of how best to supply the teaching aids, equipment, specimens and the like to the entire school system. Resources are not always adequate to the task.

In summary, some parts of the new curricula are better implemented than others. The division of the responsibilities of planning and implementation between the different departments has its advantages and disadvantages. Efforts are made to minimize the disadvantages which endanger the curriculum reform.

Joint curriculum centres with universities

Simultaneously with the establishment of the Curriculum Centre of the Ministry of Education, other Centres were established. The Centre for Science Teaching has been working on projects for developing new curricula for the elementary and senior levels. The Hebrew University of Jerusalem, the Weizmann Institute of Rechovot, the University of Tel Aviv, and the Ministry of Education and Culture are all involved in its work.

Recently the Centre for Teaching the Humanities and Social Sciences was established. This, too, is a joint Centre involving the Hebrew University of Jerusalem and the Ministry of Education. Joint projects operated by the universities and the Ministry exist in Tel Aviv, Bar Ilan, and Haifa. The processes in all these Centres are based on team work and include formative evaluation.

Social science: an example of curriculum development

The new curriculum for social science may serve to illustrate the demands and constraints of a new programme. In the elementary grades 1–4 the old curriculum combined the study of the community and the region through biology, geography, language and topics in history. This organization was influenced by the German concept of 'Heimatskunde'. In the grades five to eight, history and geography were studied as separate subjects. History was taught chronologically from pre-history to the 1960s. Geography dealt with Israel, sample studies of other countries, and general geographical concepts. In the grades nine to 11 (12), a second course of history was studied dealing with a selection of the main periods, with special emphasis on more recent times. In the last grades of secondary education, contemporary social, political, and economic problems of Israel were studied. Elective courses were given in political science, sociology, and economics.

The planning of a new curriculum for the social sciences represented a difficult assignment, mainly because it concerns issues of public concern. Israeli society assigns great importance to the study of Jewish history. Many believe that Jewish history has vital lessons to offer the new generation in Israel and should be retained. But this was not the only problem; the subject-centred preparation of teachers as well as their readiness to change had to be taken into account. Clearly there were limits to change. Indeed teachers would have accepted great changes in learning and teaching methods in preference to changes implied in the integration of their disciplines in a social sciences course.

In the event the new curriculum had to accept the strength of teacher opinion and develop the new social science curriculum in

terms of the disciplines. Thus, for grades two to four there is integration combining elements of geography, history, anthropology,
civics, and archeology in the study of the family, community and
region, but from grade five onwards the division is according to the
disciplines:—geography, history and civics.

The course in geography consists of three groups of topics. The
geography of Israel, studies according to the regions for four years
which includes field work; sample studies of selected regions of the
world; and special topics in physical, economic and urban geography.

The course in history also has three stages. An introductory stage
which deals with some elementary concepts is followed by a chrono-
logical sequence of four years for grades six to nine (11 weekly
periods altogether), starting at biblical times and moving up to the
last decade, and finally selected topics from history which deepen
the understanding of a historical period or case. In each grade from
10–12, three such topics will be handled, two for all students with
an elective in the third year.

The civics programme is similarly in three parts: an introductory
elementary stage, a course in the seventh grade dealing with the
political order and structure of the State and its main functions,
and in the eleventh grade a course on the social, political and
economic problems of Israel is offered. From six topics, three or
four have to be selected.

The principal aims of all these courses are to provide knowledge
of the main events and facts, and introduce basic concepts, to develop
skills and ways of thinking and learning characteristics of the
relevant disciplines, cultivate understanding and tolerance towards
the feelings, traditions, and ways of life of different peoples and
nations, and to foster the identification of the student with his
people and his country.

The methods of learning and teaching used in these courses are
varied. An effort is made to bring in the inquiry method to a case
studies approach, simulation, the analysis of controversial issues,
and to use programmed instruction.

These Social Science Courses deal with many controversial and
delicate problems which may arouse feelings among parents and in
the community. But this does not mean that controversial issues will
be avoided; rather the opposite. Materials expressing different
points of view are introduced and their analysis is encouraged. The
teacher is advised to be careful in expressing his own personal views
so as not to give offence and with the aim of creating a tolerance
for differences of attitude, opinion and habits in others.

It is not an easy assignment. From time to time there are complaints in the newspapers and in Parliament. Even so the new

curriculum seems to be succeeding in not rousing too much antagonism and in cultivating a tolerance of differences. The preparation of materials is still going on; so far the materials produced have been well received by teachers and students. The final outcome of this new curriculum, however, will not be clear for some time.

The future

The preparation of new curricula is an ongoing process. The 'plans' (syllabi) for the junior high school (which had priority because of structural reorganization) have been prepared, but the learning materials have yet to be developed. Work is needed on the development of curricula for both the elementary and senior high schools, and much is in hand.

Changes in curricula were influenced by the so-called 'new curriculum movement', especially in science. But because of the many needs of a school system undergoing structural reform, the process of curriculum change followed a 'meliorative' model and not an 'optimal' once. Projects were started largely because there was manpower to hand and, once started, every project concentrated on its own problems—of content, methodology, process and implementation, but seldom the general problems of schools, of the young generation or changes in society and its possible future.

'Second generation' curricula developments are expected to start only after a thorough analysis of the general problems of schools, the needs of society and students, as well as an analysis of the philosophic assumptions behind the interpretation of these needs. New priorities, differences of emphasis, new styles of learning, new topics, changes in time allocation, modifications to the climate of the school—all of which derive from ideas about man, society and what is desirable—have to be discussed long before preparation for the 'second generation' of curricula can be put in hand. As the work on the 'first generation' of the new curricula continues so preparatory work for future curricula is already under way.

In the 'second generation' project teachers may have more autonomy though just how much depends on a reasonable standard of entry to the teaching profession being maintained; and an improved training, the existence of a variety of materials, with different versions to suit different ability levels, a range of topics from which a selection can be made, and training in the development of materials.

In a country where the number of students and teachers grew almost tenfold within 25 years, all the conditions for teacher autonomy in curriculum development are still to be achieved.

However, with a steady improvement in the existing centralized system of curriculum development it is hoped to find ways in which to combine the preparation of materials in their various stages of development with the training of teachers in modifying them to suit the needs of their students, and in helping them to develop their own teaching materials.

The first step in developing and strengthening the autonomy of the teacher may be to help teachers to choose, from a variety of materials, those which are the most appropriate for their students in meeting their stage of readiness, their abilities, interests and backgrounds. To develop such materials is an enormous task for a small country, especially one whose language is not spoken elsewhere.

Individualized instruction, the integration of subjects, the structure of the disciplines, the ideas of progressive education all strive to find realization in curriculum development. At the same time there are the problems raised by attempts to plan and implement a whole range of curricula.

Few curriculum planners doubt that the implementation of a new curriculum can be separated from its planning, and to saddle a National Curriculum Centre which is currently involved in more than 30 projects with the responsibility for both planning and implementation could in time make the Centre responsible for the entire learning process of a school system. This could mean that planning might be limited by the urgent short-term needs of the schools which tend to influence the 'new' curricula at the stage of implementation. The problem is how to retain freedom to concentrate on planning and still secure implementation of the programmes that are planned.

Not only is there the press of the school and its needs but also the task of finding ways to cooperate with departments of a Ministry without limiting the initiative and activities of those departments while at the same time retaining the purposes and priorities of a programme. Such problems have yet to find solutions—solutions which recognise that the role of a school is related to the needs of the society which it serves. A voice for 'deschooling' may express the frustration of an individual in a developed society with its schools. In developing countries the role of schools is critical. In a country where mothers learn the mother-tongue from their children, schools play a crucial role in building up a nation. What happens in a school depends not only on the teacher but also on the tools which are at his disposal. The curriculum is his main tool. In renewing it lies the challenge of curriculum development.

References

BENTWICH, J. S. (1965). *Education in Israel*. London: Routledge and Kegan Paul.

BLOOM, B. S. (1966). 'The role of the educational sciences in curriculum development', *Internat. J. Educ. Sci.*, **1**, 5–16. (This paper is in part based on a report submitted in 1963 to the Government of Israel about the organization of a National Curriculum Centre.)

BLUM, A. (1971). 'Science teaching in developing societies. Some psycho-social determinants', in *New Trends in Integrated Science Teaching*. **1**, 318–22.

COMMITTEE ON EDUCATION AND LABOUR, HOUSE OF REPRESENTATIVES, 91ST CONGRESS (1970). *Education in Israel: Report of the Select Committee on Education*. Washington: US Government Printing Office.

CURRICULUM CENTRE, MINISTRY OF EDUCATION AND CULTURE, ISRAEL (1969a). *The Structure of Matter, Outline of the Physics-chemistry Course for Grade 7*. Jerusalem:

(1969b). *The Animal and his Environment, Outline of the Biology Course for Grade 7*. Jerusalem:

(1971). *Let's Grow Plants, Agriculture as Rural Science. A Curriculum Project for Grades 7 to 9*. Jerusalem:

EDEN, S. (1972). *The Curriculum Centre of the Ministry of Education and Culture, Israel*. Jerusalem: Ministry of Education and Culture.

EDEN, S. (Ed.) (1971). *New Curricula* (Hebrew). Tel-Aviv, Ma'alot.

CHAPTER 9

Curriculum Development in Scotland

Ian R. Findlay

What curriculum means in Scotland

No outside observer can fully understand an unfamiliar school system and its curricular structure without contextual knowledge of its past and present environment, especially of those stronger influences which have created its individual character. To that rule Scottish education is certainly no exception. While the limits of a chapter do not permit a full account of Scottish educational history and contemporary evolution, (this may be found by the interested reader in the bibliography suggested later), some brief sketch of dominant moulding influences seems necessary as a prelude to study.

For over 400 years, since the initiative taken in the *First Book of Discipline* by the Protestant Reformer John Knox and his colleagues, the idea of a planned system and a grimly purposeful curriculum has been deeply characteristic of Scottish schooling. The planning objective was 'a school in every parish' which also indicates the historical importance for three of these four centuries of the Church of Scotland and other religious agencies. The original plan was a pyramidic one involving a parish elementary school (ages five to eight), grammar schools in any sizeable towns (eight to 12), education in classics, logic and rhetoric in larger burghs (12 to 16), a University Arts course from 16 to 19 and a final peak of five years of either Medicine, Law or Divinity from 19 to 24. Although scarcity of resources in the subsequent two centuries did not allow such provision, this original 'pyramid of academic elimination' remained as the motive power and spirit of all school development in the 17th, 18th and 19th centuries, and the same period actually saw a determined striving towards the 'school in every parish' ideal. In fact, when the State took over as provider from the various churches in the late 19th century, it looked out on a small country well covered with a network of fairly accessible schools. It also inherited a tradition in which many of these parish schools provided not only elementary schooling, but for academically promising boys a measure of pre-university secondary education designed to lead into University study in the mid-teens. The 'grim purposefulness' of the curriculum derived from its dominant concern with academic values and prowess and with the moral good, indeed 'godliness' of the individual. While the second concern has faded very greatly in a secular society, the first remains important even in an era of comprehensive schooling. State involvement in 1872 ushered in a period in which the Scottish curriculum undoubtedly suffered from the application of English principles and financial rules to a totally different system, but after the emergence of an autonomous 'Scotch' Education Department in 1885 a machinery of interconnected levels and types of school gradually appeared, retaining its basic characteristics quite continuously until the mid 1960s. These 'basic characteristics', needless to say, included a strong underpinning of the value of academic excellence. In 1888 the Leaving Certificate was introduced as the curricular goal of a five-year academic secondary course and an indicator of fitness for university study, this being taken by suitable 17-year-olds in carefully specified 'full secondary' schools. The 1890s felt pressure for expansion of the number of secondary centres eligible to prepare pupils for this examination, so that in effect the old Scottish tradition of providing secondary as well as elementary education in the parish schools revived after its temporary subjection to English influence. From the turn of the century to the Education Act of 1908, an 'intermediate' form of lower secondary education was gradually created under the strong guiding hands of successive energetic Secretaries of the Scotch Education Department and given its final curricular linkup in 1908 by being constituted a prerequisite for a course leading to the Leaving Certificate. Thus a ladder with clearly fixed rungs was provided for the selected and the academic. But parallel to this, what had been a purely terminal 'extended elementary' schooling for the majority in the 1890s was gradually, from the 1900s to the 1930s, given a semi-secondary form by general/vocational two-year courses (leading to a certificate at age 14) successively known as Advanced Departments (1899), Supplementary Courses (1903) and Advanced Divisions (1923). This tradition evolved into the 'Junior Secondary School' idea in the 1936 Education Act which also intended that the non-academic Junior Secondary curriculum should lead to an appropriate certificate at a raised minimum leaving age of 15. The Certificate never materialized and the extension of schooling to 15 was postponed until after the Second World War. But at least the idea of seeing all post-12 education as postprimary (or secondary) had emerged in Scotland a decade earlier than in England, probably because of the separate

Scottish process of unification and evolution described above. In legislation on Scottish (almost simultaneously with English) schools immediately after the War, this idea of a three-year Junior Secondary non-academic curriculum took further shape. Therefore characteristically the school system in the period until the mid-1960s consisted of a seven year primary (five to 12) and, after selection at 12 (not, as in England, at 11), a five-year academic 'Senior Secondary School' programme leading to what was now the 'Scottish Leaving Certificate' and a parallel three-year Junior Secondary non-academic course terminating in various local authority certificates. An important point to clarify for the less familiar reader is that 'Junior' and 'Senior' in the Scottish context have *never* implied as in some countries a lower and upper secondary respectively. Both began at age 12 and followed longer and shorter paths from that same point, the distinction being between the academic and non-academic content of their curricula. This had certain implications for their higher and lower prestige in the eyes of Scots generally and perhaps explains to some extent the later move towards elimination of such status levels in comprehensive schooling.

The picture gains a further dimension if a distinction is drawn between urban and rural secondary schools. In the cities, the parallel five- and three-year curricula described above were provided in separate schools, the Junior Secondaries serving local areas and the Senior Secondaries accepting a fixed percentage of the academically selected from a wider catchment area. But in the rural areas (and this is a crucial point in understanding the subsequent evolution of comprehensive schools and curricula) both Junior and Senior Secondary courses were provided under the same roof although with a fairly rigid barrier of class organization, curricular difference and indeed teacher attitudes imposed between the two. Obviously transfer could happen and did in some cases take place more easily in rural than in urban schools. Also, the remoter the rural area the more likely it was that a large percentage found its way into the academic 'certificate' courses, a figure of 35 per cent being by no means abnormal. This could be explained by a combination of reasons, notably the academic tradition itself (at its strongest in the rural areas), rural parental respect for educational values and encouragement to the child, and the need to gain certificates as entrance tickets to higher education and employment in more urban settings.

In the 1950s, despite an important report of 1955 which took a strong line on 'education for life' instead of the watering down of academic curricula for the Junior Secondary pupil, the Junior Secondary school gradually lost ground as a visible form of school, largely because of its lower academic and social status. But it must be said in fairness that the philosophy of the 1955 report (emphasizing the wider needs of the non-academic pupil in social and vocational education, and the use of pupil centered methods, and the individualization of teaching) was a clear signpost towards the thinking of curricular documents of the following decade, both before and after the beginning of official comprehensive school policy. The difference in the late 1960s and early 1970s lay in the application of such a wider view to all pupils, not just the 'non-academic'. The slow death of the Junior Secondary was accelerated by the introduction in the fourth secondary (15–16 year) of the Ordinary Grade SCE (Scottish Certificate of Education which now replaces the Scottish Leaving Certificate). This provided a lower academic certificate at which a greater number of pupils could aim, and has since then been a major cause of increased voluntary staying-on in Scottish schools.

Vocational education also received attention in the following year in the Brunton Report which placed its faith in the interest claimed as generated for the average pupil by work-related curricula e.g. carcraft, building and other similar options.

The advent of a British Socialist government in 1965 and a strong central advocacy of comprehensive secondary unification (which became four years later an attempt to compel local authorities to submit comprehensive reorganization schemes) gave added urgency to the questions raised about the curriculum by Brunton. This urgency was underlined in 1965 by the setting up, under the chairmanship of the Secretary of the Scottish Education Department, of the national Consultative Committee on the Curriculum (CCC) to act as a means of surveying and coordinating curriculum development at all levels of the school system. Its Curriculum Papers (particularly the so called 'Ruthven Report' of 1967 on the Organization of Courses Leading to SCE) together with the Scottish Education Department's publications of 1966 and 1970 on the curricular implications of the forthcoming raising of the school leaving age to 16 (now a fact since 1972/73) have contributed to a swift development of thinking.

Main concerns were: (a) a period of 'common course' orientation for all pupils in Secondary 1 and 2 (12 to 14), (b) the development in Secondary 3 and 4 (14 to 16) of vocational, social/moral and leisure-oriented curricula of a non-examinable type alongside SCE-directed courses, together with greater flexibility in the guidance of individual pupils into whatever combination of these should prove most suitable for him or her, and (c) the beginnings of change in Secondary 5 and 6 (16 to 18) towards 'minority time' studies, purposeful learning and the growth of independent thinking: since 1968 a Certificate of Sixth

Year Studies (CSYS) has existed at post-SCE Higher level to promote such objectives as these.

From 1971 official policy has produced in secondary schools a new force of teachers holding various types of responsible posts in the field of Counselling and Guidance, the obvious intention being to promote the smooth operation of such an increasingly flexible curriculum as well as to provide careers information and deal with personal problems. It would be fair comment to say, however, that this has all the characteristics of infancy at present.

So far little has been said about the primary school stage. General agreement can quite readily be found among Scottish educationists that most of the trends already mentioned are flowing into and changing the secondary school from an already vastly altered primary school curriculum. The so called 'infant stage' (Primary 1 and 2, age five to seven) is safely described as steeped in the philosophy and practice of child-centred, play-centred discovery learning and the process of socialization. This is the most 'progressive' section of the system in every way. The primary school proper (age seven to 12) has also changed tremendously (especially in the last ten years of comprehensive school policy and under the stimulus of the report 'Primary Education in Scotland' of 1965) towards an integrated, thematic type of curriculum employing discovery learning and with the inclusion of areas such as Mathematics, Science and a foreign language formerly regarded as secondary preserves. In fact, a feeling can be discerned among both primary and receiving secondary schoolteachers that there is now not sufficient emphasis on the once traditional Scottish elementary skills of reading, writing and number —and the Scottish Education Department is trying through its inspectors to swing the pendulum back to the centre of the Scottish academic tradition.

The style of Scottish curriculum development

In Scotland, those with the longest and strongest influence on curriculum development have been, Her Majesty's Inspectors (HMIs). Particularly since the first appointment of a separate Secretary of the Scottish Education Department (SED) in 1885, they have had access to every corner of the school system and acted as the main force for change, for the maintenance of minimum standards and the evolution of the system under the guidance of SED policy. Their job has traditionally been to examine pupils, assess the professional competence of teachers, survey the working conditions of both and report back with recommendations to the centre. As such, they gained in the eyes of the teachers of the past something of the image of 'snoopers' or policemen. Happily this has changed in the postwar years. The HMI has become an adviser, a helper, a teachers' guide and what might be termed a 'curriculum development stimulator'. The last mentioned is further explained by reference to the work of the Inspectorate in organizing conferences, initiating local teachers' development groups and centres in co-operation with local education authorities and serving on national committees concerned with important problems of, for example, research, the development of audio-visual aids, teachers' in-service courses etc.

The contemporary educational stage, however, exhibits some other newer actors. The already mentioned Consultative Committee on the Curriculum has since 1965 been the main Scottish agency for coordination of all effort in this field. It is representative of all those with an interest—universities, colleges of education, teachers, Directors of Education, further education and industry, and the HMIs themselves—and has 24 members. Within its concern is not only such a general overview as already mentioned, but the identi-fication for the Secretary of State of any priority or specialist curricular areas needing attention from expert sub-committees or 'working parties', and the provision of a considered view to him on any recommendations produced by these groups. Although the SED officially tends to shy away from claiming direct control over the curriculum, and takes the attitude that headmasters are free to decide within their schools what to teach, it has in fact now in the CCC (under the chairmanship of the SED Secretary, and guided at all levels by HMIs) a strong measure of central direction—or at least pressure—over the nationwide application of curricular recom-mendations.

Circulars and Memoranda which appear as a result of aspects of CCC work are in effect official policy documents, and have prestige in the schools and strengthen the hands of HMIs. Obviously there-fore, in newer ways the HMI remains a powerful and influential figure in the area under consideration. The status of the Consultative Committee on the Curriculum contrasts with the independence from department control of its counterpart in England, the Schools Council. The close link in Scotland between central government and the main national curriculum development body is criticised by some as unlikely to encourage more than a carefully screened curriculum innovation process, and taken by others as simply proving a regrettable continuity of the tendency of Scottish schools, as in the past, to look to the SED as 'knowing best'; to continued paternalism. But a fair estimate should also indicate that it is a settled policy of the Department through its HMIs to encourage local initiative to grow wherever the soil is fertile. Abolition of small local education authorities and transition in 1975 to regional control of education with a greater financial power in nine regional and three district centres may well swing Scots away from the excessive centralization of the past—and in particular strengthen local participation in curriculum development.

Such local participation has indeed grown in recent years in 'Teachers' Centres' (now to be found in all areas), sponsored by the local education authorities. The main purpose of these certainly include curriculum development, through meetings, conferences and in-service courses for staff. Perhaps the most valuable group engaged in promoting the fullest possible use of these centres has been the corps of primary and secondary 'advisers' or 'organizers' now to be found in the service of all the local authorities. Like the Inspectorate (but regionally rather than nationally) the 'Advisorate' is to be found involved in every type of course, conference and working party concerned with curriculum change—and working in partnership with HMIs, college of education lecturers, and 'teachers with ideas' for the benefit of the schools.

In the rural areas, expecially in the remoter communities of the Highlands, the primary school advisers in particular have been the main agents in the communication of curricular trends to teachers in one- and two-teacher schools, and consequently in raising the quality of the school curriculum to at least minimally acceptable levels. They have in fact done much to end the 'professional isolation' which used to be typical of the teacher in such schools. When it is added that a very recent count showed 335 one-teacher schools still operational in Scotland, the extent of the advisers' curricular impact and the size of their workload is revealed. This task will continue, because the geography of much of the north and west of Scotland (as in Norway) necessitates the continuance of many such schools. But lest the impression should be given that the quality of teaching in remote areas is low, it must be said—and the writer is strongly of this opinion—that many small schools in Scotland provide some of the best primary education to be had anywhere in the country. This is of course because of the high creativity and imagination of the teachers involved, rich curricular fare in a family grouping situation, an integrated day and week, and a small number of children. A greater localization of in-service provision for teachers, fertilized by ideas from other areas and national sources, could not but improve this quality further.

Similarly, the growth of secondary advisers or organizers has contributed to a situation in which subject specialists are continually meeting together in the discussion of new ideas, alternative syllabuses and new forms of assessment. Some examples of these will be mentioned later.

The Colleges of Education also play an ever increasing part in curricular change, mainly through the provision of in-service courses and conferences, but also through the continuous visitation of college lecturers to student teachers in practice and the indirect effect of this upon the experience of school colleagues with whom students are working. This is added to by the trend in the colleges themselves towards shorter college service and quicker return to schools by the lecturing staff, and by continuous involvement while in college with chosen schools. Again, however, as with most curriculum development, in-service training is something which the colleges share with the local education authorities. The main discernible trend is towards provision of short courses by the authorities, and organization of those lasting a minimum of one month by the colleges. A further step in the same direction is the identification of certain chosen courses as 'Open' or 'National' courses designed to present key personnel in the schools with ideas aimed at some kind of curricular 'breakthrough'.

Attached also to the larger Colleges of Education are four national curriculum development centres. These are not strictly speaking part of the host colleges, but owe allegiance directly to the Scottish Education Department. Their purpose is to disseminate information on four major curricular areas—English, Mathematics/Science, Social Subjects and Modern Languages—and to promote experiment in these subjects in the secondary schools.

The role of Scottish universities in curricular development, however, must be described as a very indirect one indeed. Historically, there has been almost no direct involvement by universities in the school system, participation being rather through individuals and representatives on national and regional educational bodies, (on the CCC for example). It is true nowadays, however, that some larger scale pieces of university research affect the system in a broad way. For instance, research on the age of primary-secondary transfer has contributed to radical rethinking on the nature of the later primary and earlier secondary curriculum, and current research on the relationship between education and depopulation in the Highlands may produce implications for the curriculum of rural primary and secondary schools.

Decision and implementation

The best way to begin to understand how curricular decisions are taken in Scotland is to appreciate the relationship between the central and local authority. This is quite simply one of partnership between (a) a central authority which does not make decisions directly binding on schools, but has responsibility for regulation and supervision of all that happens in education locally and (b) a local authority which, through its education committee and sub-committees, advised professionally by the Director of Education and his colleagues, has wide responsibility for decisions on all aspects of the school system in its area. In short the SED supervises and the education authority provides.

In curricular questions, this naturally implies that central activity, the work of the CCC and its publications, the Inspectorate and their school contacts for example, does not have *direct* effect in the schools, although as already indicated it has much prestige and influence in creating a national mainstream of curriculum development and a body of norms within which local decisions can be taken. It is the individual education committee which decides that such and such a curricular policy will actually be implemented in its schools.

Good examples of important areas of recent concern are the provision of a common course for orientation in Secondary 1 and 2, the development of 'ROSLA' (raising of the school leaving age), courses in Secondary 3 and 4, and the questions of moral education and education for leisure. It will readily be understood from this that there is some variation in the enthusiasm shown in the implementation of such curricular policies, perhaps because of the smallness and financial weakness of a particular county, or because of differences in political colouring between county council or city corporation and central government. It may be that curriculum development will be easier to align with central guide-lines when Scotland has a much smaller number of larger education authorities taking a more objective overview of regional schooling. On the other hand, a powerful region at variance with the party in power at the centre could constitute a difficult political problem.

Even so we do not have the full extent of the truth about devolution of decision in curriculum and its implications. The First Report of the CCC, published in 1969, states that education authorities will decide what is taught in the schools '*acting with the advice of the heads of their schools and their teachers*'. This is essentially an acceptance of the fact that the individual Scottish school staff—and particularly the headteacher, who has always been more powerful in Scotland than in many countries—have the right to be something more than mere robot operators of official policy. The situation has of course its advantages and disadvantages. It means above all that the 'curricular style' of a school is very much bound up with the outlook of the headteacher. The more conservative 'heads' resist the evolution of some major trends, while the more liberal tend to keep the school—

and indeed their junior staff colleagues—abreast of contemporary policy. Another less obvious dimension of this difference is the extent to which 'heads' with differing outlooks involve their middle level and less experienced colleagues in decisions on curriculum and other educational matters. Central pressure is being applied to encourage such 'devolution' by the vast new policy of appointing Assistant Headmasters or Headmistresses with specific broad tasks, one of these being in many schools that of curriculum development.

Perhaps the best example of a curricular variation in Scottish schools resulting from this inter-school diversity is the present situation of the 'Common Course'. Officially, this is a period of two years' orientation from age 12 to 14 in the secondary school. But only in some schools can such a pattern be found. Others apply the policy for one year or less, while some schools—which are, in the context of their local planning, 'neighbourhood comprehensives', still organize their first year intake on an academically graded basis.

Implementation of curricular decision is therefore ultimately a matter for the teaching profession, so that a high degree of professional awareness is a vital necessity now and in the future for Scottish teachers. They, like any others, nevertheless need guidance for their thinking, and they receive this perhaps most powerfully through documents and reports of working parties produced on a local level by individual education authorities—within, of course, the broad lines of central policy.

Notable examples of such work have been suggestions for 'ROSLA' planning in Glasgow and the central belt, and in the North East reports on Moral Education and Guidance Counselling. But we return inevitably to the teachers with the thought that whether such recommendations bear fruit in the schools depends in the final analysis on the headmasters and staffs in the schools—together with advice and persuasion from their advisers and organizers. In view of the centrality of the profession in Scottish education, therefore, what seems highly important now is to ensure recurrent provision for their professional development through in-service training. At the moment the provision of courses on all aspects of the primary and secondary curriculum is a growth area in both colleges of education and local authorities, and the sheer number of teachers attending is rising fast. But the danger remains of 'preaching to the converted'. In the long term this problem may be solved by a combination of such measures as: sabbatical terms for teachers if the profession reaches the surplus envisaged by recent White Papers; the possible introduction of some days of compulsory in-service training within the school year; the increase of the principle of linkage between in-service and qualifications relevant to promotion; some form of sandwich training instead of a year after university for post-graduate secondary school teachers. All or any of these would contribute to professional awareness of the centrality of curriculum development in educational growth. Some start has already been made along this path by the provision of courses for heads of school subject departments in secondary, and headmasters of primary schools, the next step being a proposal for similar courses involving secondary assistant headmasters and presumably headmasters also.

Influences, constraints and other problems

Such a portrayal of the system at work would not be complete without a mention of some of the peculiarly Scottish factors which help or hinder. A random sample should suffice.

On the credit side, the very smallness of the Scottish school system produces some advantages. It is relatively easy to know and have contact with most of the influential people in one's professional field. Innovations are relatively well known throughout the system and information is reasonably easily disseminated. Central authority can maintain good contact with the periphery, and headmasters' conferences are quickly convened.

But some adverse characteristics are there too. As a general rule primary teachers have always tended to be too professionally docile and lacking in willingness to 'think policy'; and too ready to accept the latest 'dictates' of 'authority'. This is betrayed in many conversations which show rigidity of thinking on 'old' and 'new' methods and a deep set assumption that there must always of necessity be some 'official' thinking which the rank and file have to follow. Recently in some quarters this characteristic has shown itself in discussion of open plan primary schooling which has now spread to quite an extent in Scotland. The tendency has been to polarize thinking into the 'approvers' and 'disapprovers'. The idea that success or failure of this—or indeed any other—innovation depends on teachers' attitudes, talents and creativity has to be very forcibly stated to be heard at all.

There is still something of a gulf fixed in most places between the primary and the secondary school, although notable experiments are being undertaken here and there to bridge it. A need is evident for primary and secondary teachers to understand each others' curricular patterns, objectives and methods, and to ensure a smooth continuity of curriculum for children in the middle years. Especially is it urgent that secondary teachers understand the new, freer, discovery-oriented atmosphere in which the children have lived, and learn to adapt their curriculum accordingly at least in the earlier years. The 'common course' must gradually be seen as something of an extension of primary education.

Some difficulties of adequate curricular provision there are, and they stem from shortages of staff. Two differing examples of this are the huge shortage of all categories of teachers in Glasgow and the west, and the difficulty of implementing a 'common course' in island schools through lack of continuity in such subjects as French and the sciences.

Perhaps one of the dominant considerations in attitudes to the curriculum in Scotland is the pressure felt from the approach of examinations. This carries over into a tendency to take more seriously that which is examinable. Hence proposals for non-examinable or 'minority time' studies (either as 25 per cent of the 'ROSLA' week or as part of Sixth Year or post Higher time) tend to make slow, difficult progress. One recent emergence of this attitude was in the painfully hammered out compromise proposal by the Millar Committee on Moral and Religious Education that Religious Studies should be examinable, but only at the Sixth Year level.

Some recent and current curriculum developments

As examinations of the annual 'blue book' reports of the Secretary of State for Scotland will show, the early 1970s have been a time in which very many curricular developments have appeared in Scotland, too numerous to mention in a chapter of this scope. The interested reader would be well advised to go to these reports for a full picture. But some of the most significant must feature here.

In the field of nursery and preschool education (before the compulsory starting age of five) much attention has been given under an Urban Development programme dating from 1968 to an expansion of the provision of early education into deprived areas, and discussion has grown on the enrichment of the curriculum for nursery children by the involvement of the home in the process. The latter development has been sparked off by a report of the Scottish Education Department, entitled *Before Five* and published in 1971.

The most notable lines of advance in primary education have been in environmental, thematic and community studies of all kinds which have gained much ground through the excitement and the interest generated everywhere in young children by integrated discovery, the methods which they employ. The production of mathematics material and the mounting of pilot projects in mathematics by numerous groups throughout the country, particularly by a national working party using 14 schools and evaluating results with the help of teachers and headmasters has had its effect, as has the improvement of music and art both by the training of the class teacher and the planned use of visiting specialists. The attempt to remedy deficiencies in the teaching of primary French, and where possible to consolidate and expand it, perhaps even to add German as a second language, has also become commonplace in Scottish primary schools.

Secondary curriculum development is perhaps best described through a synthesis of the picture presented by a study of annual reports since 1970. Primary-secondary transfer of pupils and curricular continuity is seen nationally as a weakness needing attention and more liaison between schools, but encouraging exceptions are mentioned where individual secondary schools are operating 'transition' or 'bridge' curricula designed to combine continued primary integration and some degree of secondary specialist enrichment. There is in fact a single area where plans are being made for a full scale 'middle school' curriculum for age 10 to age 14—but against opposition from the teachers' organization representing graduates in secondary school who see such a move as allowing non-graduates to teach in the secondary years—a most un-Scottish practice!

The report of 1972 'The First Two Years of Secondary Education' continues to criticise the lack of two-way contact between primaries and secondaries, but indicates a continuing trend towards mixed ability organization of first year intakes into secondary schools across a wide subject range and the integration of subjects. But it also raises doubts on the part of modern linguists and mathematicians as to the possibility of teaching their subjects in mixed ability classes, and uncertainty as to the best length of a 'common course'.

The third year of secondary school (14 to 15) is becoming regarded as an extension of general education, vocational choice being increasingly a matter for Secondary 4. The raising of the school leaving age to 16 ('ROSLA' implemented in session 1972/73) generated great curricular activity in the early 1970s. The report of 1970 lamented that most schools still made rigid divisions between certificate (examination-orientated) and non-certificate lines in the later years, but applied pressure for change in this area towards 'bridging' (partly 'O' Grade, partly non-examinable) courses. Since then progress has been made nationally in this direction.

Resources centres have been set up by progressive local authorities such as Dunbarton and Fife to devote time and money to the production of materials relevant to ROSLA curricula (indeed to common course and 16 to 18 aids as well) and the success of these is attested in the report of 1972. Also in urban areas of varying sizes like Edinburgh and Inverness a very successful and encouraging link has been established between the local further education (technical and commercial) colleges and secondary schools, ROSLA pupils being given the opportunity of spending up to 50 per cent of curricular time in vocational options offered by the colleges. The most significant feature of this has been the raised morale of a group of pupils which could have continued to be an unwilling captive audience, as were some of their predecessors.

In the various subject areas some trends and changes are evident.

English. In English the priority has been 'ROSLA', the development of oral work in meaningful situations and the choice of literature suitable to all abilities.

History. History has turned much more towards the depth study of limited themes, the use of primary evidence, individual investigation (under the influence of the philosophy accepted for Certificate of Sixth Year Studies (CSYS) since the late 1960s) and to the use of more Scottish and modern topics.

Geography. The stimulus of the CSYS in geography has led to a growth of field studies, much use has been made of closed circuit television and of audio-visual aids. A '14–18' Geography development group linked with the Schools Council in England has begun work, teachers have experimented with simulation and role play and Geology has appeared as a 'minority time' study.

Modern Studies. What is called in Scotland 'Modern Studies' (integrated civics and international studies) is described as a 'popularity growth area' with some expansion of SCE Higher curricula.

Language. Language developments include investigation of group teaching and the provision of language options in Secondary education, including Gaelic in Highland schools, greater emphasis on audio-visual methods and on communication fluency. There has been official encouragement of Gaelic through CSYS and 'O' Grade in the sixth year and the organization of 'Gaelic camps', and a Classics policy of substituting non-linguistic 'Greco-Roman civilization' studies in Secondary 1 and 2 and postponing Latin until the third year.

Mathematics. Mathematics groups have studied the application of alternative syllabuses to mixed ability groups of pupils and the construction of a four-year course for 16-year-old leavers, while statistics and computer studies are also being introduced.

Science. Under the stimulus of the CCC's now internationally known 'Curriculum Paper 7' (Science for General Education) integrated science courses have spread rapidly in Secondary 1 and 2, and Biology has become widely chosen up to 'O' Grade; Individual research in Secondary 6 is now normal and objective tests have been introduced.

Economics and Business Studies. The relatively new area of business studies and Economics has seen modernization in technique (e.g.

audio-typing rather than shorthand) and in content and assessment (to meet changing industrial needs), while the growing attractiveness of Economics is reflected in new proposals for 'O' Grade certificates in economic history and accounting, and in successful seminars for pupils on mangement problems and opportunities.

Art. The place of Art in the curriculum is growing not only in increased numbers taking SCE 'O' and 'H' examinations, but through a significant contribution to 'use of leisure' courses for ROSLA and other older 'non-examinees'—all this being given focus by a 1970 working party report and by Curriculum Paper 9 of the CCC.

Music. Logically, a working party has also just been formed to examine Music, in which the areas of advance have been expanded instrumental instruction, more schools involved in choral performance, extracurricular musical appreciation groups, some experiments in programmed learning and an alternative 'O' Grade syllabus—the 'leisure significance' of the subject being naturally similar to Art.

Technical Subjects. Inclusion in the common course, diversification into all branches of wood, metal and plastics technology and recommended extension to girls have been the main features of the technical education scene.

Home Economics. Home economics now moves towards the same curricular position as a technical subject and, places more emphasis on scientific knowledge, projects and problems with less on the traditional aspects. Also, it forms links with other subjects, involves primary schools and caters for boys.

Physical Education. Physical education, more accurately to be regarded as 'physical recreation' (in the context of the well established 'education for leisure' philosophy and a working party report) increasingly extends its horizon and its activities to prepare pupils for active life beyond school years and to develop imagination and initiative during them in the schools' year-by-year multiplication of options for self expression and the outdoors pursuits.

It will readily be understood that the unifying motive power behind all these changes is the strongly felt need to create a curriculum which has relevance to the increasingly diverse employment avenues of a modern society, makes wide provision for intelligent use of leisure in an era of growing 'free time' and encourages more young people to spend lengthened school years in taking advantage of both. Change and expansion carry with them, of course, respectively the major problems of (a) ensuring that the teaching staff involved are fully abreast of all that happens, and (b) the ever-growing expenditure on education which is a certain bequest to the new regional education authorities.

A word on the future

It is at this point that speculations are as likely to prove wrong as to hit the mark, but at least some possible features of the future curricular scenario could be suggested. Perhaps the safest beginning is to point out the ways in which the Scottish curriculum development machinery could improve.

Given some years of growing strength in regional curricular experimentation, the present need for such a tightly centrally controlled body as the Consultative Committee on the Curriculum could lessen. Although the role of this kind of purposeful central machinery is defensible at present (given the past conservatism of Scottish teachers), change in grassroots curriculum planning could remove the necessity for so much centralization. The greater participation by school staffs in curriculum planning seems by no means an impossibility, if schools generally become organizations in which 'top and middle level management' learn the art of leadership, consultation and joint policy formulation at school and departmental levels. Such a situation may come to pass through the expansion of professional and staff colleges in-service training for 'the promotees and the promoted' who matter so much, and this linkage of in-service with promotion would take the process further.

But other less obvious needs exist: the need for continuous international comparison between Scots and their colleagues in other national systems on specific curricular aims and problems: and the need for better communication of research results to the classroom—some future statutory requirement of annual in-service training may help here.

But there are some changes which seem predictable both nationally and regionally. These include (a) the introduction of new curricular subjects in the Social Sciences range and in European studies; (b) the expansion of health, sex education and guidance facilities; (c) the increased examinability, optional status and specialist teaching of Religious Studies; (d) the provision by regional authorities of their own resources centres operating some sort of schools' mail order service in teaching aids, films, video-tapes and the like; (e) the use of educational technology for 'self-education' purposes in the schools; and (f) the emergence of all these into a world where schools will increasingly participate in permanent and recurrent education for an adult population given to more 'educational consumption'.

Scottish education has always been famed for a high, if narrow, academic excellence. It remains to be seen whether it can, through its present time of change, achieve high quality in *every* kind of curricular option for vastly expanded numbers of pupils with every from of ability.

References
A. General References
FINDLAY, I. R. (1973). *Education in Scotland*. Newton Abbot: David and Charles, and Hamden, Connecticut: Archon Books, World Education Series.
HUNTER, S. L. (1968). *The Scottish Educational Service*. Oxford: Pergamon Press.
KERR, A. J. C. (1962). *The Schools of Scotland*. Glasgow: McLellan.
KNOX, H. M. (1953). *Two Hundred and Fifty Years of Scottish Education*. Edinburgh: Oliver and Boyd.
MORGAN, A. (1927). *Rise and Progress of Scottish Education*. Edinburgh: Oliver and Boyd.
NISBET, J. D. and KIRK, G. (Eds.) (1969). *Scottish Education Looks Ahead*. Edinburgh: Chambers.
OSBORNE, G. S. (1968). *Change in Scottish Education*. London: Longmans.
RICHMOND, W. K. (1971). *The School Curriculum*. London: Methuen, pp. 127 ff.
SCOTLAND, J. (1969). *History of Scottish Education*. Vols. 1 and 2. London: ULP.

B. Curricular Policy, Reports etc.
PUBLIC SCHOOLS COMMISSION (1970). *Second Report Vol. 3* (Scotland). London: HMSO.
SCOTTISH CERTIFICATE OF EDUCATION (SCE) EXAMINATION BOARD. *Certificate of Sixth Year Studies*. (Annual reports since 1968).
SCOTTISH EDUCATION DEPARTMENT (SED) (1947). *Secondary Education*. A report of the Advisory Council on Education in Scotland. Edinburgh: HMSO.
SED (1955). *Junior Secondary Education*. Edinburgh: HMSO.
SED (1959). *Report of the Working Party on the Curriculum of the Senior Secondary School*. Edinburgh: HMSO.
SED (1960). *The Post 4th Year Examination Structure in Scotland*. Edinburgh: HMSO.
SED (1961). *Technical Education in Scotland*. (Latest published at time of writing 1972). Edinburgh: HMSO.
SED (1963). *From School to Further Education*. Edinburgh: HMSO.
SED (1965). *Primary Education in Scotland*. Edinburgh: HMSO.
SED (1966). *Raising the School Leaving Age: Suggestions for Courses*. Edinburgh: HMSO.
SED (1968). *Guidance in Scottish Secondary Schools*. Edinburgh: HMSO.
SED (1969). *French in the Primary School*. Edinburgh: HMSO.
SED (1970). *Raising the School Leaving Age: Organization and Development of Courses*. Edinburgh: HMSO.
SED (1971). *Before Five*. Edinburgh: HMSO.
SED (1972). *The First Two Years of Secondary Education*. Edinburgh: HMSO.
SED (annually). *Education in Scotland*. (Latest published at time of writing 1972). Edinburgh: HMSO.
SED Curriculum Paper series of the Consultative Committee on the Curriculum (CCC) Annually, especially 'Ruthven Report 1967'. Edinburgh: HMSO.

CHAPTER 10

Curriculum Development in Sweden

Urban Dahllöf

Curriculum development and school reforms

In 1950 the Swedish Parliament took a decision to convert its traditional European dual school system into a nine-year comprehensive school. After an experimental period during the 1950s in a number of communities, the new school was introduced on a national level from 1962. Meanwhile planning concentrated on the secondary school level in order to meet the increasing demand for secondary schooling and higher education. Thus, after a series of reforms, the most important of which was taken in 1964, there has been a unified secondary school since 1971. In the secondary schools there are about 20 'tracks', most of which offer a two-year vocational training programme. There are also three tracks offering a three-year university preparatory programme and another two lines which offer professional training programmes for economists and engineers while at the same time leading to qualifications for general university entrance.

The structure of the old system is shown in Figure 1, and the new system in Figure 2. In both cases an approximation is made to the relative size of the age cohort entering the different school forms before 1950 and in 1970. The enrolment to secondary schooling, preparatory to university entrance, has increased from about eight per cent to about 30 per cent. The new secondary school now has a capacity to take 95 per cent of all 16-year-olds.

The past 20 years have thus seen a great expansion and profound structural changes in the major part of the school system. It goes without saying that curriculum development has been so closely connected with the reform of the whole system that it is extremely difficult and perhaps not meaningful to separate them. Both at the comprehensive and at the secondary school levels the reforms aimed at enrolling a much broader population in further studies. At the same time the basic philosophy of schooling was subject to revision.

School reforms were initiated as an important means for bringing

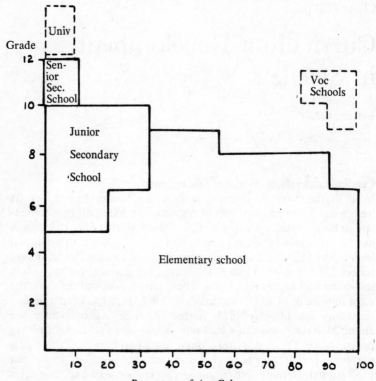

Percentage of Age Cohort
Figure 1. *The school system of Sweden just before* 1950

about long-term changes in society in the direction of greater social, economic and regional equality. Thus, most curriculum development activities in Sweden during the period 1950–1970 have to be regarded as a set of means in an over-all social strategy.

There are, however, some exceptions to this generalization. There was for example, a revision of the comprehensive school curriculum in 1969 after the new system had been in operation for a number of years which was not related to any changes in the goals of comprehensive education. Its purpose was largely to up-date and revise subject matter and teaching methods. In this respect the 1969 curriculum revision might be regarded as a more 'normal case' of curriculum development *per se*, but it is still not typical of the type of 'rolling reform' that took place after the initial period of extensive structural reforms. The reason for this is, that this first wave of rolling reform was in fact accompanied by quite important changes in the option and track system in the upper comprehensive school; in

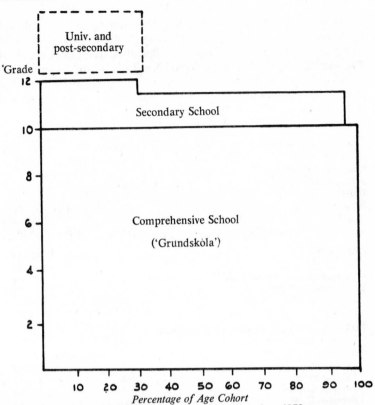

Percentage of Age Cohort
Figure 2. The school system of Sweden about 1970

grades 7–9. There is thus, from Sweden, no clear-cut example of curriculum development within a given organizational structure, except for those minor changes of subject content, sequencing and teaching methods that may take place within the boundaries set by a given framework of schooling.

The national context

Sweden's school system is highly centralized. One has, however, to bear in mind that the country is small. It has only eight million inhabitants, 5·7 of whom live in cities. Roughly one-third live in the big cities of Stockholm, Göteborg, and Malmö. But the general population density is low, 51 inhabitants per square mile, and in the northern part there are vast sparsely populated areas.

Sweden is often said to be one of the countries on the verge of the post-industrial era. Economic development has been rapid. Agriculture now accounts for only seven per cent of those gainfully employed, with service industries now the most important. Political life in Sweden is characterized by a strong emphasis on social welfare policy and public responsibilities for education. The Gross National Product amounts to $4,640 per head. (See Table 1) and some data on the distribution of resources is given in Table 2. It can be seen that education takes about 16·6 per cent of government expenditure, and more than is spent on defence.

Table 1: *Some Indicators of the Economic Status of Sweden*

GAINFULLY EMPLOYED	1930	1950	1971
		per cent	
Agriculture	36	20	7
Industry	32	41	37
Service	32	39	56
	100	100	100
GNP (millions $)		6,660	37,723
GNP per capita (in $)		945	4,640
Passenger cars per 1,000 of pop.		36	291
Telephones per 1,000 of pop.		239	570

Table 2: *Government Income and Expenditure*

CENTRAL GOVERNMENT BUDGET	1949/50	1970/71
Revenue Sources	(million $)	
Direct taxes	423	3,466
Indirect taxes	458	4,423
Total Expenditures	1,094	10,035
Social welfare	300	2,859
Defence	199	1,313
Education	111	1,757

Curriculum definitions and decision levels

Taking Johnson's (1967) definition of curriculum as a 'set of intended learnings' as a starting point, the documents which convey these intentions in Sweden are the official curriculum guides for the comprehensive school and the secondary school respectively, and are issued by the National Board of Education (NBE) an institution separate from the Ministry of Education, the main duties of which are the planning of teaching, administration, and evaluation of the school system. The curriculum guide contains both mandatory prescriptions, which in turn are subject to approval by different agencies, and recommendations by the National Board of Education aimed to guide the teachers in methods of instruction.

The contents of the curriculum guide may be broken down into units, reflecting the different decision levels in the following way:

Curriculum Issue	Final decision by
Overall structure of system (options, tracks)	
General goals and aims	
Subject structure and numbers of hours a week for each subject	Parliament
Rules about number of pupils per class, sub-groups, etc.	
Main objectives and content units within subject	Ministry of Education
Recommendations about teaching methodology	National Board of Education
Textbooks and teaching aids	Local school board
Sequence, method of instruction, selection of content within main units	Teacher

A distinction is necessary between the more general term 'curriculum' and the notion of 'syllabus' that denotes the main objectives, contents, and strategies prescribed for a given subject matter area (Dottrens, 1962). This distinction does not necessarily imply a restriction to the traditional academic subjects, but is also used to refer to broad subject fields, e.g., the science area, which at the comprehensive school level is organized as an integrated study of physics, chemistry, biology, and earth sciences under the label of Understanding Science to give a general educational background. The humanistic and social science subjects are similarly grouped. Within each block the students take different working-units or interest areas. These may not necessarily be the same for all students in the class, even though this often is the case in big classes where it is difficult for the teacher to individualize his teaching.

Change in curricular balance as part of a school reform

What is the role of curriculum development in school reforms which are part of attempts at social change? It would lead too far to answer that question in detail but let us take some examples from the comprehensive school reform in 1962 and the secondary school reforms of 1964. In both cases the most important contribution is made by a change in the balance of the total curriculum i.e., a revision of the relations between main goals and subjects for the total programme.

The background of the comprehensive school reform has been described by Paulston (1968) and further details are given by Marklund and Söderberg (1968; cf. also, Husén and Boalt, 1968; Mallea, 1970; Marklund, 1971). The secondary school reform has been described by Dahllöf, Zetterlund and Öberg (1966) and Dahllöf (1966).

The comprehensive school reform aimed, among other things, at creating a common frame of reference for all Swedish children. Thus, the old parallel, selective, school system with its early selection of an élite was abandoned in favour of a much later selection by a gradual introduction of options from grade seven onwards. The option system was made flexible, so permitting the late developer to enter a secondary school preparatory programme at an even later grade (cf. Andrae, 1973). The main objective of this change was to get away from the social bias that was connected with early selection (see Husén 1960, 1962, 1971; Husén and Henrysson, 1959).

What did this mean in terms of curriculum changes? First of all, there was only one curriculum common to all children from grades one to six in all subjects and in grades seven to nine in most subjects except the options. Thus, there is no longer any elite curriculum that is more rigorous in most subjects, based on a 'pass-fail' principle. Second, the general goals of the school were broadened to include a stronger emphasis on the social and personal development of the whole child to accord with a progressive educational philosophy, first proposed by the 1946 school commission (SOU 1948: 27). In order to promote these ends, the teachers were urged to rely less heavily on the authoritarian question and answer pattern of teaching in favour of an activity-centred instruction emphasizing groupwork as well as individual teaching. Third, mainly to promote social equality but also to 'open a window to the world' for all citizens of Sweden, English was introduced as a compulsory foreign language. Fourth, besides the changes in the general background subjects already mentioned, both theoretical and practical vocational and study guidance was introduced. Fifth, the whole balance was changed in favour of a greater emphasis on communication skills especially in Swedish and mathematics (SOU 1961: 30).

Another set of decisions had as their main purpose to help the teachers to adapt their instruction to the much greater heterogeneity of the pupils. The comprehensive class was regarded as the ideal for creating a common frame of reference and for training the pupils for life in a democratic society. In the upper section of the new comprehensive school, most of the teachers were, however, trained for and accustomed to teaching classes selected by ability. Because it was expected that individualization in comprehensive classes would lead to difficulties, optional courses at two levels of difficulty were introduced and a corresponding streaming was permitted in such 'heavy subjects' as mathematics and English. Another way of promoting individualization was to develop self-instructional packages, e.g. in mathematics and physics, based on the principles developed within educational technology.

Although the primary motives for curriculum changes were of the social kind the school reform did also imply a modernization of the syllabus within each subject. An attempt was made to combine an up-dating of subject matter in different areas with an adaptation to the demands and expectations for learning which is relevant to the practicalities of everyday life. In some subjects a research programme was undertaken to collect relevant information on the state of affairs in these respects with the upper forms of school in mind. One of the findings in mathematics, for example, was that there was a great variation between curriculum units in respect of the extent to which adults retained what they had learnt at school. Considerable gains were found in units in every-day use in approximations and per cent calculations, while losses were great in general fractions and geometry. One of the outcomes of these studies (Dahllöf, 1960; Husén and Dahllöf, 1960, 1965) has been not to overload the easier course in mathematics, another to strengthen understanding of the basic concepts. Another study by Bromsjö (1965) focused on a content analysis of textbooks in civics with similar findings.

At the secondary school level a corresponding development took place some years later (SOU 1963: 42. 1963: 50, 1966: 3). The total balance of the curriculum was affected by the need to decrease the number of tracks and to avoid 'dead-ends' in relation to further studies at the post-secondary level. Thus, the programme was often broadened. Examples of this are the introduction of science in the humanistic and social science sector, the inclusion of geography and social economy into civics, and the diminished role of Latin in further humanistic studies at the university level. These changes rested to a great extent on findings from a co-ordinated research programme, in which students' attitudes and reactions to the choice of subjects and study programmes (Hårnqvist and Grahm 1963) were set against the demands and expectations of different kinds of consumers of education, the universities as well as industry, trade, and the civil service (Dahllöf 1963). Contrary to the investigator's anticipations, the different sets of data did in fact support each other in a way that made it easier not only to integrate them into a general curriculum model and its basic philosophy, but also to draw practical conclusions. (For a more detailed summary, see Dahllöf, 1966; cf. also Dahllöf, 1969, Dahllöf, Lundgren and Siöö, 1971).

Curriculum development strategies

As a consequence of the social goals of the school reforms, most systems and curricular changes have been introduced 'from above'. The initiative has in the great majority of cases been taken by politicians. Although teachers also can be found among those who have advocated the need for school reforms, most of their contributions have been channelled through the political parties. In Parliament there has been broad political support among most of the parties—with the exception of the right-wing party in the case of the differentiation of the upper section of the comprehensive school—although a number of compromises have been made in the planning phase.

The planning has generally been carried out by *ad hoc* governmental planning committees, chaired by prominent politicians or top administrators and with a considerable number of politicians as members. The secretariat has often been led by senior officers in the National Board of Education, assisted by a number of experts. Some of these have been undertaken research studies for the committees, but most of them have been well-known teachers who have been given responsibility for planning the curriculum in detail.

As may be expected, considerable resistance to the changes was shown by secondary school teachers, who both at the comprehensive and the secondary school levels had to adjust to a much broader enrolment, and attempt to individualize instruction to meet the needs of heterogenous groups. Especially at the upper secondary level, the 1964 reform also forced teachers to take up new subjects or parts of subjects. For example, a great number of teachers of Latin and Greek had to start teaching French, Spanish, Italian, or general linguistics, while teachers trained mainly in political science and history had to extend their instruction in civics to geography and social economy. Science teachers with university studies in one or two of the subjects had to include a third or even a fourth one in the new integrated study mentioned above.

The reforms have generally been launched on the heels of the final decision by Parliament, with a consequential lag in the supply of new textbooks and appropriate teaching aids. This has been a controversial issue in the public debate. As regards the comprehensive school, it has on the one hand been argued that the final decision in 1962 was preceded by a public debate lasting for more than 20 years (the first planning committee started on an expert level in 1940 and was succeeded by the 1946 Parliamentary Commission) and by a 12-year period of experimentations in many districts which had considerable impact on the debate.

On the other hand it might be said—and has in fact been said—that, in its crucial details and in spite of the long experimental period comprehensive school reform was not well prepared. There are several indicators pointing in this direction. One of them is that the experimental period actually concentrated mainly on organizational problems, little attention being paid to the problems of teaching mixed ability classes. This, in turn, was due to the fact that in spite of directives from the Ministry of Education, most local communities organized the upper section of schools in the traditional way, creating selected classes according to the pupils' choice of optional courses. In the event, the National Board of Education (Skolöverstyrelsen, 1959) blamed the local communities for making use of their freedom in too one-sided a way. However, the responsibility in this matter of the NBE has also been questioned (Dahllöf, 1967).

There are indications that the planning committee did underestimate the difficulty of individualizing instruction in classes of mixed ability, especially for teachers who did not have any specific training for it. Support for a somewhat optimistic attitude in this respect was in turn given by interpretations of the only research study on the effects of ability grouping on academic achievement (Svensson, 1962) that was published just before the reform decision. This study made use of traditional standardized achievement tests and showed—as usual (cf. Goldberg, Passow and Justman, 1966)—almost no significant differences, when the students' initial ability and social background were kept constant. This study has been subjected to a re-analysis by Dahllöf (1967, 1971a), who showed that the tests had low content validity. They did in fact cover only the most elementary curriculum units. There were also considerable time differences, in terms of a much more rapid progression in the selected classes. The ratio of time differences in unit coverage were considerable—about 1:3. These findings point once again to the problems related to the basic patterns of teaching which tend to persist no matter what reforms are instituted. A model to help understand these patterns better has been developed and further tested by Lundgren (1972; cf. also Dahllöf and Lundgren, 1970) and the relationship of these findings to the mastery learning model of Bloom (1968, 1971a-c) has been discussed by Dahllöf (1971a, 1973a, 1973b).

In any case when the reform started, there were in fact very few, if any, suitable teaching aids for individualized instruction, and very few inservice training courses had been given up to that time. It is true that the National Board of Education launched a big training and development programme in connection with the final decision but it could not be expected to have much, if any, immediate effect.

Even though the Swedish strategy of reform may be criticized for its deficiencies in the implementation phase, the present author is not prepared to join those critics who argue that the centralized national reform approach should be entirely abandoned in favour of teacher-initiated reform along English lines. The different strategies do not seem to lead to the same type of innovation. The teacher initiated reform approach 'from within' is no doubt very effective for bringing about a renewal of the syllabus within a certain subject matter area, but it is doubtful if it can ever lead to any profound change in the total balance of the curriculum, at least not within a limited period of time.

Follow-up problems

Unfortunately there are very few good follow-up studies of recent curriculum reforms in Sweden. It is no doubt true that the central approach described above has produced considerable tension among former secondary school teachers. They have, nevertheless, been very loyal. As regards effectiveness, a distinction should be made between changes in content, e.g., teaching new or partly new subjects to student groups of about the same general characteristics, and changes in teaching methods, which demand individualization within mixed ability classes. Although many teachers had a difficult time preparing themselves for the new situations—a period that was also filled by a conflict between the government and the teachers' union—one gets the impression that they have been quite successful in implementing the first type of curriculum reform. The changing of teaching methods to suit a broadened population within the same class has been much more difficult to achieve, especially in the city areas. Team teaching and open schools have had varying success and are still not well established.

Perhaps the greatest success has been the quantitative expansion of the system from a seven-year programme to an 11-year programme for about 90 per cent of the population. Much of the planning effort was concentrated on achieving a greater social and regional equality. There is no doubt that the opportunities for secondary and higher education have increased immensely in the rural areas in general and in the sparsely populated northern part of Sweden in particular. Early studies by Boalt (1947) and Husén (1947; cf. also Husén and Boalt, 1968) revealed great social bias in enrolment for secondary schooling, and several studies, especially by Härnqvist (1958, 1960, 1965, 1966) aimed at investigating the reserve of talent, and the psychological bases for choice of studies. The success of the new system in evening out the differences between social strata in enrolment for further studies have been moderate. So far, one can say that the general education standard has been raised considerably by prolonging schooling for all, but that the social enrolment pattern still remains, albeit at a higher age level. A study by Härnqvist and Bengtsson (1972) has shown, for example, that when enrolment in higher education within the different social strata is taken as a whole, there are even greater differences than before, favouring the highest social groups. A more detailed analysis shows, however, that the social bias has almost disappeared at the highest levels of performance. Thus, even in lower social strata, more than 90 per cent of the pupils with high comprehensive school marks enter secondary education programmes.When it comes to lower levels of achievement in the comprehensive school, the tendency is, however, the reverse: upper class children with low marks have increased their share of the total enrolment considerably, which affects the overall mean in the negative way mentioned above.

Present trends and probable future changes
In modernizing the curriculum, the governmental committees already mentioned made use of teacher expert groups, often affiliated to the National Board of Education. They formed working groups and drew heavily on their personal experience as teachers or inspectors when making their proposals. When published, the proposals are generally remitted to the teacher unions, who circulate them among their members and report back to the Ministry or the National Board. The proposals are also sent to other types of organizations, such as the universities and the parent-teacher association. The reports from this circulation form the foundation for the final decisions. Since the school sector recently has been subject to great expansion and profound changes in its basic structure, the Ministry of Education has announced that the time for large scale reforms is now over and that future changes will be introduced according to the principle of 'rolling reform'. The National Board of Education will be held responsible for such a programme. As mentioned above, the first example of this is the 1969 revision of the comprehensive school curriculum (Skolöverstyrelsen, 1967). It seems, however, that this policy has at the same time resulted in something of a regression to an older pattern of curriculum planning carried out mainly through teacher working groups, with very little systematic evidence about the actual functioning of the curriculum (cf. Dahllöf, 1971b).
In the long run, however, there are good reasons to expect increased

interaction between curriculum revision activities and the research
and development programme within the National Board of Education
(Cf. Alkin and Johnson, 1972). Since different student groups and
regions often have varying needs, there are also indications of a
greater flexibility and freedom for the local communities. The
consequence of this is less formal uniformity but, it is hoped, a
greater adequacy. Changes like these will no doubt be followed by a
greater stress on local initiatives from schoolboards, teachers and—
why not?—students and teachers in collaboration. Non-grading in
the upper level or small rural schools in sparsely populated areas
(Andrae and Dahllöf, 1973) may be cited as an example of locally
initiated development programmes.

References

Official curriculum guides for the comprehensive school
Läroplan för grundskolan 1962. Kungl. Skolöverstyrelsens skriftserie 60.
Stockholm: Skolöverstyrelsen.
Läroplan för grundskolan 1969. *Allmän del.* Stockholm: Utbildningsförlaget.

Official curriculum guides for the upper secondary school
Lärplan för fackskolan 1965. Kungl. Skolöverstyrelsens skriftserie 81.
Stockholm: SÖ-förlaget.
Läroplan för gymnasiet 1965. Kungl. Skolöverstyrelsens skriftserie 80. Stockholm:
SÖ-förlaget.
Läroplan för gymnasieskolan 1970. Allmän del. Stockholm: Utbildningsförlaget.

Other References

ALKIN, M. C. and JOHNSON, M. (1972). 'Some observations on Educationa
Research and Development in Sweden', *Scand. J. Educ. Res.*, 16, 41–60.
ANDRAE, A. (1973). *Late-bloomers and alternative courses of study at the senior
level of the compulsory comprehensive school and qualifications for academic
education at the upper secondary level.* Project Compass 54. Göteborg: Reports
from the Institute of Education, University of Göteborg No 26. Mimeo.
BLOCK, J. H. (Ed.) (1971). *Mastery learning. Theory and practice.* New York:
Holt, Rinehart and Winston.
BLOOM, B. S. (1968). 'Learning for mastery', UCLA-CSEIP *Evaluation comment*
2, 1. 1971a: 'Mastery learning', in: *Block* (1971) ch. 4, 47–63.
BLOOM, B. S. (1971b). 'Individual differences in school achievement: A vanishing
point?', *Education at Chicago*, Winter 1971, 4–14.
BLOOM, B. S. (1971c). 'Mastery learning and its implications for curriculum
development', in: GISNER, E. W. (Ed.) (1971). *Confronting Curriculum Reform,*
Boston, Mass: Little, Brown and Co.
BOALT, G. (1947). *Skolutbildning och skolresultat för barn ur olika samhälls-
grupper i Stockholm.* Akad. avh. Monografier utgivna av Stockholms kommu-
nalförvaltning.
BROMSJÖ, B. (1965). *Samhällskunskap som skolämne.* Akad. avh. Stockholm:
Scandinavian University Books.
DAHLLÖF, U. (1960). *Kursplaneundersökningar i matematik och modersmålet.*
Diss. 1967 års skolberedning III. SOU 1960: 15. Stockholm: Ecklesiastik-
departementet.

DAHLLÖF, U. (1963). *Kräven på gymnasiet.* 1960 års gymnasieutredning II. SOU 1963: 22. Stockholm: Ecklesiastikdepartementet.

DAHLLÖF, U. (1966). 'Recent reforms of secondary education in Sweden', *Comparative Education,* 2, 71–92.

DAHLLÖF, U. (1967). *Skoldifferentiering och undervisningsförlopp.* Göteborg Studies in Educational Sciences 2. Stockholm: Almqvist and Wiksell.

DAHLLÖF, U. (1969). 'Materials and methods of implementation in the development of the curriculum. Outline of a model and some illustrations from Sweden', in: HOLMES and RYBA, R. (1969) *Curriculum Development at the Secondary Level of Education.* Prague: Comparative Education Society in Europe, 88–9.

DAHLLÖF, U. (1971a). *Ability grouping, Content Validity and Curriculum Process Analysis.* New York: Teachers College Press.

DAHLLÖF, U. (1971b). *Svensk utbildningsplanering under 25 år.* Lund: Studentlitteratur.

DAHLLÖF, U. (1973a). *Data on Curriculum and Teaching Process: Do they make any difference to non-significant test differences—and under what conditions?* Address to division B of the American Educational Research Association, February 27, 1973. Göteborg: Institute of Education, University of Göteborg. Mimeo.

DAHLLÖF, U. (1973b). 'Rahmenfaktoren und zielreichendes Lehren'. in: EDELSTEIN, W. and HOPF, D. *Bedingungen des Bildungsprozesses,* Stuttgart: Ernst Kiett, 271–84.

DAHLLÖF, U. and LUNDGREN, U. P. (1970). *Macro and micro approaches combined for curriculum process analysis: A Swedish educational field project.* Project Compass 23. Göteborg: Reports from the Institute of Education, University of Göteborg 10. Mimeo.

DAHLLÖF, U., LUNDGREN, U. P. and SIÖÖ, M. (1971). 'Reform implementation studies as a basis for curriculum theory: Three Swedish approaches', *Curriculum Theory Network,* 7, 99–117.

DAHLLÖF, U., ZETTERLUND, S. and ÖBERG, H. (1966). *Secondary education in Sweden.* Stockholm: National Board of Education.

DOTTRENS, R. (1962). *The primary school curriculum.* Paris: UNESCO.

EDELSTEIN, W. and HOPF, D. (Eds.) (1973). *Bedingungen des Bildungsprozesses.* Stuttgart: Ernst Klett.

GOLDBERG, M., PASSOW, H. and JUSTMAN, J. (1966). *The effects of ability grouping.* New York: Teachers College Press.

HOLMES, B. and RYBA, R. (Eds.) (1969). *Curriculum Development at the Secondary Level of Education.* Proceedings of the Comparative Education Society in Europe, Prague, 1969.

HUSÉN, T. (1947). 'Begåvningsurvalet och de högre skolorna. En undersökning rörande rekryteringen till de högre skolorna från de olika tätortsgrupperna', *Folkskolan—svensk lärartidning,* 1, 124–37.

HUSÉN, T. (1960). 'Loss of talent in selective school systems', *Comparative Education Review,* 4, 2.

HUSÉN, T. (1962). *Problems of differentiation in Swedish compulsory schooling.* Stockholm: Scandinavian University Books.

HUSÉN, T. (1971). 'The comprehensive versus selective school issue: Introductory remarks', *International Review of Education,* 17, 3–10.

HUSÉN, T. and BOALT, G. (1968). *Educational research and educational change. The case of Sweden.* Stockholm: Almqvist and Wiksell and New York: Wiley.

HUSÉN, T. and DAHLLÖF, U. (1960). *Mathematics and communication skills in school and society.* Stockholm: The Industrial Council for Social and Economic Studies.

HUSÉN, T. (1965). 'An empirical approach to the problem of curriculum content', *International review of education*, 11, 51–76.
HUSÉN, T. and HENRYSSON, S. (Eds.) (1959). *Differentiation and guidance in the comprehensive school*. Stockholm: Almqvist and Wiksell.
HÄRNQVIST, K. (1958). 'Beräkning av reserver för högre utbildning', I *SOU* 1958: 11, 7–92.
HÄRNQVIST, K. (1960). *Individuella differenser och skoldifferentiering*. 1957 års skolberedning II. SOU 1960: 13. Stockholm: Ecklesiastikdepartementet.
HÄRNQVIST, K. (1965). *Social factors and educational choice*. Göteborg: Reports from the Institute of Education, University of Göteborg No 3. Stencil.
HÄRNQVIST, K. (1966). 'Social factors and educational choice', *International Journal of Educational Sciences*, 1, 87–102.
HÄRNQVIST, K. and BENGTSSON, J. (1972). *Educational reform and educational equality*. Contribution to a reader on Social Stratification ed. by R. Scase. Göteborg: Reports from the Institute of Education, University of Göteborg No 20.
HÄRNQVIST, K. and GRAHM, A. (1963). *Vägen genom gymnasiet*. 1960 års gymnasieutredning I. SOU 1963: 15. Stockholm: Ecklesiastikdepartementet.
JOHNSON, M. jr (1967). 'Definitions and models in curriculum theory', *Educational Theory*, 17, 2, 127–42.
LUNDGREN, U. P. (1972). *Frame factors and the teaching process*. Project Compass Göteborg Studies in Educational Sciences 8. Stockholm: Almqvist and Wiksell.
MALLEA, J. R. (1970). 'The implementation of Swedish educational policy and planning', *Comparative Education*, 6, 99–114.
MARKLUND, S. (1971). 'Comparative school research and the Swedish school reform', *International Review of Education*, 17, 39–49.
MARKLUND, S. and SÖDERBERG, P. (1968). *The Swedish comprehensive school*. New York: Humanities Press.
PAULSTON, R. G. (1968). *Educational change in Sweden: Planning and accepting the Comprehensive School Reforms*. New York: Teachers College Press.
SOU (1948: 27). *1946 års skolkommissions betänkande med förslag till riktlinjer för det svenska skolväsendets utveckling*. Stockholm: Ecklesiastikdepartementet.
SOU (1961: 30). *Grundskolan*. 1957 års skolberedning VI. Stockholm: Ecklesiastik-departementet.
SOU (1963: 42). *Ett nytt gymnasium*. 1960 års gymnasieutredning IV. Stockholm: Ecklesiastikdepartmentet.
SOU (1963: 50). *Fackskolan. Betänkande avgivet av fackskoleutredningen*. Stockholm: Ecklesiastikdepartementet.
SOU (1966: 3). *Yrkesutbildningen*. Yrkesutbildningsberedningen I. Stockholm: Ecklesiastikdepartementet.
SKOLÖVERSTYRELSEN (1959). *Försöksverksamhet med nioårig enhetsskola. Sammanfattande redogörelse för läsåren 1949/50—1958/59*. Kungl. Skolöverstyrelsens skriftserie 42. Stockholm: Kungl. Skolöverstyrelsen.
SKOLÖVERSTYRELSEN (1967). *Läroplansöversyn. Grundskolan. Förslag till Kungl. Maj: t angående översyn av läroplan för grundskolan*. Stockholm: SÖ-förlaget.
SVENSSON, N.-E. (1962). *Ability grouping and scholastica chievement*. Diss. Stockholm Studies in Educational Psychology 5. Stockholm: Almqvist and Wiksell.

CHAPTER 11

The Development of Certain Key Curriculum Issues in the United States

Herbert M. Kliebard

To a large extent, the ferment that characterized the educational world at the turn of the century in the United States centred on curriculum. To be sure, virtually every earlier effort to treat educational issues in a serious way had somehow involved consideration of the curriculum, but never before had the curriculum been such a direct source of study and controversy. National commissions were formed to recommend curriculum change and bitter debates emerged as to the impact on curriculum of the burgeoning high-school population. Condemnations of an outworn and anarchistic curriculum were commonplace. In particular, those who identified themselves as Herbartians, fresh from their experiences in Germany with Ziller at Leipzig and Stoy and Rein at Jena, questioned not only the theory of faculty psychology, but its counterpart in curriculum theory, mental or formal discipline. Although the leading Herbartians like Charles De Garmo, Charles and Frank McMurry, and C. C. Van Liew were never to agree fully even among themselves as to a suitable substitute, they did succeed in drawing critical attention to certain critical issues in curriculum development such as the relationship between the child's interest and the subjects of study, the correlation of studies within the curriculum, and the relationship between method and subject.

The direct influence of the American Herbartians was, perhaps, short lived—the National Herbart Society quickly evolved into the National Society for the Study of Education—but out of the ferment they helped create arose an unparalleled effort to reform the curriculum. Although the reformers were to disagree violently among themselves, they did have in common an overwhelming sense that the curriculum needed, not simply to be changed, but to be transformed. The urgency one senses in the calls for overhauling education in general and the curriculum in particular seems rooted in a feeling that a transformation had taken place in American society during the 19th century without a corresponding revolution in the way the children in that society were being educated. But more than that, many of the reformers became convinced that the particular social changes that had taken place had special meaning for the school as a social institution and for what should be taught. The influence of urbanization on the family as an institution, for example, had certain direct implications, they felt, for how the school should organize its studies.

Reform origins of the curriculum field: two early directions

It is here, however, where the reformers begin to part company. Although they shared an urgent, almost an apocalyptic, concern for reforming education, they differed widely as to what direction schooling should take. It is largely out of these differences that there arose disparate visions of what form the curriculum should take and of the role of the school as a social institution. Take, for example, the question of the relative absence of parental influence in an urban as opposed to an agrarian society. The enormously influential American sociologist, Edward A. Ross, welcomed the change. In his book, *Social Control*, he argued 'Another gain lies in the partial substitution of the teacher for the parent as the model upon which the child forms itself. Copy the child will, and the advantage of giving him his teacher instead of his father to imitate, is that the former is a picked person, while the latter is not.' The declining influence of the family, therefore, provided the opportunity for society to exercise more direct and more potent control on the child through the institution of schooling (Ross, 1901).

Only a year earlier, John Dewey also considered the educational implications of the emergence of the 'factory system' replacing the 'household and neighbourhood system'. In *The School and Society*, Dewey recognized the economic advantages inherent in the factory system and mass production, but he recognized as well that many of the household occupations that were no longer practised carried with them enormous opportunities for character building, for social cooperation, and for the training of attention and judgment—for doing things that have meaning and import as opposed to tasks artificially assigned. In Dewey's laboratory school at the University of Chicago, therefore, he reintroduced the household occupations of weaving, cooking, and working in wood or metal 'as methods of living and learning, not as distinct studies' (Dewey, 1900). Unlike Ross, then, Dewey saw industrialization and the decline of household occupations as implying that the school reintroduce those critically educative activities, once centring in the family and the community, that had become lost in a modern industrial society.

Out of these interpretations of the social role of the school, arose two major traditions in curriculum thought. One tradition saw the school as a place where useful social skills and practical knowledge are transmitted for future use: the curriculum would be geared toward particular adult roles and functions. The other emphasized present living, where children engage in activities, not unlike those that take place or once took place in the larger society; in school, however, they would occur under conditions that bring those activities to richer meaning as part of what Dewey called an 'embryonic social community'. The keys to the former tradition are prediction and control; the key to the latter is evolving intellectual independence. In some sense, both represented a major departure from 19th century theory and practice, the one in its emphasis on what has direct social or practical value, the other in its emphasis on the child's interests, needs, and problems as the starting point for curriculum development.

Coincidentally, the year 1918 saw the publication of major statements representing these two currents of curriculum thought. One was Franklin Bobbitt's *The Curriculum* (1918) and the other was William Heard Kilpatrick's 'The Project Method' (1918). Bobbitt's ideas evolved into the dominant curriculum ideology, variously called scientific curriculum development or social efficiency; much more radical in scope and implications, Kilpatrick's evolved in what came to be called the activity or experience curriculum which, although occupying a relatively prominent place in the curriculum literature of the 20th century, nevertheless had a negligible impact on the curriculum in the schools of the country.

Kilpatrick's activity curriculum was an effort to infuse into curriculum thought a theory of knowledge drawn from pragmatic philosophy. While typical curriculum thinking usually begins with some conception of what knowledge and skills are important to know and then attempts to find a means to bring children and youth to that knowledge, Kilpatrick proposed as the starting point the child's interests and needs with knowledge serving these incidentally or instrumentally. Thus knowledge would be introduced functionally —in use—as opposed to some logical and necessarily artificial form. This artificially abstract organization of knowledge, according to Kilpatrick, was not only removed from the child's natural sphere of interest and curiosity; it took knowledge out of its natural locus in human affairs. As such Kilpatrick and his adherents needed a new definition of subject matter. 'By "subject matter",' he said, 'we mean here simply knowledge conceived as instrumental to thought and endeavour' (Kilpatrick, 1934).

Kilpatrick and his associates hoped to infuse this conception of knowledge into the curriculum of the schools by transforming the unit element in the curriculum. Instead of a *subject,* Kilpatrick proposed the *hearty purposeful act.* Furthermore, an essential ingredient of a curriculum based on hearty purposeful acts was the notion of the development of the process of thought. In various versions, this may have been called problem solving, reflective thinking, or the method of intelligence, but clearly, the movement was directed toward improving the ability to think and thereby increasing the possibility of intelligence in human action. It is in this respect, curiously enough, that the radical activity curriculum shared with the traditional mental discipline curriculum a central purpose and direction, the development of thinking ability. From a curriculum perspective, therefore, mental discipline and the activity curriculum had in common a disdain for *content* and a reverence for *form.* What was ultimately important in designing a curriculum was not *what* was learned, but the form that the learning activity took— *how* one engaged in the process.

In this critical respect as well as in others, the scientific curriculum movement differed sharply from the activity movement. Paradoxically, although both were reform movements arising out of a common rejection of traditional 19th-century curriculum practices, the routes they took were widely divergent, even, one might say, antithetical. The reaction of the scientific curriculum makers to what they regarded as the non-functional character of the existing curriculum was not to reconceive the role of knowledge in the curriculum, but to prune the curriculum of its non-functional features. As the social efficiency ideology grew dominant, therefore, those elements of the curriculum that could not demonstrate a direct relevance to adult living were excised. This took the form not simply of virtually eliminating such non-functional subjects as Greek and Latin but of transforming existing subjects like English and mathematics in order to give them a more directly utilitarian orientation. Although deceptively simple, this doctrine as developed and refined by the foremost curriculum practitioners became the dominant paradigm for curriculum in the United States.

Bobbitt's two major books on curriculum published in 1918 and in 1924 included the main elements of the theory as well as the procedure by which it could be implemented. His earlier work in the area of school administration had filled him with admiration for the operation of the factory with its emphasis on ever greater productivity through ever more efficient procedures. But his study of the works of Frederick Winslow Taylor, the father of scientific management in industry, led him to go beyond merely translating the managerial aspects of factories into managerial techniques for school administration. The metaphor of the factory was carried into the techniques of curriculum development and the criteria by which curricula would be judged. The metaphor of production has become so powerful that its implications have come to be accepted almost as literal by those who are professionally socialized into the curriculum field.

'Education', Bobbitt declared in *How to Make a Curriculum* (1924), 'is primarily for adult life, not for child life. Its fundamental responsibility is to prepare for the 50 years of adulthood, not for the 20 years of childhood and youth.' This notion of education as preparation was in stark contrast with Kilpatrick's dictum that 'education be considered as life itself and not as a mere preparation for later living' (Kilpatrick, 1918). The implications of this divergence of viewpoint for the curriculum are enormous. For one thing, if the curriculum is to be directed toward some point in the future, it would become critically important to know what that future would be like. In curriculum terms, it would become important to know not simply that children grow into adults, but what kind of adults. One must have some basis for predicting the particular roles and functions that these adults would perform in a rather remote future. Furthermore, the activities of life that characterize these adult roles would have to be specified with a certain degree of exactitude. It simply would not do to prepare a future general in the same way as a future trolley-car conductor. Thus was developed, not only predictability as a key criterion of curriculum planning, but a justification for curriculum differentiation as the path to differing adult roles. As in industry, therefore, the careful prespecification of the end product as well as the standardized and efficient means for achieving it, became the key elements in curriculum design.

One major source of appeal for this curriculum doctrine was its alleged scientific character. Both the end product, the objectives of education, and the most efficient means toward their achievement were advertized as scientifically or sociologically determined. Vague and unverifiable statements of the aims of education would be replaced by a set of detailed and substantiated objectives that had been sociologically analyzed. In *Sociological Determination of Objectives in Education*, for example, David Snedden, an enormously influential figure in curriculum, could say in all optimism, 'It should ... prove easily practicable, given sufficient working resources, to analyze, classify, and, at least crudely, to evaluate the habits, knowledge, appreciations, aspirations, and ideals promotive of such values as health, wealth, sociability, and righteousness which given groups or classes of adults possess, and to trace to their respective sources in original nature, environmental influence (including by-education), and school education these various qualities' (Snedden, 1921). Thus was ultimate good and the means toward its achievement within the grasp of science. In a process which came to be known as 'activity analysis', prototypic leaders in the curriculum field, such as Franklin Bobbitt and W. W. Charters, studied the activities of adults as a basis for drawing up extended lists of objectives, and then proceeding to find the most efficient means toward their achievement. This is a conception of curriculum development, of course, which in somewhat modified form, remains dominant today.

In contrast to the mental disciplinarian emphasis on form, and its redefinition and resurrection in the experience curriculum, scientific curriculum making clearly placed its emphasis on content—on clearly specifiable knowledges and skills—as the culmination of education. The measurable product rather than the means towards its achievement became the ultimate criterion of success. The later translation of this product into behavioural terms represented a relatively minor and certainly predictable development.

Search for theoretical constructs

Two events in mid-century signalled the beginning of a possible second stage in the development of the curriculum field. One was the publication of what may be considered a summation of the accumulated wisdom in the field of curriculum, Ralph Tyler's *Basic Principles of Curriculum and Instruction*. Actually a syllabus for the curriculum course that Tyler taught at the University of Chicago, it became quickly acclaimed as *the Tyler rationale*. The rationale is based on four basic questions:

1.   What educational purposes should the school seek to attain?
2.   What educational experiences can be provided that are likely to attain these purposes?
3.   How can these educational experiences be effectively organized?
4.   How can we determine whether these purposes are being attained? (Tyler, 1950).

These questions became translated into a four-step model for curriculum development: stating objectives, selecting experiences, organizing experiences, and evaluation. The rationale's most direct ancestry is the work of scientific curriculum makers like Franklin Bobbitt, W. W. Charters, Douglas Waples, and David Snedden. It is fundamentally deterministic in character and behviourist in orientation. But Tyler succeeded also in incorporating enough of the rhetoric of the experience curriculum position as to obfuscate previously unmistakable differences in doctrine. Whatever may have been the merits of the earlier positions, their previously sharp divergence had incredibly given way to consensus. In contrast to the internal criticism that characterized the earlier period, the second stage was characterized by almost universal acceptance of the Tyler rationale.

The large number of printings required to keep Tyler's syllabus on the market would seem to indicate that a vast number of persons were socialized in the field of education in the period since 1950 in part through its use. The perspective on curriculum they developed was essentially a technological one. The curriculum was a set of particular ways to do particular things, a perspective implied by the term curriculum *specialist*. Curriculum planning in many people's minds involved a technical skill, one which excluded the non-trained professional or at least the ordinary layman from engaging in that activity. In a sense, this may have been the culmination of the field's earlier drive for scientific respectability.

The most visible present manifestation of this technical orientation of the curriculum field is the enormous effort being expended in the stating, particularly the precise wording, of behavioural objectives —the first step in Tyler's model. Textbooks and manuals along with workbooks are being produced in large numbers for the purpose of initiating future curriculum workers into the arcane mysteries of writing behavioural objectives. The objective must, of course, be measurable, and this sometimes means distinguishing between taboo and approved verbs in the stating of the objective. Often, objectives have to be 'field tested', thus making the accumulation of an appropriate set of objectives even further out of the reach of the non-trained professional. This has even led to the sale of objectives. One recent professional publication, for example, carries advertisements for objectives, one of them asking the question 'Why ask teachers to spend hours churning out behavioural objectives from scratch?'; another announces 10,000 objectives and items for sale in a variety of subject areas (Phi Delta Kappan, 1973). This attention to objectives is, of course, understandable given the technological orientation of the field. Without a visible and carefully delineated end-product, the process of education could not proceed.

The development of the curriculum field on the basis of a technological model should not be seen as motivated mainly by a desire of status and exclusivity. Probably more important is the fact that many, and probably a majority of the people working in the curriculum field subscribe to the notion that the process of curriculum development involves a set of techniques. Curriculum research has essentially taken the form of trying to discover the best way to teach the short story or quadratic equations or the concept of homeostasis. A large percentage of PhD dissertations in major American universities are orientated toward discovering not only the best routes toward the accomplishment of such conventional academic work, but in such relatively unconventional areas as intercultural relations, mental health, and world peace. Typically, a new or modified technique—programmed instruction, computer-assisted instruction, the 'discovery' method—the 'experimental', is pitted against a conventional method, the 'control'. The effort is designed to determine which is a better route to a given point. One should not assume, however, that the appearance of the Tyler rationale in itself was instrumental in pointing the curriculum field in a given direction. Rather, the work represents a dominant stream of thought with respect to curriculum in this century and elevates a rather commonsense way of thinking to the level of technological respectability.

Alongside this consolidation of curriculum thinking, however, there arose a parallel effort to look forward to the further development of the curriculum field. This effort is perhaps best represented by the publication, also in 1950, of *Toward Improved Curriculum Theory* edited by Virgil Herrick and Ralph Tyler. The book was not nearly as great a popular success as *Basic Principles of Curriculum and Instruction*, but, at least on the surface, it appeared to herald a new stage of maturity which would concentrate on the conscious development of theoretical constructs with perhaps less emphasis on an uncritical reform commitment and sheer evangelistic fervour. The monograph, a product of a conference on curriculum theory held at the University of Chicago in 1947, drew together statements by some of the most prominent persons in the curriculum field, who, besides the editors, included B. Othanel Smith, Gordon Mackenzie, J. Paul Leonard, G. Max Wingo, William Alexander and Hollis Caswell. The group represented the best known of the second generation of curriculum leaders.

The emergence of the curriculum field from its pupa stage, however, may have been more symbolic than real. Perhaps it should not be surprising that, given such diversity of authorship, little emerges in the way of a coherent statement of what curriculum theory is or what course of action should be taken in pursuing it. In commenting on the impact of the monograph, for example, Beauchamp (1961) concluded that although 'the literature has been literally sprinkled with references to curriculum theory . . . it is not readily apparent from the literature whether significant progress has been made.' As Johnson (1967) has indicated, there is still remarkable disagreement on such matters as whether curriculum theories are descriptive or prescriptive, involve the process of curriculum development (e.g. Tyler) or a particular plan for the curriculum itself (e.g. Phenix), and if the instructional process is or is not to be considered in curriculum theory. This notable absence of agreement as to notions of curriculum theory has led one prominent philosopher to question whether such a thing as curriculum theory is even possible. He may, of course be right if one were to define theory in terms of prediction and control.

Nevertheless, it may be useful to note, even briefly, what has been attempted in the way of conscious curriculum theory development. One interesting line of endeavour has been to attempt to translate relatively established theories from cognate fields, the social sciences in particular, into curriculum theories. As practised by some of Herrick's former students, this has essentially taken the form of using a general theory of behaviour or a Parsonian structure-function analysis as a model for curriculum theory (Macdonald, 1956; Faix, 1964). More recently, input-output analysis drawn largely from economic theory has gained popularity. Similar attempts at translation have been attempted by major figures in related fields such as Robert Gagné (1970) in cognitive psychology and Carl Rogers (1969) in psychoanalytic theory to adapt their theoretical frameworks to the field of curriculum and instruction.

While it should not be denied that some of these attempts at least have intellectual respectability and have even achieved some currency, it may be argued that the attempts to make such adaptations from the domain of another field to curriculum are almost necessarily inadequate. On the one hand, the commonly assumed ties between curriculum and other fields such as psychology and sociology make such endeavours apparently promising. Psychology, in particular, in a variety of its manifestations such as learning theory, theories of human development, and psychological measurement has long been thought to be a direct source for the illumination of problems that characterize the curriculum field. On the other hand, while few would deny that psychology touches in some ways on key issues in the curriculum field, the connections may not be as direct as some have assumed.

It is one thing to consider psychological aspects of certain central curriculum questions, but it is quite another matter to begin from the vantage point of another field such as psychology and address oneself to the problems of curriculum wearing the lenses of a psychologist. Even the most influential curriculum construct of the 20th century, the Tyler rationale, may be seen as conceived by someone whose primary interest is educational measurement perhaps unconsciously arranging the stages of curriculum development in such a way as to make the outcomes easily measurable. As a matter of fact, in recent years, the measurement component of curriculum design has so come to dominate thinking in the curriculum field that to develop a curriculum in which the outcomes are not precisely and easily measurable is to commit a sin of inexpressible magnitude. It could be considered an interesting example of the tail wagging the dog. The effect is so to restrict and distort the multitude of questions that might arise in the context of evolving a curriculum theory as to make curriculum development a mere adjunct of the educational measurer's art. In other words, if one were to ask the admittedly vague question, What kinds of things are important to know in the modern world?, the measurement lens would cause him to see that question as, What kinds of things are important to know but can also be compressed into discrete units of learning and which in turn lend themselves to being translated into test items on a paper and pencil test? This tends so to restrict the scope and process of thinking in curriculum as to transform the very issues that presumably give legitimacy to the field.

The same sort of problem emerges when one attempts to view the problems of curriculum from the perspective of learning theorists. Quite naturally, the learning theorist devotes much of his attention to the establishment of a concept of learning and to the conditions under which learning occurs and then, insofar as he may turn his attention to curriculum and/or teaching at all, these become merely the instruments by which learning may take place. Gagné (1970), for example, defines the teacher as a 'manager of the conditions of learning' whose job it is to arrange the appropriate combination and sequence of stimuli into the most efficient arrangement for producing the desired effect. As Gagné (1970) puts it, 'The objective of this management is to insure that learning will be efficient, that is, that the greatest change in the student's behaviour will occur in the shortest period of time, and that this change will lead progressively to increased self-management of further learning.' Like the measurement specialist, the learning theorist who views the problems of curriculum or the activities of teaching is inclined to carve out one facet of the enterprise, perhaps even an insignificant one, and present that as the whole.

The views of Carl Rogers on curriculum and teaching are equally elliptical. To call a teacher a 'facilitator', for example, singles out one feature of the teaching enterprise in the same way that calling a teacher a 'manager' does. Rogers first equates teaching with the imparting of knowledge and skill and then condemns it as unimportant or even trivial. Since what Rogers values, learning how to learn, is excluded by his own definition of teaching, he must relegate teaching to 'a relatively unimportant and vastly overvalued activity (Rogers, 1969). The process is one of giving a dog a name in order to hang him.

Perhaps, the problem of attempting to derive theories of curriculum and/or teaching from the so-called parent or foundational disciplines can be illustrated by reference to an example that Polanyi (1958) presents in his *Personal Knowledge*. If we were to take a machine, say a clock or a typewriter or a locomotive, it is best understood according to Polanyi, in terms of the *operational principle* of the machine and how its parts relate and combine to fulfil the special function that the machine performs. Although the machine operates, obviously, according to physical or chemical laws, these laws do not provide the context or the standard of excellence by which the machine may be viewed. These standards are inherent in the operational principle and purpose of the machine. Thus, a clock that keeps accurate time is better than a poorly running clock, not because it more strictly adheres to the principles of physics, but because the operational principles of machines provide what Polanyi calls the *rules of rightness*. As Polanyi expresses it, 'a physical and chemical investigation cannot convey the understanding of a machine as expressed by its operational principles. In fact, it can say nothing at all about the way the machine works or ought to work' (1958).

What Polanyi seems to be saying is that any object or perhaps any activity can be understood by the principles that are inherent in it and not by principles derived from anything external to it. A good curriculum or good teaching may be explained only by those operational principles that evolve from the activity itself. Success can be explained only in terms inherent in the activity, although failure may be explained by those related studies comparable to physics in Polanyi's example. This may be what William James meant when he said just before the turn of the century 'that you make a great, a very great mistake, if you think that psychology, being the science of the mind's laws, is something from which you can deduce definite programs and schemes and methods of instruction for immediate schoolroom use' (James, 1915). Dewey expressed this point just as emphatically five years later in *The Relations of Theory to Practice in Education*. 'We do not make practical maxims out of physics,' he said, 'by telling persons to move according to laws of gravitation. If people move at all, they *must* move in accordance with the conditions stated by this law. Similarly, if mental operations take place at all, they *must* take place in accordance with the principles stated in correct psychological generalizations. It is superfluous and meaningless to attempt to turn these psychological principles directly into rules of teaching' (Dewey, 1962).

Dwayne Huebner once indicated very perceptively another of the problems inherent in deriving methodological and theoretical constructs from other fields of study. The question that he considers also raises doubt about the extent that knowledge developed in one scholarly domain can be transferred to another. Using Polanyi's term, 'society of explorers', to describe a field of study, Huebner (1968) pointed out that 'when knowledge is taken out of that society of explorers and used by other men in other occupations it is yanked out of its self-correcting context and has the possibility of becoming dated and misused. The user risks reifying it, when all he meant to do was to make it an instrument'. Borrowing theoretical constructs, then, is much more difficult and complex a process than we may have thought at first.

A prospectus

The foregoing has attempted to conceptualize the development of the curriculum field in essentially two stages. The first was characterized by an almost universal spirit of educational reform which focused to a large extent in a call for curriculum change. The kind of change advocated by educational leaders in the United States differed radically, but, ultimately, a dominant ideology for the curriculum field emerged. It drew its dominant metaphorical construct from the factory, focusing essentially on developing standardized means to achieve predetermined ends. Both the means and the ends were to be achieved 'scientifically'. Key points of emphasis were predictability, control, and efficiency.

In what might be called the second stage of the curriculum field's evolution, there was perhaps less emphasis on sheer missionary zeal for reforming the curriculum. It was a period, however, where the technological model for curriculum design became entrenched as embodied, principally, in the Tyler rationale. It was also characterized by a modest but conscious attempt to develop theoretical constructs that could serve as a more orderly basis for the development of curriculum as a field of study. At least some of the serious attempts to develop a curriculum theory took the form of attempting to translate theories from related fields into curriculum terms. These attempts have not been notably successful.

Perhaps it should be pointed out that the massive curriculum reform efforts in the United States during the 1960s were undertaken with hardly any participation by those who were identified with the curriculum field. The key figures in the post-Sputnik era of curriculum change were drawn largely from the academic disciplines. This may have been related to the particular kind of reform that characterized the period, but it may also be indicative of the failure of a technological rationale for the curriculum field. At least, the National Science Foundation and other well financed and powerful agencies that were interested in instituting curriculum reforms did not turn to those identified as curriculum specialists either for their technical expertise or for their theoretical grasp of curriculum problems and issues.

It would be hazardous to predict what form a third stage might take, or even if there will be a third stage, but it may be useful to speculate as to what directions may prove to be the more promising ones. These directions may be seen as (1) an extrapolation of the key problems and issues that characterize the field of curriculum; (2) the development of a distinctive perspective from which to view these problems; and (3) the identification of alternative metaphorical constructs to serve as a basis for theory development.

On the first issue, it would seem hazardous, perhaps even disastrous, to proceed on the assumption that the study of curriculum may be reduced to the single question of how to produce desired educational ends most efficiently. This is a thin reed indeed. A more fruitful direction would be an attempt to identify and anlyse the critical and persistent questions around which a field of study such as curriculum may be built. This need not take the form of trying to establish a consensus as to what the curriculum is. It could take the form of H. L. A. Hart's seminal study, *The Concept of Law*. In that book, Hart (1961) asks the question, 'What is Law?' in the same way the people have asked the question, 'What is the curriculum?' One of his basic assumptions, however, is that given such a question as 'What is Law?' 'nothing concise enough to be recognized as a definition could provide a satisfactory answer to it'.[1] Hart's attempt to define law, therefore, is not a search for a consensus. Instead, he attempts to answer this question in terms of what he calls the 'persistent questions' that have characterized the field, questions such as, 'How does law differ from and how is it related to orders backed by threats?' 'How does a legal obligation differ from, and how is it related to moral obligation?' and 'What are the rules and to what extent is law an affair of rules?' (Hart, 1961). Hart does not claim that the search for definition is wholly a useless endeavour; in fact, he thinks by addressing oneself systematically to the fundamental questions that characterize a field such as law one can ultimately identify a central set of factors which form a common part of the answers to such questions. A search for the persistent and fundamental questions that

---

[1] To my knowledge, Jane Roland Martin first noted the possible relationship between Hart's approach and curriculum issues in her introduction to *Readings in the Philosophy of Education: A Study of Curriculum*, Jane Roland Martin (ed.), Boston: Allyn and Bacon, Inc., 1970.

characterize the curriculum field along with a throughgoing analysis of the kinds of answers that might be provided to them could provide needed theoretical constructs, and in the long run, lead to a form of definition that would prove useful.

Secondly, in contrast to the apparent direction of the field of curriculum toward establishing itself as yet another field of specialization within education, the study of curriculum may be advanced as a field of generalization; that is, the most distinctive and useful role for persons associated with the curriculum field may be a synoptic one. This notion is derived from Lewis Mumford's description of the function of a generalist in the field of pre-history: 'The generalist has a special office, that of bringing together widely separated fields, prudently fenced in by specialists, into a larger common area, visible only from the air. Only by forfeiting the detail can the overall pattern be seen, though once that pattern is visible new details, unseen even by the most thorough and competent field workers digging through the buried strata, may become visible. The generalist's competence lies not in unearthing new evidence but in putting together authentic fragments that are accidentally, or something arbitrarily, separated, because specialists tend to abide too rigorously by a gentleman's agreement not to invade each other's territory' (Mumford, 1967). The fields of specialization within education have multiplied during this century. Each of these specialities, as already indicated, tends to view education from a distinctive perspective and, presumably, can shed light on educational problems. The curriculum generalist can serve the function of attempting to bring together some of these widely separated fields into reasonably unified conceptions of the educational process with a particular emphasis on how these unified conceptions can be translated into school programs.

Thirdly, on the question of curriculum theory and how it is derived or constructed, one might consider alternatives to the process of borrowing from related fields. Referring to the metaphor of 'growth' in the work of such educational theorists as Rousseau, Pestalozzi, and Froebel, Max Black (1944) suggested that 'the time has come to experiment with alternative "root metaphors" '. As suggested here, the metaphor of 'production' with its technological implications has come to dominate thinking in the curriculum field. A search for theory, then, may take the form of developing and analysing those metaphorical elements of language and thought in curriculum that give promise of new direction. In associating theory with metaphor, however, one should not assume that this relationship is distinctive to curriculum or even to education generally. As Mary Hesse (1970) has indicated, the development of theory even in the natural sciences may be more closely associated with metaphorical thinking than is commonly assumed. In this relatively unexplored avenue, however, one may find the direction that has been lacking in other efforts to develop theoretical constructs for the curriculum field.

References

BEAUCHAMP, G. A. (1961). *Curriculum Theory.* Wilmette, Illinois: The Kagg Press.

BLACK, M. (1944). 'Education as art and discipline', *Ethics,* 54, 4.

BOBBITT, F. (1913). 'Some General Principles of Management Applied to the Problems of City-School Systems.' *Twelfth Yearbook of the National Society for the Study of Education,* Part I. Chicago: University of Chicago Press.

BOBBITT, F. (1918). *The Curriculum.* Boston: Houghton Mifflin.

BOBBITT, F. (1924). *How to Make a Curriculum.* Boston: Houghton Mifflin.

Phi Delta Kappa, Vol. LV, No. 1 (September 1973), p. 95.

DEWEY, J. (1900). *The School and Society.* Chicago: University of Chicago Press.

DEWEY, J. (1962). *The Relation of Theory to Practice in Education.* Cedar Falls, Iowa, The Association for Student Teaching, (Reprinted from *Third Yearbook of the National Society for the Scientific Study of Education.* Chicago: University of Chicago Press, 1904).

FAIX, T. L. (1964). 'Toward a Science of Curriculum: Structural Functional Analysis as a Conceptual System for Theory and Research.' Unpublished PhD dissertation, University of Wisconsin.

GAGNÉ, R. M. (1970). *The Condition of Learning.* New York: Holt, Rinehart and Winston. Second Edition.

HART, H. L. A. (1961). *The Concept of Law.* London: Oxford University Press.

HERRICK, V. E. and TYLER, R. W. (Eds.) (1950). *Toward Improved Curriculum Theory.* Supplementary Educational Monograph No. 71. Chicago: University of Chicago Press.

HESSE, M. B. (1970). *Models and Analogies in Science.* Notre Dame, Indiana: University of Notre Dame Press.

HUEBNER, D. (1968). 'Implications of Psychological Thought for the Curriculum', in UNRUH, G. G. and LEEPER, R. R. (Eds.), *Influences in Curriculum Change.* Washington, D.C.: Association for Supervision and Curriculum Development, NEA.

JAMES, W. (1915). *Talks to Teachers on Psychology: And to Students on Some of Life's Ideals.* New York: Henry Holt and Company.

JOHNSON, M. (1967). 'Definitions and models in curriculum theory', *Educational Theory,* 17, 2, 127–40.

KILPATRICK, W. H. (1918). 'The project method', *Teachers College Record,* XIX, 4, 319–35.

KILPATRICK, W. H. (1934). 'The essentials of the activity movement, *Progressive Education,* 11,

MACDONALD, J. B. (1956). 'Some Contributions of a General Behaviour Theory for Curriculum.' Unpublished PhD dissertation, University of Wisconsin.

MUMFORD, L. (1967). 'Technics and Human Development': *The Myth of the Machine, Volume One.* New York: Harcourt, Brace.

POLANYI, M. (1958). *Personal Knowledge.* Chicago: University of Chicago Press.

ROGERS, G. R. (1969). *Freedom to Learn.* Columbus, Ohio: Charles E. Merrill.

ROSS, E. A. (1901). *Social Control.* New York: MacMillan.

SCHWAB, J. J. 'The practical: a language for curriculum', *School Review,* 78, 1, 1–23.

SNEDDEN, D. (1921). *Sociological Determination of Objectives in Education.* Philadelphia and London: J. B. Lippincott.

TYLER, R. W. (1950). *Basic Principles of Curriculum and Instruction.* Chicago: University of Chicago Press.

Some Additional Notes on Curriculum Development in the United States

Mauritz Johnson

Since Professor Kliebard's penetrating review of American curriculum development focused on its theoretical and ideological foundations, a brief overview of its practical aspects may be useful for comparative purposes. The US Constitution makes no mention of schools or education, but its Tenth Amendment provides that whatever powers are not delegated to the federal government or prohibited to the states are reserved to the states or to the people. Consequently, the constitution of each state provides for the establishment of a system of public schools, and the legislative bodies of the various states have enacted numerous laws pertaining to education.

To a great extent, these laws assign to local boards of education the final authority over the curricula of schools, but in almost all states, they also mandate at least one subject, and sometimes many subjects, to be studied by all pupils at a particular level or at least by those seeking a high school diploma. Probably the most widespread requirement is the study of American history and government, although English is also commonly required throughout the secondary school. The only subject that is universally prohibited is religion. Further generalization is difficult because there are, in actuality, 50 different educational systems quite independent of each other.

Curriculum development at the state level

One of the most highly centralized of these systems is that in the State of New York. The power there is vested in a Board of Regents, with 15 laymen as members, and in a Commissioner of Education appointed by that board. The State Education Department, of which the Commissioner is head, is a large bureaucracy with several thousand professional employees, and since the state's population is approximately 20 million, this Department is comparable to some national ministries.

Consistent with existing legislation and the rules and policies of the Regents, the Commissioner, on the advice of his staff, issues regulations pertaining to all aspects of school operation, including curriculum matters. These requirements can be enforced upon schools by the threat of withholding state financial aid. In addition, since New York is the only state with a system of external examinations in certain secondary-school subjects, there is an added incentive to follow the curriculum specifications in state syllabi. But the Department also promotes curriculum development positively through some funding of experimental projects, advice to schools by specialized and generalist supervisors (formerly considered 'inspectors'), and the activities of its curriculum development centre and its three bureau for curriculum development in elementary, secondary, and continuing education.

The traditional practice has been to undertake periodic reviews of the curriculum in the various subject areas by constituting committees of experienced teachers and university subject specialists. In the past these committees would prepare or revise brief syllabi indicating the educational goals to which it was claimed the subject contributed, a general outline of the topics encompassed, some suggestions on teaching approaches and instructional materials, and a bibliography of selected references on the subject. More recently the publications have become far more detailed in that concepts and generalizations included under the topics in a course are explicitly identified and supplementary information is furnished pertaining to definitions, key facts, and minimum performance requirements. Sometimes there is a companion compendium consisting of suggested learning activities, sources and descriptions of materials, and discussions of contemporary developments in the subject. Experimental courses are developed in great detail, providing the teachers who will try them not only with instructional suggestions but also actual instruction in the substantive content itself.

These publications, therefore, are not designed to be 'teacher-proof', but on the contrary to contribute to the in-service education of teachers as an essential aspect of curriculum revision and instructional improvement. Although various schools in the state served as experimental centres for the national curriculum reform projects sponsored by the US Office of Education, National Science Foundation, and various philanthropic foundations, the New York State Education Department did not adopt any of these new curricula, but chose instead to develop its own. Like the national efforts, those of the State were almost exclusively directed to the micro-curricular level, i.e., the content and format of specific courses, or at the most to the re-alignment of the sequence of courses within subject fields. Also consistent with national trends have been the emphases on contemporization of content, on conceptual organization consistent with underlying disciplinary structures, and on the use of so-called 'inquiry' or 'discovery' approaches in instruction. Leading scholars in pertinent disciplines are consulted for their recommendations and for review of tentative materials, but not, as in the national projects, to do the actual curriculum development. That task is the responsibility of the committees of teachers with staff support and leadership from curriculum specialists in the State Education Department.

The Department also arranges for the tryout of tentative versions of new or revised curricula. In the case of a recently developed comprehensive curriculum for health instruction which included units on human sexuality, systematic efforts were also made to acquaint the public with the included content and to secure public endorsement of its use in each locality.

Local curriculum development

Even in New York State, much curriculum development occurs at the level of the local school district or individual school. To be used as a basis for high-school graduation, locally developed secondary-school courses must be submitted to the State Education Department for approval. In most of the other states, this is not necessary, there being much more local autonomy over curriculum.

Throughout the country, including New York, it is common in all but the smallest school districts to assign responsibility for curriculum matters to a staff member carrying some such title as assistant superintendent for curriculum and instruction, or director (or co-ordinator) of curriculum or of elementary or secondary education. This person may coordinate and facilitate such activities as the efforts of citizen advisory committees to clarify school goals and review curriculum offerings, the work of district-wide teacher committees on the overall curriculum, course revision in a particular subject department or at a grade level, resource and media centres, and in-service training courses, workshops, and conferences. Some of the incumbents in these leadership positions have been trained as educational administrators or are experienced teachers without administrative training, but increasingly they have received specialized training at the masters or doctoral degree level from departments of curriculum and instruction, which are found in the schools of education of most American universities. Professors in these departments are brought together with the curriculum leaders in the schools through the 13,500 member Association for Supervision and Curriculum Development (ASCD) by means of journals, yearbooks, special publications, and annual conventions at the national, state, and regional levels.

National curriculum reform

Compared with the scholars who dominated the 'national curriculum reform movement' of the 1950s and 1960s, the curricular interests of ASCD members are more permanent, broader, and more responsive to social and cultural changes, particularly as they affect children and youth. That the two groups were never brought into close cooperation with each other was a shameful misfortune for American education. The academicians made an important contribution in the efforts to rid the curriculum of its accumulation of obsolete, inert, poorly arranged content. Only such experts can interpret the significant developments at the frontiers of scholarship, assign priorities, and indicate structural considerations imposed by the assumptions, substantive relationships, and methods of scholarly work within particular disciplines. But they were politically naive to believe that in a nation of 50 autonomous and largely decentralized state educational systems they could achieve substantial and continuing curriculum change without close collaboration with the leadership group represented by the ASCD membership.

As it was, the involvement of the scholars was short-lived, perhaps in the main because of the reduction in federal funding, but in any event their impact was almost entirely micro-curricular, with little attention to the 'orchestration' of their separate fields into a total programme. Except for a general concern for 'national security or prestige', they gave little attention to the curricular implications of societal trends and issues outside their particular scholarly specializations, such as those relating to the status of minority groups, the alienation of youth, the quality of the environment, the impersonalization of life, the unresponsiveness of governments and other social institutions, the effects of economic deprivation and insecurity, the impact of electronic media and the popular arts, increasing automation and shifting employment patterns, and the mobility and growth rate of the population.

The national curriculum projects centred at various American universities during the past decade were so numerous and widely publicized that they will not be identified here. Best known were those in mathematics, the natural sciences, and modern foreign languages, but some projects were eventually launched in English and social studies, with less notable success. Two conclusions generally accepted by those involved in these projects were that the successful introduction of new curricula depended on their being embodied in material form and on the re-training of teachers for the task of teaching them. Consequently, special institutes were offered at selected universities, during the summers and the academic year, for carefully chosen teachers, who were supported through federal stipends. There they were familiarized with the vast arrays of text-books, films, equipment, manuals, supplementary reading, and other materials produced by a particular project. Although referred to as *curricular* projects, most of them devoted so much attention to instructional procedures and instrumental content that it is often difficult to identify from their materials just what learning outcomes were in fact intended to result. Much disappointment was expressed over the fact that many teachers who were exposed to the new content and the preferred instructional procedures at the institutes returned to their classrooms to teach the new curriculum by traditional methods. The assumptions that subject matter experts are necessarily best qualified to decide the most effective instructional procedures and that in any event there is a single best procedure may have been unfounded. The importance of distinguishing between curriculum and instruction is emphasized by the experience of these projects.

Textbooks and the curriculum

Nevertheless, a new approach to the development of instructional materials evolved out of the national projects and others devoted to the production of programmed instruction units, 'learning activity packages' (LAPs), and other individualized programmes. Its key feature is the repeated testing of materials with students, followed by formative evaluation and revision of materials, as many times as necessary to achieve desired results in summative evaluation. The textbook has always had a dominant role in American education, sometimes determining, rather than following, the curriculum. But, unlike the newer materials whose effectiveness can be certified as a result of the development procedures followed, the traditional textbook was (and still is) written by one or more authors, usually having university affiliation, without its being subjected to systematic testing in classrooms.

The nation-wide marketing of text books tends to make the curricula of the separate state systems remarkably similar. New curricular content can be rapidly and widely introduced through textbooks, but they also exert a conservative influence on curriculum due both to the expense to school districts in changing, and to publishers in revising them and also to the eagerness of the latter to conform to the specifications of those states which approve textbooks for use in their schools or even adopt them for state-wide use. It should be noted, however, that in most states, the selection of textbooks is a local prerogative, which in some instances provides teachers with one of their few opportunities to participate in curriculum decisions.

The federal role

In exercising their responsibility for curriculum development, states and their localities are not free of coercion from the government in Washington, even if it has no constitutional authority in the matter. The influence is exercised primarily through funding policies. There is a powerful vocational education 'lobby' in the United States, and since 1917 the federal government has provided increasing financial support for vocational education. Even at the cost of distorting the balance with general education, the states and local districts find it impossible to refuse the available money. The federal support for academic subjects during the 1960s did benefit general education, but the underlying motive was again vocational, i.e., to provide an adequate number of well-trained scientists, mathematicians, and translators. Around 1950 the US Office of Education offered encouragement (but little financial support) to a 'Life Adjustment' movement aimed at applying the vocational philosophy to general education by converting it into specific training for all facets of everyday life. In the late 1960s some attention was given to the humanities in the form of a National Foundation (and Endowment) for the Arts and Humanities, and an emphasis was placed on literacy, both in the schools and in continuing education (Right-to-Read Programme). But by the early 1970s, under an administration strongly committed to the 'work ethic', federal policy again returned to a familiar theme under the slogan of 'Career Education', designed to cast all education from the kindergarten through the secondary school into one continuous preparation for work.

Thus, the federal government, lacking ultimate responsibility for education and any authority over curriculum, cannot be relied on for any consistent philosophical direction or financial support, except with respect to its long-favoured cause, vocational education. The newly established National Institute of Education may develop a coherent policy with respect to research support, but what priority will be given to research pertaining to curriculum remains to be seen. Meanwhile, curriculum development in most states is largely in the hands of teachers with little special training for the task and little time either, except insofar as a small number are employed during their summer vacations for that purpose. Where teachers' unions are growing more powerful, they are beginning to demand a greater voice for teachers in curriculum decisions. At the same time, proponents of 'open education' in the elementary school and of 'alternative schools' at the secondary level favour an increasing role for students in determining their own curricula. It is not easy to say just how curricula get developed in the United States today, and it may be even more difficult to do so in the future.

CHAPTER 12

Toward an Overview

Philip H. Taylor

Introduction

A nation should not be judged by its utterances alone. One must also look at its style, at how it makes its policies, takes its decisions, implements them and evaluates the results. Nowhere is this likely to be more true than in the way in which a country decides what it is proper to teach the young, and goes about developing the means to give reality to its policies through what is taught and learned in its educational institutions. In some cases the larger role will be played by central government. In others it will be devolved to the region, the locality or even to the individual school. Whatever the case a curriculum will have been developed which within acceptable limits reflects the meanings and values which each society wishes its young to acquire, understand, appreciate and be responsive to. There will also be reflected, though not always clearly, the contradictions, the tensions, the ambiguities and the uncertainties with which all policy-making must attempt to cope, and which are made tractable by compromise, by rationalization or simply by letting rest decisions of an earlier time.

Style is essentially qualitative. It is not about what things are put together but about how they are put together. It resides more in relationships, and in what results from them than in the parts that are related. In this final Chapter we shall look at how different countries use their institutions and those who serve them to realize their educational intentions and at how both the intentions and the roles of those who serve them give them meaning in schools and classrooms, are changing. Of special interest will be the relationships between intention, institution and the roles played by individuals in the education system and in society generally. It is here that distinctive styles of curriculum development are to be found. It is here also that what is common to all countries will be seen.

There is, however, one overwhelming impression: curriculum development is a political activity in every sense. It is caught up with values, with what it is worthwhile, beneficial and useful to teach the young, and with how best to distribute educational resources both human and material. It is a process which frequently has to make its way between contending and competing claims, tread carefully, respect certain social beliefs unquestioningly, and struggle to free itself from the sterility of decisions made for reasons no longer relevant. Nor is it ever entirely free from the need to find justification for its activities in ultimate principles, impermanent and uncertain though these may prove to be. Curriculum development has this need because the curriculum in its practical and operational aspect, in the way in which it shapes what is learned, influences what the young are taught to think and value and who they may conceive themselves to be. It also shapes their view of what it is like to be human in a particular society at a certain point in time and how they should regard others both in their own and in other cultures.

As an enterprise curriculum development depends not only on cosmology (Douglas, 1973) but also on the arts of the practical through which teachers are given a framework within which to engage the young and are provided with a blueprint for the learning system by which to monitor their teaching. It is between the purpose and meaning to be given to life and the awakening of an awareness in the young to all that life is that curriculum development must shuttle, and shuttle even faster as customary values shift and change ever more rapidly and less confidently in the modern world.

Criteria of comparison

In Chapter 1 (p. 11) six questions were posed and will be re-stated here in a somewhat different form, and examined for the role each might play in a comparative evaluation of curriculum development:

1. *Who decides what purposes the curriculum will serve and the degree of emphasis each shall receive?* The curricula of educational institutions serve many purposes, both social and educational. They serve to ensure social continuity and give support to the life of the mind, and additionally they may enable the individual to take something from them which is purely personal and which frees the individual in some degree from the tyrannies of the social order into which he was born. Whoever decides what benefits are to be distributed to the young exercises very considerable powers, and to know where this power lies and how it is used could well cast light on the degree to which a nation lays store by and depends upon what is taught to its young. It is in this respect that the criteria will be used.

2. *Who decides what shall be taught so as to achieve curricular purposes?* Subject matter is the agent of educational purposes. It is the medium that conveys the messages; messages which are frequently latent, hidden, difficult to discern and sometimes unintended (Dreeben, 1969) as well as messages made plain in the rhetoric of

education, and in the prospectuses of schools and colleges. Those who select subject matter, whether it is the informal experiences of the nursery school or the formal subjects of the pre-college curriculum, exercise great influence on what the curriculum can achieve. It is at this point that *de facto* control over the system can be secured (Young, 1971). What are the limits of this control, what checks and balances are built in to avoid too easy a distortion of intention? To know answers to such questions is to know how different curriculum systems monitor their input of aims and give them substance through what is taught.

3. *Who decides what specific learning outcomes in relation to general curricular goals shall be selected?* The intended results of curricular experiences may be cognitive, having to do with the mind and the intellect, or affective, having to do with the feelings and with states of awareness. Yet again they may have to do with social competencies and roles. Whatever is intended, some result is expected, and one that is congruent with the larger purposes which the curriculum serves. These intended outcomes of learning serve as units by means of which the system can be monitored and may well vary from country to country.

4. *Who directs what teachers will teach and how they will teach it?* Teaching, like other professional and semi-professional activities, is not entirely free to follow where it will. It must respect what is expected of it by its clients and it must honour its traditions. And more than this, it is not free from the influence of the many social and educational agents and agencies which serve society (Taylor, Reid, *et al.* 1974). The degree to which teachers are free to make decisions about what to teach and how to teach it is a measure not simply of professional autonomy but also of the extent to which they legitimate the purposes their teaching will serve. Societies differ in the degree to which teachers are afforded such authority.

5. *Who advises teachers?* All professions have their 'experts' both in the theory and the practice of what they engage in. Teaching is no exception, and teachers look to those experts for advice. They perhaps look most to those who have practical suggestions to make because theirs, they believe, is a practical art, and least to experts who are 'theoretical' and 'scientific'. But advice comes not only from expert sources, it also comes from elsewhere. And it does so because education is a functional part of those moral concerns with which all societies must grapple. In dealing with them meaning is given to such terms as 'equality of opportunity', 'the welfare of the individual', 'standards of performance' and 'the quality of life'. Just how open to advice teachers are and from what sources may well vary country

by country, and the variations may indicate qualitative differences in the ways in which the curriculum is made real and given relevance.

6. *Who decide on the conditions in which curricula will operate and on how they are to be evaluated?* The quality of curricular experience depends on the conditions under which the curriculum has to be transacted; not only on the physical conditions but also on the psychological and institutional conditions. The level of resources made available, both physical and human, may well be crucial for the quality of result. Teacher education both initial and further, educational technology, teaching materials and the state of the plant in which teaching takes place all play their part in the total system. Those who influence the sub-systems also influence what the curriculum results in, what is taught and learned.

Equally influential are those who evaluate the curriculum, and of considerable interest are the criteria which they use. To be responsible for estimating the 'efficiency' of any system means that in some degree those who estimate will have an effect on its operations, will either confirm its activities or push it in one or other direction. It is at this point that the risk of distortion is the greatest for the relationship between 'purpose' and 'output' is not always clear, especially in systems whose function is to deal with people (Kreisemberg, 1968). How different countries cope with these problems, if at all, is of interest, and their processes of evaluation may be increasingly critical as the pace of change and innovation rises.

Some comparisons

No attempt will be made in what follows to be exhaustive, even if it were within the abilities of the authors to be so. In the foregoing ten contributions are data which can be processed in many ways, from many perspectives and with different ends in view. To provide these data was one of the main objectives of this book. A main objective was not to be definitive about any one mode of comparison. But it may be of interest to explore the issues which our six questions raise.

1. *Curricular purposes*

A recurring issue in many accounts is the quality of educational opportunity, and a frequent theme, the implementation of comprehensive education to achieve it. But such a major issue is accompanied by a parade of minor issues, each of which seeks and finds its own claim to justifiable recognition. Each becomes a demand to be attended to. A demand for more effective social education, for the continuing redevelopment of science education, for a greater commitment by the young to what education has to offer, and for improved levels of achievement.

For the larger issues the central government in many countries holds itself responsible, sets the arena, provides the framework, and determines 'the rules of the game' within which implementation of policy will take place. In some instances, Sweden for example, the schools and teachers are cast as functionaries, the tactical arm of government there to produce the results which will represent the policy makers' intended outcomes. In others the meshing of policy-making with implementation will be less exact, and may even be morally ambiguous as for instance, in England, where the rhetoric of 'the freedom of the teacher' forces central government into shifts and procedures which are less than direct. Here the larger purposes to be served by the curriculum development process are subjected to the assessment of teachers to a greater extent than seems apparent elsewhere. Negotiation is diffused throughout the many levels of the system and yet does not seem to be the only mechanism by which curriculum development is guided. Ideologies also play their part though more overtly in some countries than in others. For the Federal Republic of Germany, possibly because of its recent history, the role of beliefs is seen as a central one in determining the part which curriculum development will play in the implementation of policy. Similarly, though to a lesser extent ideologies play their part in the Canadian and Israeli context at least in terms of the thrust toward national identity.

2. *Implementation of purposes*

On the broad front where educational purpose and social purpose merge into a common continuum of moral concerns governments are prominent, and in some countries remain prominent as educational purpose is given meaning in pedagogic practices. Between purpose and practice, decisions about what to teach have to be made. It is at this point that the experienced teacher, the subject specialist, the educational adviser and the educational specialist begin to play their part. Most frequently they play it under the controlled circumstances of the nationally appointed committee or commission. Less frequently, as in England and Scotland and the United States, they play their part in direct relation to the schools at the local level, though seldom without the general guidance of national recommendations from a central advisory body. In the United States Congressional enquiries will serve this function and in England it will be played by the Central Advisory Council for Education.

In whatever way seems legitimate, governments will find means for influencing that crucial process of curriculum development, the translation of educational purpose into stipulations about what should be taught in the schools. However, the style will differ in some degree country by country and the result will be to enhance or diminish the part played by the practising teacher. He may be cast, as in Sweden and Germany, in the role of the tactical arm of education, there to serve the plans for teaching laid down by national ministeries, or as in England and the United States, the autonomous professional, using his own initiative to interpret the educational purposes as he sees them. Whichever is the case, and the distinctions are never as marked in practice as a literal reading of the context seems to suggest, it is at this point in the process of curriculum development that the risk emerges of creating a tension between the national interest in education and educational interests as construed by the teachers. In England it was out of such a conflict that the Schools Council grew (p. 68). In Sweden it was reduced by industrial dispute to an issue of reward for the expanded competence of teachers (p. 164). Whichever way it is tackled, this conflict of interests is potentially the most dangerous for the process of curriculum development. It can stultify the process, render it weak by compromise and sterile through antagonism. Each country seeks means for avoiding such outcomes sometimes by control of teacher education both initial and further in-service education and sometimes by the deliberate involvement of teachers and teacher organizations in debating the issues of what should be taught in the schools.

3. *Specific learning outcomes*

The selection of subjects to be taught or educational experiences to be provided is only one part of the complex process of curriculum development. As important is the nomination of the learning outcomes to be achieved in transacting them in schools and classrooms. If this stage in the process of curriculum development is not dealt with explicitly, then the chances of subject matter, the content of the curriculum, being used to serve ends other than those intended become greater. The recognition of this issue depends partly on the adequacy and completeness of the concept of curriculum employed and partly on the cultural context in which it is set. It is evident that in Belgium, Denmark and Holland a more extended concept of curriculum is coming to be needed if the curriculum is to serve educational policies and not merely reinterpret them in terms which do little to redevelop the conventional curriculum.

In England, on the other hand, despite the availability of a more extended concept of curriculum, it is the culturally embedded belief that it is the individual and his needs that are more important than society and its needs which pre-empts major decisions about the learning

outcomes to be served by the curriculum and makes discussion of
them opaque to many teachers who see no point in debating an issue
already settled or in justifying the self-evident. (p. 60)

The specification of learning outcomes or curriculum objectives
as an aspect of the process of curriculum development has its
strongest grip in the United States and in Sweden. In both countries
major curriculum developments in recent years have been initiated
outside the schools and have to a degree been related to central
national concerns, economic, technological or social.

It is through the specification of objectives that the curriculum
may be most readily shaped to serve particular ends, or so it is
believed, becoming in the process a controllable and assessable
learning system. Such a view has had some currency in Germany
(p. 97) but, has been severely criticised. Nevertheless, it is used as
part of the curriculum development process, as it is in Sweden, and
in some English projects.

4. *Teaching: content and method*

In the last analysis, none of the countries surveyed stipulates
precisely what its teachers will teach and how they will teach it,
though in all, the teacher, with his attitudes and expertise is seen as
crucial in the curriculum developmental process, and the issue of
how best to bring the teacher into the process of changing what is
taught, a central one. Weaning teachers away from their dependence
on text books, which are a potent influence on what is taught in
Belgium and Holland, for example, and equipping them with the
abilities to construct their own teaching materials, as seems to be
the desire in Israel, and to make choices among teaching materials
competing for their attention which seems to be reckoned important
in England and Scotland, is the heart of the problem.

Even though each country struggles to provide some freedom for
the teacher, recognizing that at the limit the teacher has at least a
strong negative sanction which he may apply to what he is called on
to teach, each country brings influence to bear on directing what
teachers should teach. This influence frequently takes the form of
legitimating the claim made as to what should be taught. Sometimes
it is the claim of legal status, as in Denmark, sometimes of professional repute as with many of the English curriculum projects,
and sometimes, as in Canada, the call of community expectations,
which underwrites the claims made about what the teacher ought
to teach.

Influence on the teaching methods adopted by the teacher is much
less apparent, and only becomes an issue when there is a press toward
homogeneous grouping or 'open' education against the expressed

wishes of the teachers. At present there seems little evidence of this, though the experiences of Sweden in this respect ought to be salutary.

5. *Advising the teachers*

In one form or another, either as 'inspectors', 'advisers' or 'supervisors', most of the countries surveyed have a system for advising the teachers on curriculum developments, encouraging them to experiment with them and to implement them. The same individuals will also take an active part in the curriculum development process and even be prominent in initiating curricular changes as they have been, for example, in England, Holland and in Scotland.

Sources of advice are, however, many and varied, and increasingly there is an attempt to provide means for co-ordinating them. The creation of the Schools Council in England and its counterpart in Holland as agents of curriculum change are instances of this. In the United States the new National Institute of Education may develop a similar role. In Canada some provincial governments have established similar agencies, among which the Ontario Institute for Studies in Education has been eminently successful.

Generally speaking, there would seem to be a concern for a greater co-ordination of those with an interest in the curriculum and for a planned approach to curriculum development, though just how extensive planning for curriculum development can become may be dependent on both the national context and the persistence of the desire to reform what is taught.

6. *Curricular context and evaluation*

The curriculum is given operational reality in schools and class-rooms. If it 'works', it does so out of the transactions which constitute teaching and learning. It is in the context of this teacher-learning relation that the process of curriculum development reaches its conclusion, though not necessarily its intended ends. Here also is one baseline for curriculum evaluation: the learning outcomes achieved.

Control of the context in which curriculum development is implemented is, in most of the countries reviewed here, moved to the margins of control exercised by those who initiated and developed the curriculum. It is here that negotiation with teachers, and increasingly with students, has to take place. It is at this point that curricular issues, including those of evaluation, are subsumed within the larger issue of the purposes schooling is to serve. This is so in Denmark, the United States, Israel, Canada, Holland and Scotland. It is implied both in the concern in Germany for an adequate theory of curriculum evaluation and, more directly, in the plea for 'school-centred theories of curriculum development'.

This search for a wider context within which to set the curriculum development movement, which in its very language offers meanings in metaphors which have yet to be extensively examined (Jenkins, 1973), may be no more than a search for a means to attach educational change to more general social and political change, change which is becoming increasingly less predictable and which makes one cautious about predicting the future of curriculum development, the form it will take and the theory which will guide it.

References
DREEBEN, R. (1969). *On What is Learned in Schools.* New York: Rand McNally.
DOUGLAS, M. (1973). *Natural Symbols.* Harmondsworth: Penguin.
JENKINS, D. (1973). 'The Moving Plates of Curriculum Theory'. In: TAYLOR, P. H. and WALTON, J. (Eds.) *The Curriculum: Research, Innovation and Change.* London: Ward Lock Educational.
KREISENBERG, L. (1968). 'Internal Differentiation and the Establishment of Organizations'. In: BECKER, H. S. *et al. Institutions and the Person.* Chicago: Aldine Publishing Co.
TAYLOR, P. H. *et al.* (1974). *Purpose, Power and Constraint in the Primary School Curriculum.* London: Macmillan for the Schools Council.
YOUNG, M. F. D. (Ed.) (1971). *Knowledge and Control.* London: University of London Press.

Notes on Contributors

Frank Achtenhagen is Professor of Education at the University of Göttingen. He taught educational theory at the Free University of Berlin and is the author of several publications. His main research interests are in the fields of didactics, curriculum theory and teaching methods.

Urban Dahllöf is Professor of Education at the Institute of Education at the University of Gothenberg. He played an important role in the Swedish School Reform, and is the author of many research reports. Currently he is engaged on fundamental research in curriculum theory, and has lectured in many parts of the world.

Klaas Dornbos is Director of the School Advisory Centre in Arnhem with special interests in curriculum development, he is the author of several research reports dealing with children's learning difficulties, educational selection and the determinants of school achievement.

Shevach Eden is Director of the Curriculum Centre and Curriculum Division of the Ministry of Education and Culture, has studied in Poland and the United States, and taught in a wide range of educational institutions. He is the author of articles and books in the field of social education, teaching and curriculum.

Ian R. Findlay is a Senior Lecturer in Education at Aberdeen College of Education with interests in the history of education and comparative education. He is the author of *Education in Scotland*, and is engaged on research into the influence of the Scottish Education Department in the first quarter of this century.

John Herbert is Associate Professor of Educational Theory at the University of Toronto and at the Ontario Institute for Studies in Education. Previously he was the Director of the graduate programme of teacher preparation at Reed College, Oregon, and for many years a school teacher and administrator. He is the author of many articles and books, and is the Founding Editor of the *Curriculum Theory Network,* and a member of the Editorial Board of the *Journal of Curriculum Studies*. Currently he is conducting research on classroom environments and is active in the genesis of the new Canadian Association for Curriculum Studies.

Mauritz Johnson is Professor of Education with special responsibility for curriculum and instruction at the State University of New York at Albany, and has taught in schools and colleges. He is the author of a wide range of publications including major contributions to curriculum theory, and has been director and consultant to a wide range of projects.

Herbert M. Kliebard is Professor of Curriculum and Instruction and Educational Policy Studies at the University of Wisconsin—Madison. He has had a wide range of teaching and research experience, and published many articles mainly in the field of curriculum theory and evaluation. His books include *The Language of the Classroom* of which he was co-author.

Tom Olsen is a Senior Lecturer at the Royal Danish School of Educational Studies and a member of the Board of Educational Experimentation. His main area of teaching and research is in curriculum theory and methods of teaching.

Joslyn Owen is Chief Education Officer of Devon and formerly a Joint Secretary of the Schools Council for the Curriculum and Examinations. He has taught and held several posts in educational administration, and been a consultant to several governments in Europe and North America. He is the author of many articles and recently published the *Management of Curriculum Change*.

Philip H. Taylor is Professor of Education and Head of the Division of Curriculum and Method at the University of Birmingham. As well as holding a variety of teaching posts he was for three years Director of Research for the Schools Council. He is the Founding Editor of the *Journal of Curriculum Studies*, author of many articles and several books including *How Teachers Plan their Courses*. He has directed Research projects for the Department of Education, the Schools Council and the Social Science Research Council.

R. Vandenberghe is now Junior Lecturer at the University of Louvain (Institute of Education). In 1970, he obtained his masters degree in education with a thesis on educational innovations and the planning of change in education. His main research activities are centred around the same topic and he has published several articles about educational change.